"Araceli Cab Cumí has lived almost all of her life on the half block where she was born in Barrio Tres Cruces, Maxcanú, Yucatán, Mexico. The house in which she was born and the one in which she lived with her paternal grandparents are just across the street from the house where she and her husband lived, reared two children, and where she still resides. . . .

"Yet the achievements of Araceli Cab Cumí extend beyond the boundaries of her barrio, hometown, state, or nation. In a place and time where women are still underrepresented in partisan politics, indigenous people a rarity, and indigenous women hardly a presence at all, Araceli is a successful longtime Maya woman politician. A grassroots leader and political party activist since 1960, she is the only indigenous woman to have ever been elected to the Yucatecan State Congress. She has in fact served two terms in the Congress, once in the mid-1970s and again in the early 1990s.

"But Araceli Cab Cumí is also exceptional because she is a writer. Over the past thirty years she has written the political speeches and position papers expected of a politician, but she has also composed essays, poetry, and personal narratives. She has delivered many of the political speeches and position papers in the Yucatecan State Congress or at other political events. Her essays, poetry, and personal narratives, however . . . , were unread by anyone other than Araceli until she and I began this book."

—from *Discarded Pages*

Discarded Pages

Discarded Pages

Araceli Cab Cumí, Maya Poet and Politician

Kathleen Rock Martín

University of New Mexico Press • Albuquerque

© 2007 by the University of New Mexico Press
All rights reserved. Published 2007
Printed in the United States of America
13 12 11 10 09 08 07   1 2 3 4 5 6 7
Library of Congress Cataloging-in-Publication Data
Martín, Kathleen R.
Discarded pages : Araceli Cab Cumí, Maya poet and politician /
Kathleen R. Martín.
p. cm.
ISBN 978-0-8263-4066-5 (CLOTH : ALK. PAPER)
1. Cab Cumí, Araceli, 1932–
2. Yucatán (Mexico : State)—Politics and government.
3. Politicians—Mexico—Yucatán (State)—Biography.
4. Poets, Mexican—20th century—Biography.
5. Maya women—Mexico—Yucatán (State)—Biography.
I. Title.
F1376.C14 2007
305.48'8974207265092—dc22
[B]

2007014093

Book design and typesetting: Kathleen Sparkes
This book was typeset using Minion Pro OTF 10.5/14, 26P
Display type is Brioso Pro OTF

In Memoriam

To Maria Isara Cumí Carbello with the best homage I can give her

To Román Èk, Donato Dzul, and Isamuel Zi
with honor and respect to our race

To Guibaldo López Lara as a symbol of teaching

To Dominga Cen and Maestra Paula Cruz Estrella

To Elvia Carrillo Puerto and Felipa Poot[1]

To Don Pablo del S. Patrón Cih[2]

—Araceli Cab Cumí

To my two beloved grandmothers, Martha Ethel Whitney Jones and
Margaret Cecilia Tierney Rock. Gramma Jones was a woman of dignity,
love, and endurance. She is grievously missed by all of our family.
But also much remembered for the happiness, wisdom, and love she
brought to our lives. Gramma Rock died too young for me to know her.
Yet I feel her graceful and enduring presence living in our family memory.
And to my beloved Aunt Margaret, who gave us a lifetime of humor and
love. She taught us happiness in the most humble of life circumstances.

—Kathleen Rock Martín

Dedication

To Othón Baños Ramírez, Beatriz Castilla Ramos, Beatriz Torres Góngora, and Juan Castillo Cocom, Universidad Autónoma de Yucatán; Kathleen Rock Martín, Florida International University; Allan Burns, University of Florida; Sharon Mújica, University of North Carolina. To the primary school, "Doctor Montessori" of Maxcanú, to the Cultural Missions of my state, to the National Institute of Adult Education. To my brother and sisters, Hugo, Dalia, and Maria. To Aidee Ventura, Carmela Dzul, Martina Catzim, Edelmira Catzim, Teodora Rodriquez, Isidra Chan, Ernestina Lopez, Cristina Ku'mul, Maria Candelaria Uc, Ismelda Ventura, M. Teresa Canto C., Rosalia Pinzon R., M. Elena Martinez, Margarita Tun; to Emilia Cime and to Nidelvia Ventura R.[1]

—Araceli Cab Cumí

As Araceli says, "Death does not exist." So I dedicate this book to my father, Robert Francis Rock, for a lifetime of kindness, faith, and love, and to my husband, William Alexander Martín Gonzalez. Memo, you are my light and my reflection.

—Kathleen Rock Martín

Contents

Original Writings of Araceli Cab Cumí

Acknowledgments

To Othón Baños Ramírez, Beatriz Castilla Ramos and Beatriz Torres Góngora, and Juan Castillo Cocom of the Universidad Autónoma de Yucatán; Kathleen Rock Martín of Florida International University; Allan Burns of the University of Florida; and Sharon Mújica of the University of North Carolina, who, motivated by the search for anthropological knowledge and investigation, looked for me in order to give me the opportunity of knowing myself. My respects to life, to destiny, that we may find ourselves in the historic rock of our roots.

Never was it pretension or vanity. Never did I have the elements to support these things, something such as a social position by name or lineage, much less the capital to buy what was preferable.

This, yes, . . . always I have desired profoundly, to improve my knowledge, to have the necessary studies to strengthen my [intellectual] preparation, something that I have not been able to obtain.

As I could explain, without falling into vanity, the satisfaction that now I restrain, when I remember the way in which I learned what the great Universities harbor. The circumstances, the avatars, the unforeseen . . .

I don't pretend to be a renowned intellectual with drums and cymbals but I want to do something, perhaps posthumously, but well, which will serve the heritage of my people and all who believe in good intentions. I am assuming my right, completing my obligation. If in the course of the experience, in the school of life, or in the rugged roads of politics or for reasons of social struggle, I have said offensive words or I have had aggressive attitudes, to my fellow citizens, . . . to my people, . . . I ask forgiveness, I ask pardon. My attitude or aggressive words were and continue to serve to defend my cause as a cause of all of the women of my race. In human terms all women whether they are poor, rich, good, bad, ugly, or pretty, we go through the circumstances of poverty, abandonment, frustrations, deceptions, marginalization, misunderstanding, chastisement, unjust challenges, the burden of guilt and great ingratitude.

With such behavior it is possible that we have great defects, failures, mischievousness, or sad mistakes that as a consequence have left us troubles, pain, sorrows, and tears. But . . . we know how to say: "blessed are the tears that renew me and clean my sorrow, that console me and make sweet my troubles."

In closing I am one of many, . . . I am a discarded page, a fallen leaf that would like to remain in the world of flower gardens; I do not wish to be broken by the dark spines of the thistles or become dust of an arid region, . . . I do not wish to be unknown dust, . . . I do not wish to be anything.[1]

—*Araceli Cab Cumí*
original pages on page xvii and xviii

I thank Araceli Cab Cumí profoundly for allowing me to become a witness to her richly lived life. I continue to treasure our years of friendship and intellectual dialogue. I also appreciate the support of Araceli's family for this project. Thanks to her wise and gentle husband, Pablo, who encouraged his wife in her political career and also in the production of this book. Thanks to Zazil Espinosa Patrón, one of Araceli's four granddaughters, who has long contributed her insightful, sensitive analysis of her grandmother and her work. My thanks also extend to Eneyda May Canul, Araceli's daughter-in-law whose family shares the house compound with Araceli and Pablo. She has sometimes taken care of the household duties while Araceli and I worked on this book. And additionally I would like to thank Zoila Espinosa Patrón and Edna Patrón May, two of Araceli's talented granddaughters, for allowing us to include their short stories in this book. Thanks to Araceli's fourth granddaughter, Ana Maria Quintal Patrón, for her assistance as well.

I also wish to thank my colleagues and friends in Yucatán. I owe to "the three Beatrices," Dra. Beatriz Castilla Ramos, Dra. Beatriz Torres Góngora, and la Secretaria de SEDESO, Beatriz Zavala Peniche, many, many thanks for years of friendship, support, and intellectual companionship. You are my best colleagues. The world of Yucatán is brighter for your presence. Thanks also to my friend and colleague Dr. Othón Baños Ramírez, the consummate professional whose straightforwardness, philosophical humor, and thoughtful analysis I always appreciate. A thank-you also to Othón's delightful, sparky family, Alejandra, Othón, and Carolina with whom conversation has been a learning experience. Thanks again to Dr. Juan Castillo

Cocom, colleague, friend, and former student, for his luminescent analysis of Yucatecan themes. And to my many colleagues at the Unidad de Ciencias Sociales and the Facultad de Antropología e Historia (especially La Mafia) at the Universidad Autónoma de Yucatán—thanks for the grand pleasure of your company. I wish to thank Sr. Juan Rosado Alcocer, owner of the Hotel Santa Lucía and the Hotel San Juan where I have stayed during my trips to Yucatán and where Araceli and I worked on this book. My deepest thanks for your knowledgeable conversations about your homeland and for giving us a quiet professional ambience in which to work. And my lifelong appreciation for two special friends in Yucatán, Sister Terry and Thomas Gerhard (Sr. Tom)—my fullest thanks for your many hours of companionship.

Among my stateside colleagues, I thank Dr. Eduardo Gamarra, director of the Latin American and Caribbean Center at Florida International University, for his critical support of this project. To Dr. Mark Rosenberg, chancellor of the Florida State Universities, founder and former director of the Latin American and Caribbean Center at Florida International University, I give my thanks for his support and interest in my work in Yucatán. Thanks are also due to Dr. Steve Fjellman, who during his tenure as chair of the Department of Sociology/Anthropology at Florida International University was genuinely helpful in some difficult times. Also thanks to my colleagues Dr. Barry Levine of the Department of Sociology/Anthropology and Dr. Ana Roca of the Department of Modern Languages for their assistance. I wish to thank Juanita Mainster for her professionalism and dedication in double-checking my translations of Araceli's work. Any errors in translation or interpretation are my own. I owe thanks as well to Dr. Suzanna Rose, director of Women's Studies at Florida International University, for providing support to have my photographs scanned to appear in this book. My neighbor Dan Watts I thank for fine-tuning my photographs.

To the North-South Center, External Research Grant Program at the University of Miami I also owe thanks for their support of my work. In particular I would like to acknowledge their funding of two projects that aided in the production of this book: "Women's Participation in Democratization: Transforming the Mexican State," with Dra. Beatriz Castilla Ramos, codirector (1993), and "Indigenous Engagement in Political and Social Change: The Yucatec Maya Case," with Dr. Juan Castillo Cocom, codirector (1995).

And finally, I wish to thank again my family. Thanks to my parents, Robert and Barbara Rock, for their lifelong encouragement and support of my life's dreams. Thank-you to my sister Cynthia for listening and laughing. You are the world's best sister. To my brother-in-law Wally, thanks for your humor and ever-clear perspective. And thank you, my dear husband, Memo, you remain my light and my reflection. Thanks to all of you for listening to yet another story about Yucatán and viewing once again dozens of photographs of places you have never been.

—*Kathleen Rock Martín*

Trabajos realizados del r
al 8 de Febrero de 1999

Agradecer y......

Othón Baños, a Kathleen Martin, a Alan Burns a Sharón
Méjica, Beatriz Castilla, Beatriz Torres, Juan Castillo Cocom,
a las Universidades de la Florida y de Gainesville, que moti-
vados por los conocimientos sociológicos y de investigación me bus-
caron para darme la oportunidad de conocerme a mi misma,
por lo cual me inclino respetuosamente, ante la vida, al poner en
el camino del destino, que nos propició, tropezarnos en la piedra
histórica de nuestras respectivas raíces, para encontrar yo, la
conyuntura que me concede ocupar un rinconcito del Universo
Literario.
Nunca fué,.. ni pretención, ni vanidad. Nunca tuve los (s) elementos que a-
limentan esas cosas, algo así como la posición social por nombre o
linaje, mucho menos capital para comprar preferencias.
Eso si... siempre he deseado en lo profundo, superar mis conocimientos, tener los estudios necesarios que fortalezcan mi preparación, cosa que no pude obtener.
Cómo podría explicar, sin caer en la vanidad, la satisfacción que ahora me embarga, cuando recuerdo la forma en que conocí lo que
albergan las grandes Universidades de la Florida y Gainesville.
Las sircunstancias, los avatares,.. el azar.......?
No pretendo ser intelectual de renombre, con bombo y platillos, pero
quiero hacer algo, póstumo quizá, pero bueno, que sirva de heredad
a los míos, y a todo aquel que crea en las buenas intenciones.
Estoy tomando mi derecho, cumpliendo con mi obligación.
Si en el trancurso de la experiencia, en la escuela de la vida, o en
los abruptos caminos de la política, o por causas de lucha social,
dije palabras ofensivas,.o tuve actitudes agresivas,... a mis

Agradecer y . . . (Acknowledgments), page 1. See pages xiii and xiv.

Conciudadanos,.. a mi pueblo,... pido disculpas, pido perdón mi
actitud o palabra agresiva fué y seguiran siendo para defender
mi causa, como causa de todas las mujeres de mi raza.
En términos humanos las mujeres todas sean pobres, ricas, buenas
malas,...feas o bonitas pasamos las sircunstancias de......
pobreza,... abandono, frustaciones, decepciones, marginación, incomprensión ... hostigamiento,.. retos deshonestos, carga de culpas....
y grandes ingratitudes....
Con tales comportamientos, es posible que tengamos grandes defectos,
fallas, pícaras o tristes equívocos, que como consecuencias nos
dejan sinsabores, penas, pesares y hasta lágrimas,
Pero.... sabemos decir: "benditas son las lágrimas que me refrescan,..
y lavan mi pesar, que me consuelan y hacen dulce mi sinsabor."...

En fin soy una de tantas,... soy una hoja suelta, que quisiera
estacionarme en un mundo de vergel, no quisiera ser rota por
los espinos oscuros de los abrojos, o volverme polvo en las regiones
áridas,,.no quisiera ser polvo desconocido,....no quisiera ser..nada.

Agradecer y . . . (Acknowledgments), page 2. See pages xiii and xiv.

"I Begin These Essays Today"

I begin these essays today, August 28, 1994.

And . . . well, what can I say about myself. . . . It is 1994 . . . , at this moment of the day, it is 10 AM, on Sunday, August 28 . . . and I am 62 years old.

I was born December 9, 1932, in the middle of a poor family. At that time by custom my grandmother was the authority in the family who ruled her daughters-in-law.

Well, because of our poverty in my childhood we didn't have the things that rich families did. There were families of my town that were socially privileged because of their color, their economic position, and family names . . . Torres, Gonzáles, Castillos, Garcías, Novelos, León, etc.; these families lived on a street that they called the "royal street" that ended in the plaza of my town . . . Maxcanú.

The children of these families, well, they were privileged children and the youth of these families were important social figures.

Therefore, what could my sisters, brothers, and I be within this society?

Could we consider ourselves as important participants in such a world, born as we were poor in Maxcanú?

—Araceli Cab Cumí

The following pages provide the answer to this question . . .

—Kathleen R. Martín

Empiezo estos ensayos hoy domingo 28 de agosto - 1994.

Y... bueno, que puedo decir de mi...,
estoy en el año de 1994..., en este momento del día, son como las -
10 AM, es domingo 28 de agosto... ya cumpli 62 años.

Nací un nueve de diciembre del año de 1932 en el seno de   -
una familia pobre, en el tiempo donde todavía, le tocó a mi mamá
ser la nuera gobernada por la costumbre en que mi abuela pater -
na mandaba los actos de las nueras.

Sos pues fruto de esa costumbre, y por lo tanto mi niñez fué -
carente de esas cosas que sólo podrían tener las familias privile --
giadas, que en mi pueblo por aquel entonces se les conocían como
la gente que prevalecía en la sociedad por su color, su posición -
económica y por sus apellidos..., Torres, Gonzáles, Castillos, Gar-
cías, Novelos, León, etc. ...; que vivían desde una calle que le   de-
cían, calle real, hasta el centro de mi pueblo... Maxcanú.

Los niños de esas familias, pues eran niños privilegiados, y -
los jóvenes eran relevantes de figura social.

Por lo tanto, que podía ser yó junto con mis hermanos; ¿esta-
bamos dentro de esa sociedad?, ¿podiamos decirnos considerados
como parte importante participativa de este mundo, por ser naci- -
dos pobres y en Maxcanú.

Introduction

A Maya Poet and Politician, Araceli Cab Cumí

Leaning against the wall of her grandparents' abandoned home, Araceli gazes past me, and my camera, perhaps to a middle distance of memory. Fleetingly a quieter Araceli replaces the talkative, outgoing politician. As she looks beyond me, I wonder why she has such a thoughtful, somber expression? The moment passes and I never know. Yet at seventy-five Araceli Cab Cumí has had an eventful and unusual life upon which to reflect.

Araceli Cab Cumí has lived almost all of her life on the same half block where she was born in Barrio Tres Cruces, Maxcanú, Yucatán, Mexico.[1] The house in which she was born and the one in which she lived with her paternal grandparents are just across the street from the house were she and her husband lived, reared two children, and where she still resides. Her hometown is an hour's bus ride south of Mérida, the capital and largest city of Yucatán state.

Yet the achievements of Araceli Cab Cumí extend beyond the boundaries of her barrio, hometown, state, or nation. In a place and time where women are still underrepresented in partisan politics, indigenous people a rarity, and indigenous women hardly a presence at all, Araceli is a successful longtime Maya woman politician.[2] A grassroots leader and political party activist since 1960, she is the only indigenous woman to have ever been elected to the Yucatecan State Congress. She has in fact served two terms in the Congress, once in the mid-1970s and again in the early 1990s.

But Araceli Cab Cumí is also exceptional because she is a writer.[3] Over the past thirty years she has written the political speeches and position papers expected of a politician. But she has also composed essays, poetry,

Araceli Cab Cumí at former home of her grandparents.

and personal narratives. Many of the political speeches and position papers she has delivered in the Yucatecan State Congress or at other political events. Her essays, poetry, and personal narratives, however, stored in folders placed in a bookshelf by her kitchen, were unread by anyone other than Araceli until she and I began this book.

Meeting Araceli Cab Cumí

In 1993 Araceli Cab Cumí was serving her final year as a congresswoman in the Yucatecan State Congress. As a congressional representative Araceli was part of the political resurgence of Yucatecan women notable in the early 1990s—a resurgence from which they have never retreated very far.[4] In Yucatán during this time women held the three most important state offices: governor, Dulce Maria Sauri de Riancho; mayor of Mérida, Ana Rosa Payan Cervera; and chief justice of the State Supreme Court, Ligia Cortez Ortega. Such an obvious presence of women in powerful political positions was unusual for Mexico where men have long dominated the public political arena. Although Mexican women have a long history of political engagement, their election to public office has only become more common in the past twenty years.[5]

Convinced that women's increasingly greater public political presence represented a sea change in Yucatecan politics, my longtime friend and colleague Dra. Beatriz Castilla Ramos and I began a project that soon led us to meet Araceli Cab Cumí.[6] During the summer of 1993, as we made our way around the political circles of Yucatán interviewing women activists and politicians, our colleague Dr. Othón Baños Ramírez suggested we interview Congresswoman Cab Cumí.[7] Having met the congresswoman during his own work among the rural farmers of Yucatán, Othón regarded her as a thoughtful and capable politician, especially for someone with her modest formal education. He generously set up an interview with her for us.

On the day of the interview Othón and I met Araceli in her office in the Yucatecan Congress.[8] The interview with her was in its duration and intensity like few others we had that summer. Once we had seated ourselves in Araceli's unadorned office, Othón explained that I was an anthropologist who wished to interview her. He got no further than that. Araceli began an enthusiastic and prideful lecture about Maya stories, legends, and language. I found it impossible to interrupt her.

After some ten minutes Araceli hesitated briefly, appearing to collect her thoughts. Sensing that this was my best chance to redirect the interview, I interjected a question about her political career. Araceli nodded and picked up the new thread of the interview. She spoke forcefully and at length in response to my questions. Even years later reviewing the tapes from this first interview I am struck by the passion of Araceli's answers.

Ultimately we ran out of time to complete the interview. I requested that we finish it several days later. Araceli agreed and we made an appointment for the following week. At the end of this first interview Araceli commented that she enjoyed talking to me.

When I returned the next week, Araceli and I seemed familiar with each other as though we had known one another longer than the length of an unfinished interview. At this second interview, as in the first, Araceli was expansive, knowledgeable, and sometimes humorous in her responses to my questions. After the interview ended, I invited her to have a soft drink with me in the café outside the Congress building. I needed to wind down from the intensity of the interview and wanted to prolong my time with Araceli since I found her so engaging.

In the calm that followed our second interview Araceli and I walked slowly to the café chatting about nothing in particular. Once seated, Araceli's presence seemed as strong in the open outdoor café as it had confined to her small office. Some reporters had trailed us from the Congress and began to pepper Araceli with questions. She bounced their questions back, bantering easily with them in Spanish. Araceli then leaned over and whispered sidebar comments to me about the reporters. She then turned and ordered her lemonade, speaking Yucatec Maya to our waiter who seemed to know her. "A born politician!" I thought. I wanted to stay in touch with Araceli; her vitality, intellect, and self-assurance drew me. For her part Araceli seemed to enjoy my company.

From that day Araceli and I have remained in contact. Our common interest in politics and the lives of indigenous women has given us a grounding point for our relationship. Over the years we have also helped each other—Araceli by setting up interviews for me with other women politicians in Yucatán and me by advising her about international funding sources for her projects with women in her hometown of Maxcanú.[9] Over the years since we met Araceli and I have spent hours talking together in the cafés of downtown Mérida. We have occasionally traveled the roads of Yucatán to visit the ruins of ancient Maya cities, admiring their echoing beauty. Ultimately we worked together on this book in the quiet rooms of the Hotel Santa Lucía and Hotel San Juan in Mérida.

But I especially treasure the times I have spent with Araceli, her family, and her circle of women supporters in Maxcanú. Sometimes the experience as we talk around her dining room table is all-enveloping. I am especially impressed by the admiration Araceli's longtime supporters have for her. She speaks for these women. They embrace her intelligence and regard her as their leader. Araceli is a woman of their town, of their life, but one who has succeeded in the distant world of state politics as no other indigenous woman from Yucatán has. She is their beloved "Doña Ari," as they call her and as I address her, a title of both respect and affection.

Araceli's Archive

I don't remember, in the eleven years that we have known each other, when Araceli first told me that she wrote anything other than political speeches or that she kept an archive of her writings. I do remember seeing thick folders and notebooks wedged together in the bookshelf by her kitchen, part of the household scenery.

In a visit to her home in June 1996 Araceli mentioned that some years earlier an acquaintance from the Yucatecan state government had read some of her speeches and thought they should be published. But nothing had ever come of the idea. I picked up the thread, thinking that publishing Araceli's writings was an idea worth pursuing. Although I had heard her deliver impressive speeches and lectures, I had never read anything that she had written. Consequently I asked Araceli if she wished to select a sample of her writings for me to review for possible publication. She agreed and chose four pieces. Araceli selected a diarylike essay, "I Begin These Essays Today," August 28, 1994 (the opening selection of this book), and two political speeches, one focusing on women ("Women Have Always Been an Example of Self-Denial," Congressional Speech, 1974) and one concerning indigenous people ("The Solidarity of Indigenous People," Congressional Speech, 1992).[10] Since Araceli also writes poetry, she added a recently composed poem ("I Begin by Smiling to the Day," 1996) to the selection.

When I translated these four pieces into English, I was impressed with the directness and originality of her essay and political speeches. They transcended the awkwardness that sometimes comes from translation. But it was her poetry that convinced me that Araceli's writings should be published. Her poems spoke with a fine literary quality, evocatively human and rich in symbols of the natural world. Consequently, I suggested to Araceli that her writings, framed within the context of her life narrative, would make a valuable and interesting book. She agreed and we began our collaboration to write a book about her life accompanied by my translations of her writings.

An Organic Intellectual

In this book I maintain that Araceli Cab Cumí can appropriately claim an identity as an "organic intellectual," a concept developed by the late Italian philosopher, political theorist, and activist Antonio Gramsci.[11] Gramsci wrote within the context of a pre–World War II industrializing Europe where economic crisis, class conflict, and the rise of Fascism much affected him and other philosophers of the day. Because of his political activism, especially as a Marxist, he was imprisoned and wrote much of his work under the close scrutiny of prison censors. He had no experience with indigenous peoples and considerations of gender were not common in the sociopolitical writings of his time. Nonetheless I think that his concept of the organic intellectual is elastic enough to have application to other times and social contexts. In particular I think that Gramsci's concept of the organic intellectual is relevant to understanding Araceli, her writings, and her political career.

Gramsci considered all intellectuals to be part of a social group; that is, intellectuals, as a distinct, independent social category, did not exist.[12] He further distinguished between two kinds of intellectuals: traditional and organic. Gramsci defined as traditional intellectuals those employed in readily distinguishable institutional positions in literary or scientific organizations such as universities or state agencies.

Gramsci's theoretical innovation, however, was his notion of the organic intellectual. He defined organic intellectuals as the thinkers and organizers of a particular social group who were embedded within their group's living dynamic. By recognizing another category of intellectuals aside from the traditional, Gramsci gave notice to those gifted, articulate, reflective, and dedicated activists who labored not in literary or scientific organizations but within their own communities.

Thus to Gramsci, organic intellectuals are not defined as intellectuals by their employment or post within an institution. They are distinguished as intellectuals as those able to articulate the worldview of the social group to which they belong and within whose context they conduct their lives.

Gramsci maintained that from their locus within a social group, organic intellectuals are able to communicate the worldview of their group to those outside it. They are also able to position their group and individuals within it vis-à-vis the worldview they elaborate, a form of mediated representation. This mediated representation is enacted within a wider societal context that includes other social actors and institutions. Thus Gramsci maintained that organic intellectuals by their positioning from within their group provide a basis for social critique, leadership, and political activism.

Gramsci further considered organic intellectuals as those capable of envisioning and organizing a new cultural, moral, and political leadership within an emerging social group. He, following the revolutionary Marxism of his times, thought that organic intellectuals should be organized as the backbone of a class-based revolutionary political party. Gramsci depended heavily on the Marxist idea of class conflict as the overarching variable that led organic intellectuals to act as societal critics who could bring revolutionary change within the context of a revolutionary political party.

With or without revolutionary political party engagement, however, I think that organic intellectuals can perform the mediated representation between their social group and the society of which it is a part that Gramsci considered so important.[13] Further I think that organic intellectuals can create change-bringing ideas and initiate actions outside the context of class conflict as Gramsci envisioned it.

Since Gramsci's time, new or at least newly recognized bases of social organization and identity formation other than class have been conceptualized as important in understanding contemporary societies. In particular, ethnic, gender, indigenous, religious, and regional affiliations have emerged or at least been recognized as bases of social organization and collective identity.

I maintain that the contemporary indigenous peoples of the Americas represent one such example of emergent social groups. During the past several decades they have begun to organize as *indigenous peoples*, claiming and reshaping their identities. They have promoted cultural pride as contemporary peoples, often establishing their links to a preconquest indigenous past. They have undertaken political activism claiming their rights and demanding inclusion *as indigenous peoples* who are citizens of modern nations.

The Maya as the majority population in Guatemala and a significant minority in Mexico and Belize are an important component of the emergent indigenous peoples of the Americas. Most noticeably in Guatemala, the various Maya groups claim their identities as K'iché, Kaqchikel, or Q'anjob'al (among others) and perhaps more importantly, have begun a pan-Maya movement to link the diverse Maya peoples of the nation.[14] Similarly the Maya (principally the Tzeltal and Tzotzil) of the Mexican state of Chiapas have organized a social movement, growing out of a rebellion, in which they claim their indigenous identity and also their rights as *indigenous citizens* of the nation.[15]

Although there are Maya groups in the Yucatán Peninsula who organize and claim citizen rights as indigenous people, the Yucatec Maya have not yet established a panregional movement based upon an identity as Mayas. Currently the efforts are quite local, limited to forming groups that focus upon Maya theater and literature, those that seek state resources to better living standards for the Maya, groups that acknowledge and honor a Maya heritage, or ones that manage local resources as an identifiable Maya community.

Araceli through her writings and her longtime activist leadership may be a precursor of such a Maya-identified movement, especially among Yucatec Maya women.[16] She has positioned herself as a representative and spokesperson for the Yucatec Maya, especially Yucatec Maya women. Through her writings and speeches she movingly presents a worldview of a Maya woman, representative of other Yucatec Maya women. Most obviously as a political party member and congressional representative, Araceli has sought to mediate between her community and the sociopolitical institutions of Yucatecan society.

Araceli is a writer, poet, political activist, and politician. She, as her life circumstances have allowed her, lives an intellectual life, writing her own works and reading widely, especially books by and about women. In her community of Maxcanú she is recognized for her political success and admired for her intelligence. She is especially revered among the women who consider her their leader and spokesperson. These are the women who congregate at Araceli's home, sitting around her dining room table, listening and then voicing their thoughts, knowing they will be heard. Now at age seventy-five

Araceli seems to have become a respected elder remembered for her service in politics and sometimes consulted by local political activists.

Araceli roots her political agenda as an organic intellectual in the lived experience of Maya women. As a community leader she encourages agency especially on the part of women to take a hand in transforming their own lives. She especially stresses education as a path out of a life constricted by poverty and curtailed in hope. Although she is most directly concerned with Maya women, Araceli is a proponent for the rights of all women. Her advocacy of the rights of Maya women, however, occurs within the context of an advocacy on behalf of all Maya, both women and men.

In her agenda for the Maya, Araceli emphasizes certain fundamental points. As basic rights for the Maya she calls for socioeconomic equity and a role for the Maya in public policy decision making. She also notes that Maya women have special socioeconomic concerns as wives and mothers. But Araceli also claims new kinds of socioeconomic participation for Maya women based on enhanced educational and professional opportunities beyond their long-standing roles as wives and mothers.

As a writer, poet, and politician Araceli argues for the recognition of the humanity and wisdom of the Maya. In the following chapters she writes poem after essay after speech demonstrating a full range of emotions and experiences based on her life as a Maya woman. In her writings she portrays Maya women as individuals with an intellectual capacity and a fully fleshed emotional reality. Araceli underlines the relevancy of Maya culture to contemporary life, especially as a foundation for community-based approaches to solving problems and enhancing everyday life.

Araceli argues also for the inclusion of the Maya *as Maya* in all aspects of society in modern Yucatán and, by extension, Mexico. In her works she emphasizes the proud past of the ancient Maya as linked to the Maya present. She references the role of indigenous people, women especially, in the creation and construction of Mexico as a nation. As such Araceli argues for the recognition of the Maya as a part of the modern nation and their empowerment as citizens within the political system.

Yet Araceli's efforts to mediate between the community of which she is a part and the sociopolitical institutions of Yucatán were sometimes muted by resistance or nonrecognition of her role as an intellectual and leader. The representatives of political parties, male dominated and largely non-Maya, curtailed her career in politics. They only partly recognized her leadership and intellectual abilities, underplaying, or failing to recognize, her importance as a representative of a Maya community, particularly of Maya women. It seems that these political parties wanted her presence as a Maya woman but not her participation as a Maya leader.

Yet despite these obstacles, Araceli has lived her life as triumph; surmounting obstacles is the leitmotif of her life narrative. All her life seems to be an answer to the question in the last line of her poem that introduces this book, "Could we consider ourselves as important participants in such a world, born as we were poor in Maxcanú?"

A *MAYA* Woman

Currently scholars debate the term "Maya" and thus the legitimacy of a labeled "Maya" identity. Some scholars have argued that the term "Maya" is a scholarly invention and thus not indicative of a long-standing collective identity or a term that contemporary people in Yucatán routinely apply to themselves.[17] In contrast, others argue that there is a distinctly "Maya" culture with continuity from the past to the present.[18] Still others propose that terms such as "Maya" have currency among contemporary indigenous people because they are revalidating their own histories as a defense against their disadvantaged position as citizens of modern Latin American nations. Their revalidated history serves as a basis for new definitions of themselves as peoples and a basis for political action on their own behalf.[19]

Visitors to Yucatán would hear and see the term "Maya" as ubiquitous. "Maya" as a label is now widely used to market the ancient and contemporary cultures of the Yucatán Peninsula to tourists. In daily practice people in Yucatán use the term "Maya" to refer rather loosely to individuals thought to be of indigenous heritage or collectively to refer to the ancient peoples of the peninsula. Indigenous people themselves use the term in much the same way, recognizing "Maya" as a self-identity they would embrace in varying degrees depending upon the individual and the social context in which they find themselves.

For Araceli Cab Cumí, however, there is no ambiguity or nuanced debate about the meaning of the term "Maya" or the legitimacy of her identity as a "Maya" woman. Since the day I first met her, she has straightforwardly claimed and proclaimed her identity as a Yucatec Maya. Consequently, her self-definition is honored throughout this book. The term "Maya," or "Yucatec

Maya" in particular, is used in this book to reference the contemporary indigenous people of Yucatán or, depending on the context, their ancestors in keeping with Araceli's usage of the term "Maya."

It is especially important to acknowledge Araceli's self-identity as a Yucatec Maya. She not only defines herself as a Maya but she also constructs her political agenda as an activist from the basis of her indigenous identity. She, as have other indigenous political activists, seeks to build a collective identity as Maya and use this collective identity as a basis for political action. She seeks also to link the ancient Maya past with the Maya present. Araceli honors the wisdom of the Maya past and recalls it as relevant for today.

Throughout her career Araceli has centered her political agenda on her Yucatec Maya community, especially on Maya women. Her Maya community is the frequent subject of her writings as poems, essays, and political policy papers. The following chapters demonstrate that Araceli often links the contemporary Maya to a proud Maya past in her writings, claiming a continuity of identity. In her works Araceli also argues for the applicability of Maya cultural values to contemporary life and thus the ongoing relevance of Maya culture.[20] She particularly focuses upon Maya knowledge and collective, community-based approaches to the problems contemporary Maya peoples face. Araceli also maintains that such approaches could be productively applied to problems confronted by all Yucatecans whether or not they are Maya.

Araceli claims her identity as a Yucatec Maya, one of the seven million indigenous people of Belize, Guatemala, and southern Mexico who are termed "Maya" by common if debated practice. The majority of the Maya live in the same territory as their ancestors: Guatemala; the southern Mexican states of Chiapas, Tabasco, and Veracruz; or the three states of the Yucatán Peninsula, Campeche, Quintana Roo, and Yucatán. Smaller populations of Maya live in Belize. Collectively the Maya of these nations are the most populous group of indigenous people in North and Central America.

The Maya, however, despite the umbrella term "Maya," are not homogenous. They speak thirty-one distinct languages linked in their long ago common linguistic past of Proto-Mayan. Yucatec Maya is one of largest of these Maya languages with an estimated 1.5 million speakers in Belize, southern Mexico, and especially the Yucatán Peninsula.

The contemporary Maya dwell in a range of locales from the tropical lowlands to the temperate highlands to cities. They differ among themselves, not only in language or locale, but also in their histories and socioeconomic and political structures. From the 1500s until independence from Spain in 1821 or, in the case of Belize, independence from Great Britain in 1981, the history of the various Maya groups has been intertwined with that of the Spanish or British colonialists. After independence Maya history was forged within the nations of which they remain a part. Now the Maya face the culturally homogenizing and economically volatile processes of globalization as challenges to their lives as Maya.[21]

Before the conquest of their lands, the ancient Maya ruled much the same territory in which the contemporary Maya now live. Organized as city-states they were never unified into a single Maya nation and at times fiercely warred against one another. Long regarded as one of the great cultures of the Americas, the ancient Maya excelled in their knowledge of the heavens, devising a solar calendar more accurate than the European calendar of the same period. They created architecturally stunning cities, to the ruins of which tourists now flock.[22] The Maya also independently developed the concept of zero and a complex form of writing that was only decoded so that others could read it in the late twentieth century.[23] As a people with an agriculturally based economy the Yucatec Maya were also able to reach their culture peaks in the less than ideal environment of the tropical lowlands. They achieved their notable success by skillful land and water resource management in a challenging environment and by creating a social order that allowed them to harness human labor effectively.[24]

For five centuries Maya peoples have survived first conquest and then colonialism by the Spanish or British, followed by domination by the state of the modern nations in which they reside. Once part of the Spanish empire of the Americas, the Maya became disenfranchised citizens of the modern states of Guatemala and Mexico at their independence from Spain in 1821. Until its independence in 1981 Belize was a colony of Great Britain. Today the Maya are an indigenous minority within Belize and Mexico where they sometimes confront discrimination from their non-Maya fellow citizens. In Guatemala where the various Maya groups are a numerical majority, a protracted civil war, in part focused on winning rights for indigenous peoples, has only recently ended in an uneasy truce. Similarly an indigenous, largely Maya resistance movement in Chiapas, Mexico, began in 1994, which, because the underlying conflicts go unresolved, continues despite complicated and sporadic negotiations between the Zapatista rebels and the Mexican state.[25]

Maya cultural survival shows their strength and creativity as a people. The Maya have continued to thrive not only by cultural transformation,[26] but also by cultural resistance.[27] Contemporary Maya peoples are again bringing notice to their cultural genius most obviously, but not exclusively, in Guatemala where they have an enhanced presence as intellectuals, writers, and politicians.[28] Araceli Cab Cumí through her writings represents a part of this greater Maya cultural florescence, albeit emanating from Yucatán.

Why "Discarded Pages"?

As this book began to take form, the need for a title became obvious. In a visit to her home late in the summer of 1996, I asked Araceli what she wished the title to be. She paused and said, "Let me think about it" (*permítame pensar*). Our conversation then moved on, the matter of the title temporarily forgotten.

As we began to put Araceli's archive in order that day I noticed that Araceli's first written work dated from 1974. Yet her political participation actually began fourteen years earlier in 1960. I asked her why she began to write when she did, years after her political work had begun. Araceli answered, "Well, I did write some things then, earlier. But I didn't think anyone would be interested in what I wrote so I threw my writings out."[29]

I sat stunned. After a moment, I said to Araceli, "Please save anything you write—even so much as a grocery list!" She laughed and nodded. The thought that she had thrown away her earliest writings, thinking them of little value, sobered me for the rest of the day.

As we sat at Araceli's dining room table we continued to sort through the folders and loose papers of her archive. We had switched to other topics about the book, when suddenly Araceli exclaimed laughing, "*¡Hojas sueltas! ¡Es el título, eso!*" (Discarded pages! That's the title!).

"Hojas sueltas" is a complex phrase that can be translated several ways. "Hoja" can be translated from Spanish to English as "page," "leaf," or "sheet of paper" depending on the context. "Suelta" from the verb *soltar* has many meanings and as such can be translated variously as "to unfasten, loosen," "to throw away, discard," or "to fall, drop." "Hojas sueltas" thus becomes a complex phrase because of the interplay of the two words, each having a variety of meanings and consequently many possible translations.[30]

In the context of our discussion that day, however, "discarded pages" best encapsulates the meaning of what Araceli intended—a reference to her earliest work, that which she had thrown away. So in honor of her lost early writings, this book is entitled *Discarded Pages: Araceli Cab Cumí, Maya Poet and Politician*.

Given Araceli's love of wordplay, however, I think that she also referenced by the phrase "hojas sueltas" the writings she did conserve as well as the "discarded pages" of her lost early writings. Thus "hojas sueltas" was meant to include the loose or unbound pages of her archive spread out before us on her table that day. With this reference "hojas sueltas" would be translated as "loose pages." The wordplay of "hojas sueltas" thus can refer to both her lost writings and those loose pages of her archive. Had we not had the discussion that same day about her lost early work I would have thought that Araceli's use of "hojas sueltas" would have referred only to the papers in her archive spread out before us on her dining room table. Given the context of our discussion about the fate of her earliest writings, however, I think that "discarded pages" is a more telling translation.

Why Does a Yucatec Maya Woman Write in Spanish?

Araceli speaks, writes, reads, and understands both Yucatec Maya and Spanish. As a child Araceli spoke only Yucatec Maya. She began to learn Spanish as a grammar school student. At that time there were no bilingual Yucatec Maya–Spanish programs in her hometown of Maxcanú as there are now. While a student, Araceli and the other indigenous children were not permitted to speak Yucatec Maya at school.[31] Their literacy instruction was limited to Spanish.

Through her years of formal schooling, Araceli learned to speak, read, and write Spanish as a second language. But Araceli learned to read and write Yucatec Maya entirely through her own efforts as an adult in her forties.[32] In 1974, as a new congressional representative and the only indigenous person in Congress, she was asked to write a commemorative essay in Yucatec Maya on the anniversary of the assassination of Felipe Carrillo Puerto, the long-venerated former governor of Yucatán (1922–24).[33] Congressional leaders likely chose her to honor the former governor with a speech delivered in Yucatec Maya because, although not a Maya himself, Felipe Carrillo Puerto was an advocate for the Maya of Yucatán and spoke fluent Yucatec Maya.

Dissatisfied with her efforts to write the commemorative speech in Yucatec Maya, Araceli began to intensify her private study of the language. By studying the available Yucatec Maya books and consulting a bilingual Yucatec Maya–Spanish dictionary, she taught herself to read and write her first language.[34] The speech that Araceli wrote in honor of former governor Felipe Carrillo Puerto follows in chapter 4.

Once she learned to read and write Yucatec Maya, however, Araceli did not abandon Spanish as her language of composition. Why then, given the opportunity to write in Yucatec Maya, did she continue to write in a language long ago imposed by a colonial master? Araceli notes two reasons. First, she thinks that the current written forms of Yucatec Maya do not provide for all the nuances of its sounds.[35] Unfortunately the spelling of Yucatec Maya as a written language is still quite variable since it has not been standardized, as have the Maya languages of Guatemala.[36] Second, Araceli thinks that the expressiveness of Yucatec Maya vocabulary has been curtailed by recognizing only one meaning of a word when there are actually several.

In addition, Araceli notes that while many indigenous people in Yucatán speak and understand Yucatec Maya, far fewer can read or write it. Unfortunately, the limited bilingual programs in Yucatecan public schools stress Spanish-language literacy not Yucatec Maya literacy. Thus Yucatec Maya remains a living language but more as a spoken rather than written one. As indigenous people in Yucatán migrate to urban areas such as Mérida or Cancún, they and certainly their children find themselves in an ambience where Spanish is the dominant and most frequently used language not only in writing but also in speech.

Working in a second language, however, has not diminished the power or clarity of Araceli's writing. Other writers too, such as Joseph Conrad and Julia Alvarez, have composed in a second language, producing works of refinement and elegance.[37] As the Chilean writer Ariel Dorfman wrote, reflecting on his language choices:

> I have developed a linguistic ambidexterity that, I will be the
> first to admit, is not at all typical. Even so, it is within reach
> of others . . . this thrilling experience of being dual, of taking
> from one linguistic river and then dipping into the other,
> until the confluence of the two vocabularies connects distant
> communities.[38]

Writing about the Spanish conquest that imposed a foreign language on the Yucatec Maya, Araceli notes:

> We are not against the Spanish, given the logic of our times that the understanding, reason, equilibrium that ought to rule the world is dialogue and communication. What we expound is not enclosed in any blame for this past of slavery. What we do say, because it is our universal right, is that we protest with a dialogue, with reason and understanding. We do not blame the Spanish but rather the logic of the times or of history.[39]

So Araceli composes primarily in Spanish. But Araceli still writes occasionally in Yucatec Maya despite the awkwardness of its alphabetization and the lack of Yucatec Maya language literacy among many people in Yucatán. Of her sixty selections in this book, two pieces (a poem and the speech in honor of Governor Felipe Carrillo Puerto) Araceli composed originally in Yucatec Maya, translating them later into Spanish.[40]

Araceli also flavors her writing with Yucatec Maya words. In my translations of Araceli's writings I have italicized the Yucatec Maya words that she included in her Spanish-language text. Following each word is the English translation. Her original Yucatec Maya and Spanish writings are included in the text accompanied by my translations. Araceli rarely makes spelling or grammatical errors but as Spanish writers will note, Araceli sometimes omits accents, no doubt a consequence of learning Spanish as a second language.

Forward with *Discarded Pages*

When I met Araceli she presented herself as a Maya intellectual and political leader. She, as she is able, lives an intellectual's life, writing her own works and reading widely, especially books by and about women. Now that she has retired from an active, full-time engagement in politics, her writings have become more important to her as part of her self-definition as an intellectual.

In the following chapters of this book her writings are showcased within the context of her life narrative. Araceli outlines her life story in chapter 1, "Writing the Contours of a Life." In chapter 2, "The Poetry of Place and Community," Araceli locates herself through poetry in the community she seeks to represent. In chapter 3, "On Behalf of Women," and chapter 4, "An Agenda for the Maya," she details her efforts to mediate between her community and the sociopolitical structures of Yucatán as a political party activist and elected official. In chapter 5, "Poetry: 'Because I Have a Heart,'" she demonstrates her creativity as a poet, writing about the difficult and complex themes of human emotion from her perspective as a Maya woman. In chapter 6, "Endings?" Araceli describes her life now, as an older Maya woman facing widowhood, economic uncertainty, and a reduced engagement in the politics around which she has centered much of her adult life. This chapter also includes short stories by two of Araceli's granddaughters, Edna Patrón May and Zoila Espinosa Patrón, demonstrating an intellectual writing tradition that may continue in Araceli's family. In the "Conclusions" chapter, I discuss Araceli's writings and political career as a Gramscian organic intellectual.

In the longest and most inclusive of the three life narratives Araceli has written, she outlines her life story in the chapter that follows, "Writing the Contours of a Life."

From Childhood, When Ideas Began to Flow

From childhood, when ideas began to flow, . . .
I said within myself . . . I would love . . .
  I would like to be someone, . . .
someone who could get the attention of my family
    and the attention of others.
Only that, looking around, feeling the reality of my family,
    this desire had
remained hidden, . . . till today here it is
    —Araceli Cab Cumí, ca. 1999

De niña, cuando empecé a pluir ideas,...
me decía en los adentros .... quisiera....me—
gustaría llegar a ser alguien,.... alguien que
pueda llamar la atención de mi familia y
la atención ajena.
Solo que, mirando en derrodor, sintiendo la
realidad de mi familia, este deseo había
quedado oculto,.... hasta hoy que aquí
esta

CHAPTER ONE

Writing the Contours of a Life

Words are our Greatest Treasure.
—*Araceli Cab Cumí, February 1999*

A Life Narrative

In the opening poem of this chapter Araceli Cab Cumí expresses her desire for recognition rooted in intellectual achievement. As someone who is keenly intelligent but with limited formal schooling, as someone who writes as a fundamental form of self-expression yet files her work away, much of it unread by anyone but herself, Araceli desires recognition as a writer and intellectual. I have sometimes thought that she sees this book as her last chance for such recognition. As she once said to me, "The saints aren't going to help me, you are!" At age seventy-five, with her political career seemingly at an end, Araceli has few opportunities for her intellect to shine and limited venues for her writings to appear.

Araceli's writings reflect her forthright intelligence and rebounding spirit. Whether she writes love poetry or poems in tribute to her town, political speeches addressing women's issues or those of Maya campesinos, she evokes keenly etched worlds.[1] Yet the compositions in which she directs her attention to her own life are few and quite recent, all dating from the mid-1990s. Araceli writes about herself most directly in three life narratives and four short diarylike essays.[2] The three life narratives she wrote, one each year, in 1994, 1995, and 1996. The four diary essays she wrote in a single-year span from August 1994 to July 1995. Three of these essays she composed in late 1994 (August 28, September 4, and December 14), writing the final one seven months later on July 6, 1995.

It is perhaps understandable that Araceli wrote these life narrative compositions when she did. By the close of 1993 her last congressional term of office had ended. In the mid-1990s Araceli began to diminish her political activities at the state and regional level and concentrate her political engagement again in the smaller world of Maxcanú where her career had begun. With more time and some distance from her long political career, Araceli chose this occasion to write about her life.

Araceli's diarylike essays and life narratives are not self-analytical in the sense that many readers, more accustomed to the soul-baring style of much Western autobiographical writing, might anticipate them to be. Intense self-scrutiny may be Araceli's lifelong practice but the results of her self-examination do not necessarily yield a written discourse with herself at the center. In her diary, essays, and life narratives she places herself within a larger historical context and avoids positioning herself as a point around which all else would pivot. Nonetheless, despite the historical scope of her writing, Araceli's essays and life narrative compositions do define some of the contours of her life.

On the following pages is the longest and most encompassing of the three life narrative essays Araceli has written, "Life Narrative, Summer 1995," beginning "It was December 9, 1932."[3] She wrote it for the students of the Summer Intensive Introductory Course in Yucatec Maya sponsored by the Consortium in Latin American Studies at the University of North Carolina at Chapel Hill and Duke University. Under this program graduate students come each summer to Yucatán to study Yucatec Maya. Perhaps she wrote her most inclusive life narrative essay knowing that students studying Maya would read it. Araceli's other two narratives are very similar but shorter versions of this 1995 account.

Araceli's narrative retains the poetic format in which she often writes. My translation of her narrative is given first in its entirety. Following the narrative, I have written comments to frame the narrative and give it an explanatory context. In this section, divisions within the text and their titles are mine, not Araceli's. To help frame Araceli's narrative, a life chronology is given at the end of this chapter.

The Maya words with which Araceli salts her text are in italic type followed by an English translation in brackets or an explanatory endnote. The Spanish words whose meaning would be clouded by translation to English remain in Spanish, italicized with an explanatory endnote. As is the common practice in translations, I have occasionally inserted words into Araceli's text to make the English translation read more smoothly. My insertions are also bracketed. Since common Spanish writing convention allows for a longer sentence structure than does English, I have sometimes put periods where Araceli has commas, semicolons, or colons to ease the translation to English with its convention of shorter sentences. Although later chapters will add nuances to Araceli's story, the following is what Araceli thought important for her to tell others about her life:

LIFE NARRATIVE, SUMMER 1995
It was December 9, 1932. I lament that I could not select my name.
My family's origin is *campesina*,[4] heirs of the ancestral Maya.
My paternal grandparents were Romualdo Cab Uh and Dominga Pech Calderon.
My maternal grandparents were Enrique Cumi Banilla and Candelaria Carballo López.
My parents were Medardo Cab Pech and Isaura Cumi Carballo.
All of them are now in the eternal place.

Everyone in my family labored in the countryside.
I grew up in poverty in childhood as in adolescence, which strengthened me to live and to excel.
I went to school and learned to read and write in Spanish.

And so between the blows and unexpected events of the times I grew to adulthood.
I have a husband and children. That is to say that although I gave birth several times, they died so that I have only two children, Bertha Melisenda and Fernando Adrian.
My husband's name is Pablo S. Patrón C.

For this small family, I learned that my step[5] had to be stronger to try to have a better life.

But at the same time I had to learn to know myself in order to know who I am and who I ought to be so that I could reach some goal.

And so, little by little I learned that I could involve myself in political movements in my town.

In the path, in the process of doing my political activities I stumbled many times. First I suffered trying to understand that the voice of my anxieties had to be a force of constant strength. [My anxieties had] to defend me against the politics of closed ideas; had to open for me the way so that I could speak on behalf of others.

[Then] I began to search for the words that could serve as the instruments to defend the spirit of my fellow citizens, to rouse on high our eagerness for the search: once again the *sacbe* [white roads][6] of the Maya.

We do many things, this and that, we move from here to there, from there to here. A great motive is this value of ours: the respect that we want for this Maya land.

My ancestral race suffered slavery as a consequence of having been discovered by Christopher Columbus in the name of Spain.

A painful past. Maya women suffered in their flesh the lust of the conquerors, the white men that took possession of our land, of our lives for 300 years. Because of this, there are those among us who have light skin; green or even blue or light brown eyes as a consequence of the bloody seed that with the basest of intentions, they gave us.

We are not against the Spanish, given the logic of our times that the understanding, reason, equilibrium that ought to rule the world is dialogue and communication. What we expound is not enclosed in any blame for this past of slavery. What we do say, because it is our universal right, is that we protest with a dialogue, with reason and understanding. We do not blame the Spanish but rather the logic of the times or of history.

We cannot hate those who enslaved us because they were said to be kings and queens, since we ourselves are ancestors of queens and princesses and the only thing that differentiates us is our cinnamon-colored skin.

We are conscious of our presence in the stages of our history. The grand florescence of our people that inhabited the peninsula of Chacnobitán [Yucatán].[7]

> *The discovery of our land.*
> *The oppression of three hundred years.*
> *Independence.*
> *The Reform.*
> *The Imposed Dominion by the French.*
> *The Porfirian Dictatorship.*
> *The Revolution.*[8]

In the social movement of 1910, the abnegation and sacrifice of women in their absolute devotion to the altar of social justice was clear, as coparticipants in helping the men of the revolution struggle for the land that is by birth ours.

From then, the base of our struggle, our front of combat pulsates in our shawls, in our *huipils*,[9] in our *huaraches*.[10]

[Let] the leaders of world power know that our desire to win social struggles is because we want peace.

We want them to respect our right to elect freely our own best leaders to represent our people, those that have a true spirit of justice that social equilibrium can come if, as administrators of the nation's welfare, they can balance social power, distributing it equitably.

We continue looking for platforms for our words; we continue asking for understanding, a dialogue for justice and reason.
     We want dignity[11] in our homes, in education, in health,

and in all that constitutes well-being for our families. Honest work, a just salary.

[For] our *raza*,[12] it is clear, nothing is reserved for us, nothing is secret from us.

The sacrifice of our ancestral princesses was not in vain because with their lives, offered to the sacred cenotes,[13] they calmed the wrath of our gods. [Their sacrifice] revealed all the secrets [and] all the mysteries to claim a future with better days as what could be when this writing is published.

That is to say that as Maya women we have nothing to envy the heroines of Europe, nothing to envy Guinevere or Joan of Arc, nothing we desire of Cleopatra or Messalina or Lucrezia Borgia, Belle Otero, or Mata Hari or Isadora Duncan.[14] We have sufficient valor to raise up our own pride: Yucatán.

> *We have honor, we have querencia,[15] we have valor.*
> *We are good and bad*
> *We are calm, we are anxious*
> *We are rain, we are drought*
> *We are songs and poetry*
> *We are spring and winter*
>
> *Wind and breeze*
> *Laughter and crying*
> *Joy and sadness*
> *Richness and poverty*
> *Health and sickness*

In the great absence of our moral force, when the spirit feels vulnerable, we say:

> *Are we an exemplar of stains or devalued humans?*
> *Are we something that is nothing?*
> *Then to say:*
> *How our silence shouts in the infinity of loneliness!*

Some things that we didn't mention before:[16]

In my time as a student, my town had two public schools, as they called them then. I studied all the grades that they had at the time. There wasn't a kindergarten like now. My teachers were:

Little children [preschool][17]—Anastacia Garcia
First Grade—Josepa Coello
Second Grade—Antonio Zapata
Third Grade—Arsenio Mendez
Fourth Grade—Guibaldo López Lara
Fifth Grade—And again, Arsenio Mendez
The sixth grade I studied as an adult when adult education began.
The two schools I mentioned still exist, I suppose that they
    are more developed now.

In my time one was named "Manuel Cepeda Peraza no. 104."
    The other was called "Doctor Montessori no. 105."

Now both of them are combined into one: "Primary School 96 Doctor Montessori."

My career as a student was very difficult because my family had few resources.
    Another other thing is my political career. It began to advance, when in 1973, in the municipal elections after a quarrelsome electoral battle with many consequences, I was elected as a state congressional representative [*diputada suplente*][18] for a two-year period from 1974–75. But because of state affairs the term of office was cut short. The state political events were that the *diputado titular*[19] left to become director of the police and I being suplente, I took office for my district, the fifth [congressional district of Yucatán state] at that time.

During this period the International Year of Women was promoted and celebrated in Mexico. I attended the inaugural ceremony. I declare that I had no notion of what I could have done or said. I much lament that I didn't take the stand to defend my cause, which is the cause of all indigenous women.

I lament that I didn't cross paths with Domitila.[20]

From then on, I continued to pay attention to my uneasiness even more diligently.

I left the political party (the Partido Revolucionario Institucional)[21] in which I had been a longtime militant, because I felt my convictions crushed and beaten. But anyway, just as I had those against me there were also those who helped me in my [political] activities.

And so in more recent years I tried to affiliate with other [political] groups and now I have become again state congresswoman [*plurinominal*][22] of an opposition party for a three-year term.

I consider today that I have done very little [and] that my struggle is possibly passive.

In these times of crisis among the political forces of the country, perhaps the possibility of better opportunities will open for [my] aspirations. Although for indigenous women, I believe that margination continues and I will not say the opposite. I do not see clearly [that] respect [is] granted to all ethnic groups that still struggle to survive. [They make known] with their struggle [that] their customs and the value of indigenous wisdom go beyond the altars of modernity and the so-called progress of science and technology.

POSTSCRIPT:

I said that my childhood was sad. Poverty and indigence made this sadness. But I learned to read and my learning helped me understand the world. It made me learn to observe each day, each night, each moon, each sun, each star.

Money is important, yes, but an excess of material things makes us forget that stronger than ambition there exists a world, a universe, a life that wants, that desires our human attention.

Understanding this then I assert that thanks to the poverty and indigence of my childhood, because of these, a rosebush grew that blossomed into my feelings, illusions, ideals.

These are my riches.
This is my heritage.

original pages on pages 47–60

The following sections offer an explanatory context for Araceli's life narrative.

Opening the Story

Araceli sets the contours of her life as a story in a circle—beginning and ending with herself. But in the curves of the story she writes a capsule history of the Yucatec Maya that bends into a Mexican history and turns at the end to her agenda for a better life for her fellow Maya. Even though this is her life narrative Araceli does not dwell exclusively or even particularly upon herself as an individual. Araceli opens the narrative with a note about herself but she quickly moves off center stage to allow politics and history to become the focus.

Araceli roots her life narrative in her Maya identity and her activism on behalf of the Maya, especially Maya women. She proclaims her self-identity as a Yucatec Maya in the first line of her narrative by noting the difficulty, for indigenous people, of the not-so-simple matter of choosing a name for a child. "It was December 9, 1932. I lament that I could not select my name." She emphasizes here that she could not choose her own name.

When Araceli was baptized as a Roman Catholic, her parents chose a ladino couple as her godparents.[23] Perhaps Araceli's parents thought, as had other poor indigenous parents, that by asking a more economically advantaged and socially privileged ladino couple to be their child's godparents they would confer some sort of social advantage on their child. By linking Araceli as a godchild to godparents more wealthy or powerful than they were, Araceli's parents may have thought that her godparents might help her as their godchild, providing her with some future benefit.

So Araceli's ladino godparents chose her baptismal name. As befitting their own cultural heritage, her godparents chose a Spanish, Araceli Angelica de Jesus, not Maya, name. Had the choice been hers, Araceli would have preferred a Maya name.[24]

Name choice remains problematic for Araceli as an indigenous person. Despite Araceli's objection to her own name, she and her husband have chosen Spanish names for their children, Bertha and Fernando.[25] Araceli says that they chose such names to avoid the discrimination people with

Maya names and thus assumed Maya identities often face. Also, at the time her children were baptized, Roman Catholic Church officials customarily rejected Maya names as inappropriate baptismal names, suggesting instead that the names of Catholic saints were more appropriate.[26] Araceli's children in turn have continued the practice of giving their children Spanish names. Only Araceli's eldest grandchild (Bertha's eldest child) possesses a Maya name, Zazil ("clear light," sometimes translated as "dawn").

Araceli continues describing her ancestry and childhood.

> My family's origin is *campesina*, heirs of the ancestral Maya.
> My paternal grandparents were Romualdo Cab Uh and Dominga Pech Calderon.
> My maternal grandparents were Enrique Cumi Banilla and Candalaria Carballo López.
> My parents were Medardo Cab Pech and Isaura Cumi Carballo.
> All of them are now in the eternal place.
> Everyone in my family labored in the countryside.
> I grew up in poverty in childhood as in adolescence, which strengthened me to live and to excel.
> I went to school and learned to read and write in Spanish.
> And so between the blows and unexpected events of the times I grew to adulthood.

Poverty bounded Araceli's childhood and adolescence. Since her grandparents' time her family has lived in Maxcanú and farmed plots on the outskirts of town, raising a base crop of corn but also growing beans, chiles, squashes, tomatoes, and tropical fruits such as jicama, a crop for which Maxcanú is renowned. Her family was poor as many campesinos in Yucatán still are. But here as elsewhere in her writings Araceli notes a recurring theme of her life—her resilience tempered by adversity. She cites this resilience as the material from which she has crafted her life's triumphs. Learning to read and write in Spanish was one such triumph. Denied literacy in Yucatec Maya as a child, she took root in Spanish and made the language her own.

When Araceli writes, "And so between the blows and unexpected events of the times I grew to adulthood," she refers in particular to a sad, disruptive time in her early adolescence. When Araceli was fourteen, her father left his wife and their five children (Araceli, her two sisters, and two brothers) to start a new family with another woman. His abandonment plunged his wife and children further into poverty. Araceli, her mother, and siblings went to live with her paternal grandparents, the parents of the father who had abandoned them. As a familial obligation that they reluctantly shouldered, her paternal grandparents housed Araceli, her mother, and siblings. Sometimes Araceli was sent to live with other relatives and occasionally with her father. As such *niños abandonados* (abandoned children), Araceli thought that she and her sisters and brothers were seen as children less worthy of love and care because their father had abandoned them. As the eldest of the five children, Araceli was the adolescent witness to her mother's struggle to provide for her shattered family and endure the personal humiliation caused by her husband's abandonment.[27]

Araceli writes about her marriage and children:

I have a husband and children. That is to say that although I gave birth several times, they died so that I have only two children, Bertha Melisenda and Fernando Adrian.

My husband's name is Pablo S. Patrón C.

Araceli married Pablo when she was eighteen. In her narrative Araceli mentions their two children, Bertha Melisenda and Fernando Adrian. Araceli says that she would have liked to have more children. In repeated episodes that caused her great sadness, however, Araceli became pregnant only to have the infant die shortly after birth or be stillborn. As she later discovered, the likely cause of her traumatic pregnancies was an internal injury resulting from the difficult birth of her first child. The scant medical care available to Araceli left her injury undiagnosed and untreated.

When Araceli married Pablo they lived with his parents following a social convention of the times.[28] In less than a year, however, conditions in Araceli's in-laws' home became intolerable for the young couple. Araceli and Pablo moved into their as yet only partially completed home, so eager were they to escape ill treatment by Pablo's parents. In this house they raised their two children. And here they lived together until Pablo's death in June 2002.

Araceli and Pablo shared an enlarged two-house compound with their son, Fernando, his wife, Eneyda, and their four children. The family houses

*Araceli Cab Cumí and her husband, Pablo Patrón Cih,
in their backyard with their favorite dog.*

have the long-established oval shape of many houses in Yucatán, with plas-
ter-finish walls and intricately thatched roofs. Their houses share a common
wall with an interconnecting door that is almost always open. In their narrow
but deep backyard Araceli and her family raise some chickens, grow some
tropical fruits, and keep their pet watchdogs. Since Pablo's death, Araceli has
continued to live in the same house compound.

Throughout his life Araceli's husband, Pablo, was a corn farmer. At times
he tried also to make a living by working at other occupations. Pablo migrated
to work as a bracero (day laborer) in the United States for a time. He also
had a dry goods stall at the local Maxcanú municipal market for many years
but ultimately closed it as business declined. Pablo died in June 2002 after
several years of a debilitating illness. Araceli's homage to him appears in
chapter 6, "Endings?"

Political Awakening

While chapter 3, "On Behalf of Women," and chapter 4, "An Agenda for the
Maya," discuss Araceli's political career in detail, in the following passage
she introduces some of the most important facets of her political work:

> For this small family, I learned that my step had to be stronger to
> try to have a better life.
>
> But at the same time I had to learn to know myself in order
> to know who I am and who I ought to be so that I could reach
> some goal.
>
> And so, little by little I learned that I could involve myself in
> political movements in my town.
>
> In the path, in the process of doing my political activities I
> stumbled many times. First I suffered trying to understand that
> the voice of my anxieties had to be a force of constant strength.
> [My anxieties had] to defend me against the politics of closed
> ideas; had to open for me the way so that I could speak on behalf
> of others.
>
> [Then] I began to search for the words that could serve as the
> instruments to defend the spirit of my fellow citizens, to rouse
> on high our eagerness for the search: once again the *sacbe* [white
> roads] of the Maya.
>
> We do many things, this and that, we move from here to

there, from there to here. A great motive is this value of ours: the
respect that we want for this Maya land.

Araceli writes of the stumbling inexperience that marked her entry into
politics. She also describes the concern for her family that propelled her
into her initial political participation. By mentioning her responsibilities as
a mother and housewife, Araceli expresses a consciousness of herself as a
woman that is embedded in the supporting strands of family and community. Yet she notes that as a necessity of her political participation, she also
had to possess self-knowledge and grow as an individual and a woman as
part of her activist experience.[29] Ultimately Araceli arrives as a politician by
becoming a spokeswoman for her community and especially Maya women.
Araceli mentions here a central theme of her political career, the respect for
the Maya and their culture as contemporary peoples linked at least figuratively to the ancient Maya past.

Araceli often writes about the Maya women she has spent a lifetime
representing. In the passage below she discusses the Spanish conquest from
the perspective of Maya women:

> My ancestral race suffered slavery as a consequence of having
> been discovered by Christopher Columbus in the name of Spain.
>   A painful past. Maya women suffered in their flesh the lust of
> the conquerors, the white men that took possession of our land,
> of our lives for 300 years. Because of this, there are those among
> us who have light skin; green or even blue or light brown eyes
> as a consequence of the bloody seed that with the basest of
> intentions, they gave us.
>   We are not against the Spanish, given the logic of our times
> that the understanding, reason, equilibrium that ought to rule the
> world is dialogue and communication. What we expound is not
> enclosed in any blame for this past of slavery. What we do say,
> because it is our universal right, is that we protest with a dialogue,
> with reason and understanding. We do not blame the Spanish
> but rather the logic of the times or of history.

As Araceli expresses it, a major impact of the conquest was played out
on the bodies of indigenous women. As laborers in *encomiendas* and on

haciendas indigenous women labored in the fields and estates of the conquerors who also used them as sexual chattel. In Araceli's view it was in their violation that indigenous women became legitimate cofounders of the Mexican nation.

Araceli is certainly not alone in making such an analysis. Octavio Paz, Nobel Laureate in Literature (1990), in his classic analysis of Mexican culture, *The Labyrinth of Solitude* (1961), also traces the founding of the Mexican nation to the violation of indigenous women by the conquering Spanish. His analysis of the conquest argues that the violent birth of Mexico as a culture still shapes the gender identity and roles of Mexican women and men.

Locally in Mérida, a mural in the City Hall painted by the Yucatecan artist Lizama (part of a series illustrating the history of Yucatán state) provides a pictorial expression of this birth of a nation theme. Entitled *Mérida, Crisol de dos razas* (Mérida, the Crucible of Two Races), the mural depicts a nonviolent and purely conceived role for indigenous women in the birth of the Mexican nation. In the center of the mural a young Maya woman arises surrounded by light. She herself is not giving birth (*dar la luz*: literally "to give light," figuratively "to give birth") but by her central presence in the mural surrounded by light it is clear that *she* is the one born, but as an adult, fully-grown woman. Thus the mural places Maya women at the center of Mexico's creation but without any direct or graphic reference to rape. Lizama painted the conquest as a glorious birth of a nation absent the violation that lay at its root.

What is different in Araceli's view of the conquest and those of Paz and Lizama is that for her as a Maya woman the sexual violation of the Spanish conquest is personal, deeply felt, and direct in its pain. For Paz and Lizama the conquest is a long-distant but significant event that shaped their culture and nation.

Araceli's writing about Maya women emphasizes their value and humanity but also their marginalization and loneliness. The humanity of Maya women coupled with their feelings of separation and difference as indigenous women are major themes in Araceli's writings.

But Araceli also notes the nobility of the Maya by comparing them to the nobility of the Spanish in the passage:

> We cannot hate those who enslaved us because they were said to
> be kings and queens, since we ourselves are ancestors of queens

and princesses and the only thing that differentiates us is our cinnamon-colored skin.

Araceli argues that while the Spanish claimed nobility, the Maya also were the descendants of queens and kings—only their cinnamon skin distinguished them from the Spanish as nobles. Araceli links the subjugated Maya and Spanish conquerors together in a commonality of nobility.

During the time that Araceli was a congresswoman in the early 1970s she met another kind of European nobility when Queen Elizabeth II of Great Britain toured Yucatán. The queen's entourage visited the ancient Maya site of Uxmal not far from Araceli's hometown on February 27, 1975. On this occasion Araceli was introduced to the queen along with other political leaders and congressional representatives. A story, perhaps apocryphal, is told that the queen was introduced to a Maya leader, Gaspar Antonio Xiu, and told that he was a descendant of the royal Yucatec Maya lineage of the Xiu. The queen asked Sr. Xiu if he was really a prince. To which he is reputed to have answered, "Are you really a queen?" This humorous story is part of Araceli's vivid memory of her introduction to Queen Elizabeth II. Whether literally true or not, to Araceli the story credits Sr. Xiu's ready wit and his self-assurance as a Maya.[30] Araceli obviously appreciated the humor of the story, retelling it to me with relish.

Women's Place in History

Araceli writes Maya women into Mexican history in the following passage:

We are conscious of our presence in the stages of our history.
The grand florescence of our people that inhabited the
peninsula of Chacnobitán [Yucatán].
>   *The discovery of our land.*
>   *The oppression of three hundred years.*
>   *Independence.*
>   *The Reform.*
>   *The Imposed Dominion by the French.*
>   *The Porfirian Dictatorship.*
>   *The Revolution.*
In the social movement of 1910, the abnegation and
sacrifice of women in their absolute devotion to the altar

of social justice was clear, as coparticipants in helping
the men of the revolution struggle for the land that is by
birth ours.

From then, the base of our struggle, our front of combat
pulsates in our shawls, in our *huipils*, in our *huaraches.*

Araceli first establishes a Yucatec Maya presence in Mexican history:
"We are conscious of our presence in the stages of our history. The grand
florescence of our people that inhabited the peninsula of Chacnobitán
[Yucatán]." She follows with a commonly used periodization of her nation's
history to highlight events she considers important. She begins noting the
first landfall of the Spanish in Yucatán in 1517 and then mentions the protracted conquest of the peninsula followed by 304 years of colonial rule.
Independence from Spain came in 1821. "The Reform" refers to the mid-
nineteenth-century period when leaders of the newly independent Mexico
sought to bring their ideas of order and progress to the republic. During
this period Mexico had its first and thus far only indigenous president,
Benito Juárez, a Mixtec from the southern state of Oaxaca. In 1861 the
French invaded Mexico and imposed an imperial monarchy headed by an
Austrian archduke, Ferdinand Maximilian, and his wife, Marie Charlotte
Amélie Léopoldine. "The Porfirian Dictatorship" refers to the long rule of
Porfirio Díaz from 1876 to 1910. The Mexican Revolution from 1910 to 1920
began to set the path for the development of the modern Mexican state.

But among these periods of Mexican history Araceli chooses to highlight the Mexican Revolution of 1910, a significant event that helped establish modern Mexico. Although Mexico won its independence from Spain
in 1821, in the early twentieth century Mexico fought a revolution within
its own borders to rid itself of a feudal class structure and unite its dispa-
rate regions as a nation.[31] Many indigenous people as well as others who
were also impoverished and marginalized fought and died in what became
Mexico's most devastating war. Araceli notes women's role along with men
in the Mexican Revolution: "The abnegation and sacrifice of women in
their absolute devotion to the altar of social justice was clear, as coparticipants in helping the men of the revolution struggle for the land that is by
birth ours." Finally she feminizes this revolutionary history by referencing
women's dress: "Our front of combat pulsates in our shawls, in our *huipils*,
in our *huaraches.*"

A Maya Agenda for the Future

Araceli continues with an agenda for the future. She writes:

> [Let] the leaders of world power know that our desire to win
> social struggles is because we want peace.
>
> We want them to respect our right to elect freely our own
> best leaders to represent our people, those that have a true spirit
> of justice that social equilibrium can come if, as administrators
> of the nation's welfare, they can balance social power, distributing
> it equitably.
>
> We continue looking for platforms for our words; we
> continue asking for understanding, a dialogue for justice
> and reason.
>
> We want dignity in our homes, in education, in health,
> and in all that constitutes well-being for our families. Honest
> work, a just salary.
>
> [For] our *raza*, it is clear, nothing is reserved for us, nothing
> is secret from us.

Arising from what to Araceli are the still unrealized goals of the Mexican Revolution, she states her political platform: peace, free elections, and socioeconomic equity. She also asks for political dialogue, openings, and opportunity: "We continue looking for platforms for our words; we continue asking for understanding, a dialogue for justice and reason."

Araceli also asks that the dignity of the Maya as a people and as individuals be respected: "We want dignity in our homes, in education, in health, and in all that constitutes well-being for our families." Embedded in her request is the idea of respect for the Maya as *indigenous people* as citizens of Mexico, not as assimilated others.

She continues in her narrative by noting the Maya awareness of all that takes place in society. Perhaps from this awareness a greater Maya participation or inclusion in Mexican political life could be built: "[For] our *raza*, it is clear, nothing is reserved for us, nothing is secret from us."

Maya Women at the Center

In the next passage Araceli places Maya women within the context of Maya history once again. She begins:

The sacrifice of our ancestral princesses was not in vain because with their lives, offered to the sacred cenotes, they calmed the wrath of our gods. [Their sacrifice] revealed all the secrets [and] all the mysteries to claim a future with better days as what could be when this writing is published.

In this passage Araceli links the sacrifices of the ancient Maya princesses and the beneficial results of their sacrifice to benefits that could come if her writings were to be published. She wrote this life narrative after a government official had told Araceli that her work should be published. Unfortunately the official never acted on the idea, disappointing Araceli. She wrote this narrative a year before she and I discussed publishing her writings. Consequently Araceli's reference in the text to her writings being published is likely an expression of a wish rather than a foretelling of the future.

In the next passage Araceli compares Yucatec Maya women favorably and honorably with illustrious women from other nations and times:

That is to say that as Maya women we have nothing to envy the heroines of Europe, nothing to envy Guinevere or Joan of Arc, nothing we desire of Cleopatra or Messalina or Lucrezia Borgia, Belle Otero, or Mata Hari or Isadora Duncan. We have sufficient valor to raise up our own pride: Yucatán.

As an avid reader, especially of works about women, Araceli is well versed in women's history. She lists this rather eclectic collection of eight historically famous women about whom she has read. All of these women, however, share the characteristics of fame, power, and influence. They all lived complex, engaged lives and perhaps this is why Araceli chose to highlight them in her narrative.

By using the term "querencia" (see endnote 15) in the following stanza, Araceli roots Maya women deeply and emotionally in the Yucatecan homeland, arguing that they rightfully belong embedded in this place. In perhaps the most moving and lyrical passage in this life narrative, Araceli exalts the humanity of Maya women:

We have honor, we have querencia, *we have valor.*
We are good and bad
We are calm, we are anxious

We are rain, we are drought
We are songs and poetry
We are spring and winter
Wind and breeze
Laughter and crying
Joy and sadness
Richness and poverty
Health and sickness

Araceli completes this passage by describing the despair and loneliness that Maya women sometimes feel as indigenous women:

In the great absence of our moral force, when the spirit
  feels vulnerable, we say:
Are we an exemplar of stains or devalued humans?
Are we something that is nothing?
Then to say:
How our silence shouts in the infinity of loneliness!

The sense of separateness, difference, and loneliness that Araceli cites in this passage is a recurring theme that she also uses to describe her own state of mind elsewhere in her writings. It is significant that she writes, "Are we an exemplar of stains or devalued humans?" The stain Araceli refers to here likely represents the concept of cleansing of blood (*limpieza de sangre*). When the Spanish colonists arrived in the New World they viewed indigenous people as inferior. Thus there was great concern about maintaining the "pure bloodlines" (*limpieza pura*) of the Spanish by marriage and procreation within the Spanish community. Continuing the metaphor, any indigenous inheritance was regarded as a stain on the individual. Thus Araceli couples the idea of indigenous people as "stains" with the notion of "devalued humans" to describe the experience of Maya women.

Education

Araceli writes about her school years:

In my time as a student, my town had two public schools, as they called them then. I studied all the grades that they had at the time. There wasn't a kindergarten like now. My teachers were:

Little children [preschool]—Anastacia Garcia
First Grade—Josepa Coello
Second Grade—Antonio Zapata
Third Grade—Arsenio Mendez
Fourth Grade—Guibaldo López Lara
Fifth Grade—And again, Arsenio Mendez

The sixth grade I studied as an adult when adult education began.
   The two schools I mentioned still exist, I suppose that they
are more developed now.
   In my time one was named "Manuel Cepeda Peraza no. 104."
   The other was called "Doctor Montessori no. 105."
   Now both of them are combined into one: "Primary School
96 Doctor Montessori."
   My career as a student was very difficult because my family
had few resources.

To Araceli education is exceptionally important. Schooling taught her
to read and write Spanish and thus she learned the skills to begin a lifetime
of writing. Araceli studied as a child through the fifth grade—as far as the
schools in Maxcanú allowed at that time. At the end of her fifth year Araceli
wished to study more but she was unable to do so. Education was so important to her that even now, more than half a century later, Araceli remembers
the names of her grammar school teachers. Araceli completed the sixth and
final year of her grammar school education as an adult. She then became a
teacher herself, giving literacy classes to other adults in Maxcanú.
   The rural schoolteachers of Araceli's adult education classes encouraged
her involvement in community activities and in government-sponsored
cultural missions. These missions enabled Araceli to take guitar and singing lessons. She also joined a choral group that was ultimately disbanded
because too few women were able to participate. According to Araceli, few
women took part because of prejudice by their husbands and other family
members who were against women joining in such an activity outside their
homes, thinking that the women would neglect their household and familial responsibilities.
   Araceli's teachers in her adult education classes were also influential
in her life because they were the first to urge her to seek elective office. Her

successes in winning political posts in Maxcanú, for which the teachers had encouraged her to run, marked the beginning of her political career.

As in Araceli's life, it is important to note that rural schoolteachers in Mexico have been very important generators of change. By bringing formal education to remote or underserved rural areas of their nation they have not only educated people but also empowered them. A theme in Araceli's life is that despite the prejudice against indigenous people in Mexico many people have recognized her talent and encouraged her. The schoolteachers and the cultural missions workers in Maxcanú helped her complete her education and then become a literacy instructor herself. They encouraged her participation in art classes and musical events. These same people recognized her leadership abilities and encouraged her entrance into politics.[32]

Politics

Araceli writes about the progress in her political career:

> Another other thing is my political career. It began to advance, when in 1973, in the municipal elections after a quarrelsome electoral battle with many consequences, I was elected as a state congressional representative [*diputada suplente*] for a two-year period from 1974–75. But because of state affairs the term of office was cut short. The state political events were that the *diputado titular* left to become director of the police and I being suplente, I took office for my district, the fifth [congressional district of Yucatán state] at that time.

While the intricacies of Araceli's political career are discussed in chapters 3 and 4, she outlines her career in this passage of her narrative. She writes that her first victory beyond the local level came in 1974. Running as second on a winning ticket with a ladino politician, Carlos Jesus Capetillo Campos, from the PRI (Partido Revolucionario Institucional, the long-dominant political party in Mexico), Araceli was able to take a seat in the Yucatecan Congress when Sr. Capetillo Campos was appointed as state-wide director of police and thus had to surrender his newly won congressional seat. Araceli represented the fifth district in which her hometown of Maxcanú is located.

She continues:

During this period the International Year of Women was
promoted and celebrated in Mexico. I attended the inaugural
ceremony. I declare that I had no notion of what I could have
done or said. I much lament that I didn't take the stand to defend
my cause, which is the cause of all indigenous women.

I lament that I didn't cross paths with Domitila.

From then on, I continued to pay attention to my uneasiness
even more diligently.

In this section of her narrative Araceli refers to the United Nations
International Year of Women, which opened with ceremonies, followed by
several days of meetings, in Mexico City in 1975. Then in her first year in the
Yucatecan State Congress, Araceli attended as a representative from Mexico.
Clearly she was dissatisfied with her own silence and lack of participation in
this important international event. She especially regrets not speaking on
behalf of indigenous women nor meeting one of the best known indigenous
women at the meetings, Domitila Barrios de Chungara, the famous labor
and community leader from Bolivia, author of a well-known autobiography
(*Testimony of Domitila, A Woman of the Bolivian Mines: Let Me Speak!*).
This experience in self-censorship, however, left Araceli more watchful of
her silence.

Araceli describes her continued political involvement:

I left the political party [the PRI] in which I had been a longtime
militant, because I felt my convictions crushed and beaten. But
anyway, just as I had those against me there were also those who
helped me in my [political] activities.

In a move that would mark her departure from the political establishment of the time, Araceli left the PRI because of what she thought were the
party's manipulative policies especially regarding women. She left knowing
that she had political enemies but also still political supporters.

She writes further: "And so in more recent years I tried to affiliate with
other [political] groups and now I have become again state congresswoman
[*plurinominal*] of an opposition party for a three-year term."

As Mexico transforms from a single-party democracy that was dominated by the PRI throughout much of the twentieth century to a multiparty

democracy, other political parties have flourished. In 1990 Araceli again served in Congress, this time for a full three-year term. By the time of her second term in office, however, she had changed her political party affiliation to serve as a representative of the Partido del Frente Cardenista para la Reconstrucción Nacional (the Party of the Cardenista Front for the National Reconstruction). The PFCRN was originally formed as the Socialist Workers' Party in 1975. It adopted its new name in 1988 when joining a coalition of leftist parties that sought to challenge the long dominant PRI.

In Yucatán a dissident member of the PRI, Jose Maria "Pepe" Escamilla, left the party and organized a local affiliate of the Frente Cardenista. He came to Maxcanú to invite Araceli to join the Frente, which she did. Araceli was then elected as a member from the Frente Cardenista under the Mexican electoral system whereby minority parties are allocated seats in Congress depending upon the percentage of the total vote the party has won in state elections.

Yet Araceli's tenure with the Frente Cardenista was short. She resigned from the Frente amid her congressional term because she was disenchanted with the party's internal politics. Shortly thereafter she began to affiliate with another new political party, the left-of-center, PT (Partido de Trabajo, Workers' Party). After her term of office ended Araceli continued her membership in the PT, holding various party offices until 1995 when she left the PT in a regional dispute with the party's central leadership.

Araceli continues:

> I consider today that I have done very little [and] that my
> struggle is possibly passive. In these times of crisis among the
> political forces of the country, perhaps the possibility of better
> opportunities will open for [my] aspirations. Although for
> indigenous women, I believe that margination continues and I
> will not say the opposite. I do not see clearly [that] respect [is]
> granted to all ethnic groups that still struggle to survive. [They
> make known] with their struggle [that] their customs and the
> value of indigenous wisdom goes beyond the altars of modernity
> and the so-called progress of science and technology.

In this closing passage tracing her political career, Araceli writes from the position of one no longer involved in electoral politics. After more than thirty years Araceli has chosen to return to the political sidelines, seemingly doubtful that her career has resulted in much that benefited women, the Maya, or, in particular, Maya women.

She, however, writes hopefully that new possibilities may arise for her political participation. Her hopeful analysis of her own career does not indicate that she thinks the future will necessarily be hopeful for women or indigenous people. Araceli notes that women are still on the societal margins and that indigenous peoples do not receive respect for their culture.

In her last sentence of this passage, Araceli refers to a theme that is a central plank in her political platform: "[They make known] with their struggle [that] their customs and the value of indigenous wisdom goes beyond the altars of modernity and the so-called progress of science and technology." She maintains that the knowledge of indigenous people is timeless and thus is relevant to contemporary life. In a statement critical of modern science and technology Araceli further notes that the historical depth of indigenous knowledge extends beyond the bounds of these newer forms of knowledge.

Closing the Story

Araceli closes her life narrative by writing:

> POSTSCRIPT:
> I said that my childhood was sad. Poverty and indigence made this sadness. But I learned to read and my learning helped me understand the world. It made me learn to observe each day, each night, each moon, each sun, each star.
>
> Money is important, yes, but an excess of material things makes us forget that stronger than ambition there exists a world, a universe, a life that wants, that desires our human attention.
>
> Understanding this then I assert that thanks to the poverty and indigence of my childhood, because of these, a rosebush grew that blossomed into my feelings, illusions, ideals.
>
> These are my riches.
> This is my heritage.

In her "Postscript" Araceli expresses a repeating leitmotif of her life— her triumph over adversity, especially poverty. Intellect was her weapon, literacy her tool. As Araceli said in an interview in 1999: "I couldn't study more, I couldn't be a teacher, painter, or anthropologist. So I wrote."

Conclusions

As Araceli outlines her life story through her narrative, she has had an eventful and unusual life. Later chapters will flesh out the structure of Araceli's life as depicted in her writings, our interviews, and conversations.

According to Gramsci's definition of an organic intellectual, Araceli is embedded in the living dynamic of her community, able to articulate a worldview of Yucatec Maya women as a Maya woman herself, and a representative of such women. Through her editorials, political speeches, and position papers she expresses this view to others, in some cases to her fellow legislators, in others to a more general public, and in the case of her life narrative in this chapter, to American graduate students interested in the Yucatec Maya.

Particularly notable in Araceli's life narrative is her positioning of indigenous women within the sociopolitical context of Mexican history—a position from which they make claim to their rights as citizens. She especially notes indigenous women's painful role in the formation of the Mexican nation and their dedication to Mexico during its tumultuous early twentieth-century revolution.

In various portions of her narrative Araceli provides a critique of state policies and actions toward indigenous people. She then outlines her own policy platform, which includes socioeconomic equity, recognition of the humanity and wisdom of the Maya, and their inclusion as indigenous peoples in all aspects of the life of Mexico as a nation and a culture.

Araceli highlights her career as a community activist and then as political party participant trying to mediate between her Yucatec Maya community and the sociopolitical institutions of the state. Her statements of frustration and perhaps personal failure are tempered by her expressions of a continuing hope for a better future for the Maya.

Araceli has built her political career from a local base in her hometown of Maxcanú and then gone on to represent the Yucatec Maya, especially as a spokeswoman for Maya women. Within her community she is admired for her intellect and respected for her advocacy on behalf of the Maya. Her repeated references to education, history, and the legitimacy and relevance of Maya knowledge keynote her self-definition as a Maya intellectual. In closing Araceli highlights writing as a tool that allowed her to triumph over the obstacles she confronted.

Araceli's lifelong residence in Maxcanú has bounded her life. In the next chapter, "The Poetry of Place and Community," she describes her bond to Maxcanú and its surrounding natural world. She also honors some of the people who are part of her community. Araceli locates herself through poetry in the community she seeks to represent.

Araceli Cab Cumí

1932   Born in Maxcanú, Yucatán, Mexico, on December 9.

1950   Marries Pablo Patrón Cih.

1952   Daughter Bertha born.

1957   Son Fernando born.

1960   Begins political career as grassroots leader in Maxcanú. Volunteer adult literacy instructor.

1965   Enters partisan politics by joining the local PRI in Maxcanú.

1967   Elected to city council of Maxcanú (*regidora*).

1971   Elected to serve as principal secretary of women's interest section of PRI campesino organization.

1973   Runs as PRI candidate suplente for Yucatecan State Congress from fifth district.

1974–75   Takes seat in Yucatecan State Congress as diputada suplente and serves nearly complete term.

1975   Participant in UN Conference on the International Year of Women. Serves in various offices within PRI including Women's Committee of the PRI.

1982   Participates in presidential campaign of PRI candidate Miguel de la Madrid and is panelist in a citizen-consulting forum on municipal restructuring. Receives grammar school diploma under National Institute for Adult Education program.

1987   Resigns from the PRI and joins the PFCRN.

1990   Elected to Yucatecan Congress as member of the PFCRN.

1991   Resigns from PFCRN and joins the PT; serves out congressional term as member of PT.

1994   Ends term of office as congressional representative in Yucatecan State Congress. Runs as unsuccessful candidate for the Mexican Senate from the PT. Becomes president of the civil association Kaxan-Alabolal (Searching for Hope). Gives lecture on Maya women at Florida International University and presents paper at the "Wisdom of the Maya" conference at the University of Florida.

2002 Husband, Pablo, dies after a long illness. Joins Nueva Izquierda faction of the PRD.

2005 Begins various development projects with members of her civil association.

Estaba con fecha de Diciembre 9 del año
1,932. Lamento no haber podido escoger mi
nombre.

Mi raiz familiar es campesina, heredera de
la ancestral maya.
Mis abuelos paternos se llamaron
Romualdo Cab Utt y Dominga Poch Calderon
Mis abuelos maternos se llamaron
Enrique Comi Bonilla y Candelaria Carballo López.
Mis padres se llamaron
Medardo Cab Pech e Isaura Comi Carballo.
Todos ellos estan ya en el lugar eterno.

Toda mi familia estuvo compuesta por hombres
y mujeres laboradores del campo.
Creci en la pobreza y tanto mi niñez como
en mi adolescencia, hube de esforzarme para
vivir y sobresalir.
Fui a la escuela y aprendi a leer y escribir
en español.

Y así entre los golpes y avataros de la época,
llegué a la edad adulta.
Tuve pareja y tuve hijos es decir, tuve
partos y de ellos en la mayoría malos, solo
me dejaron dos hijos. Bertha Melisenda y
Fernando Adrián.
El nombre de mi pareja es Pablo S. Patrón C.

Por esta pequeña familia, aprendí que mi
caminar tenía que ser mas esforzado para
tratar de tener una mejor vida, pero al
mismo tiempo tenía que aprender a
reconocerme a mí misma, para saber quién
soy y como debo ser y hacia donde podría
alcanzar alguna meta.

Así, poco a poco aprendí que podía invo-
lucrarme en los movimientos políticos, dentro
de mi pueblo.
En el camino, en el proceso de mis actividades
tuve muchos tropiezos, sufrí para entender
que la voz de mis inquietudes tenían que

ser de la fuerza de la constancia firme
para, primero, dependerme de los políticos de ideas cerradas, para abrirme
el camino y poder hablar por los demás.

Empecé a buscar para encontrar. las
palabras que como instrumento que sirvan
para depender el esfuerzo de mis con-
ciudadanas, levantar en alto nuestro anhelo
de búsqueda: otra vez los caminos blancos
del mayab.

Hacemos muchas cosas, esto aquello nos move-
mos de aquí para allá, de allá para acá.
Un grande motivo hace nuestro valor:
el respeto que queremos para esta tierra
maya.
Mi raíz ancestral sufrió la esclavitud como
consecuencia de haber sido descubiertos por
Cristóbal Colon, a nombre de España.

Pasado doloroso. Las mujeres mayas sofrieron en su carne, la lojoria de los conquistadores, los hombres blancos que se adueñaron de nuestras tierras, de nuestras vidas por trecientos años.

Por eso, entre nosotros hay conciudadanos que poseen piel clara, ojos verdes y hasta azules o claros como consecuencia de la semilla sanguinea, que aun que con bajas intenciones, nos regalaron.

No estamos en contra de España dado el proceso de nuestros días, el entendimiento la razón, el equilibrio que debe regir el mundo es el diálogo, la comunicación etc. Lo que exponemos no encierra ningun dolo por ese pasado de esclavitud, lo decimos, por que es nuestro derecho universal, y protestamos con el dialo go, la razón y el entendimiento.

No culpamos a España, acaso a la lógica del tiempo o la historia.

No podemos odiar a los que nos esclavisa-
ron por decirse reyes, ya que nosotras
somos herederas de reinas y princesas y
lo único que nos diferencia de aquellos
es nuestra piel canela.

Estamos concientes de nuestra preceneia
en las etapas de nuestra historia.
La floreciente grandeza de nuestra raza que
pobló la peninsula de Chacnobitán.
Ed descubrimiento de nuestra tierra.
La opresión de trecientos años.
La Independencia.
La Reforma
El Imperio Impuesto por Francia
La Dictadura Porfirista
La Revolución.
En el movimiento social de 1,910, estuvo mas
clara la abnegación y el sucrificio de la
mujer en su entrega absoluta en aras de la
justicia social, como co-partícipe en ayudar
al hombre revolucionario, para luchar por

La tierra que por nacimiento es soya.
Desde entonces, el pié de nuestra lucha,
nuestro frente de combate, late en nuestros
rebozos, en nuestros wipiles en nuestros
varaches.

Los Líderes del Poder Mundial sepan que
nuestro anhelo por ganar las luchas sociales
es que queremos la paz.

Queremos que nos respeten el derecho de elegir
con libertad, a nuestros mejores líderes, para darles
la representatividad de nuestros pueblos, aquellos
que tengan como verdadero espíritu de justicia
que el equilibrio social pueda lograrse si
como administradores de los bienes de la
nación, equilibren la fuerza social, repar-
tiéndolo equitativa mente.

Seguimos buscando las tribunas de la
palabra, seguimos pidiendo la comprensión
el diálogo para la justicia y la razón

Queremos dignidad, en el hogar, en la
educación, en la salud y todo aquello que
sea bienestar para nuestra familia.
Trabajo honesto, salario digno.

Nuestra raíz, es clara, nada esta guardado
para nosotras, nada es secreto para nos.
Así no fué en vano el sacrificio de
nuestras ancestrales princesas que con
su vida oprendada a los cenotes sagrados
calmaran la ira de nuestros dioses, para
develar todos los secretos, todos los
misterios para ejercer un futuro con
mejores días como el que será cuando
se publique este decir.

Este decir, que dice: mujeres mayas que
nada tenemos que envidiar a las
heroínas europeas, nada le envidiamos
a Genoveva de Bravante o Juana de Arco
nada tenemos que desear de Cleopatras
o Mesalinas o Lucrecias Borgia

bollas Otero o Mata Haris o Isadoras Duncan
tenemos el sopiciente ánimo que levanta
la frente de nuestro orgullo : Yucatán.

Tenemos honor, tenemos querencia
tenemos valor.

Somos buenas y malas
somos calma, somos inquietud
Somos lluvia, somos sequía
Somos cantares y poesía
Somos primavera e invierno
Viento y brisa
Reir y llorar
Alegría y tristeza
Riqueza y pobreza
salud y enfermedad

En las grandes ausencias de nuestra
fuerza moral, cuando el espíritu
se siente descobijado decimos

¿Seremos un dechado de manchas, o
desvirtuadas humanas?
¿Somos un algo que no es nada?
   Para entonces decir:
Que grite nuestro silencio
en la mochedumbre de la soledad!

Algunas cosas que faltan:
En mi época escolar, tenía mi pueblo
dos escuelas públicas, como les decían
entonces. En las dos estudié los grados
que en aquel tiempo habían.
Mis maestros fueron:
no habían Kinder como ahora.
Párvolos — Anastacia García
Primer grado — Josefa Coello
segundo grado — Antonio Zapata
tercer grado — Arsenio Mendez
Cuarto grado — Gubildo López Lara
Quinto grado — otra vez Arsenio Mendez
el sexto grado lo estudié en edad
adulta cuan ya empezo a existir

educación para adultos.
Las dos escuelas mencionadas existen
es de suponer que actualmente, están
mas desarolladas.
En mis tiempos una se llamaba
Manuel "Cepeda Peraza" #104
La otra se llamaba "Doctora Montessori"
#105.
Ahora ambas son una sola
"Esc. Primaria #96 Doctora Montessori".
Fué muy esforsado mi camino escolar,
por la escasez de recursos familiares.
La otra cosa es que mi andar político,
se empezó a acrecentarse, cuando en
1973, en las elecciones municipales
despues de una reñida batalla electoral
con muchas consecuencias, salí electa
como diputada suplente, para un
periodo de dos años. 74-75, pues,
por asuntos de estado se recortó
el periodo.

Los acontecimientos políticos estatales
hicieron que el diputado titular, se
fuera como director de la policía, y,
siendo yo suplente, Tomé la responsabilidad de mi distrito, 5° en aquel
entonces.
Para ese período, se promovió y se
llevó a cabo en México, el Año
Internacional de la mujer. en cuyos
actos de inauguración estuve presente,
aclaro, que no se me dió ninguna mo-
ción de lo que podía haber hecho o
dicho. Lamento mucho no haber
tomado la tribuna para defender
mi causa, que es la causa de todas
las mujeres indígenas.
Lamento no haber tenido nexos con
Domitila.
A partir de entonces seguí haciendo
caso a mi inquietud en grados ya
mas avanzados.
Me salí del Partido Político en

que milite mucho tiempo, porque
sentí mis convicciones, humilladas
y golpeadas, pero así como tenía
conocidos contrarios a mí, los
hay también que asesoraron mis
actividades.
Y así en los últimos años traté
de abanderarme en otros grupos
y llegué, ahora sí por tres años, y
otra vez al Congreso Estatal, como
diputada plurinominal de oposi-
ción,
Siempre hice, considero muy poco,
ahora, mi lucha es posiblemente
pasiva,
En estos tiempos de crisis entre
las fuerzas políticas del país,
pues se abre tal vez la posibili-
dad de logros mejores para las
aspiraciones, aunque para la mujer
indígena, creo que sigue la marginación, y no diré lo contrario

mientras no vea claro, el respeto
constituido para todas las etnias,
que todavía luchan por sobrevivir,
haciendo con su lucha resaltar las
costumbres, y el valor de la sabiduría
indígena, que está siendo rebasada
en aras de la modernidad y diríque
el progreso de la ciencia y la tecnología.

P. D.
Dije que mi niñez, fué triste
La pobreza y las penurias, hicieron
esta tristeza.
Pero aprendí a leer y la lectura me
hace conocer al mundo, me hace
aprender a observar, cada día,
cada noche, cada luna cada sol
cada estrella.
El dinero es importante, sí, pero las cosas
materiales exesivas a veces nos hace olvi-
dar, que nos puente quela ambición

existe un mundo, un universo, una vida
que quieren, que desean nuestra atención
humana.
Comprendiendo esto así, entonces
exclamo,— bendita las penurias y la
pobreza de mi niñez, porque de
allí, germinó el rosal que ha florecido
en sentimientos, en ilusiones, en ideales
Estas son mis riquezas
Esto es mi heredad.

My Town, My Barrio

My town, my barrio responsible for my birth.
The street, the house that gave form to my life,
The hills, the cornfield, nature colored my *traje*[1]
My sky, my sun, my moon, the day, the night;
Spring, summer, fall, winter, the seasons
Of all the years that nourished my sentiments and thought.
That's how I am!
Maxcanú, body and soul of the province
—Araceli Cab Cumí, July 1999

Mi pueblo, mi barrio responsables de mi nacer.
La calle, la casa que dieron forma a mi vida,
Los cerros, la milpa, naturra,.. matizaron mi traje
Mi cielo, mi sol, mi luna, el día, la noche;
La primavera, Verano, otoño, invierno, las estaciones
de todos los años, que alimentaron mi sentir y
pensar.
Así como Soy!
Maxcaní cuerpo y alma de Provincia

CHAPTER TWO

The Poetry of Place and Community

Maxcanú, Body and Soul of the Province
—*Araceli Cab Cumí, July 1999*

Honoring the Home Place

In the opening poem to this chapter Araceli exalts her home, street, and barrio then circles outward to include the countryside around Maxcanú in her homage to her birth land. Araceli writes identifying herself as a Maya woman firmly rooted within her home community of Maxcanú.

Maxcanú is largely a Maya town with a population of about fifteen thousand. To visitors it appears less populated and more rural than it actually is because Maxcanú, like many towns in Yucatán, is quite spread out and well forested. Located on the southernmost borders of the old henequen zone, the town's economy is still primarily agricultural.[2] Recently, however, an assembly plant (maquiladora) opened and now employs several hundred people from the area. Maxcanú is also the county seat and an important median point on the main road between Mérida and Campeche, the capital city of Campeche, the state to the southeast of Yucatán state.

I once asked Araceli how Maxcanú got its name. She recounted a story drawn from the distant past that has two different versions. Each, however, ends with the naming of Maxcanú. As Araceli tells the story:

In Maxcanú there was a cenote (a water-filled sinkhole common in Yucatán, this one reputedly located under the main plaza of the town). One day a princess, daughter of the local chieftain, sat peacefully at the cenote watching four blue snails walk near the edge. Her boyfriend, however, who wasn't so refined, came by and killed them. To this the young woman shouted, "*max kan ul!*" meaning in Yucatec Maya, "you killed four snails!"

In the second version the princess was sleeping by the cenote that she so loved. She placed her favorite jade bracelet with its stones shaped as four moons on a rock while she slept. Her boyfriend then came along and placed his bag on her bracelet, breaking the four jade moons. She then exclaimed "*max kan u!*"—"You broke four moons!"

Both versions of the story, however, conclude with the same ending. The princess's father does not wish the couple to marry because the boyfriend is of a lesser social class. Nonetheless the princess and her boyfriend run off together to marry. But because their love is forbidden, they are not allowed to marry. The princess's father pursues them and kills them with a sacrificial stone knife. But before he kills them the princess asks that the place by the cenote be named "Maxcanú" in honor of their love. Thus the town got its name, honoring a forbidden love between a refined princess and a rather clumsy commoner.[3]

In keeping with the theme of honoring her birthplace, Araceli wrote the following two poems dedicated to her hometown of Maxcanú:

SONG TO MY TOWN
> *I reflect without end . . . such colors*
> *That embellish step by step your pathways*
> *To breathe the scent of your many flowers.*
> *To see the birds, . . . to hear trills in your beautiful branches.*
> *As the background of your grand painting*
> *The low hills with their distinct green*
> *Carpet with magic, with smooth fineness*
> *Your history made in legends, fame and song.*
>
> *Your low hills whose blurred images*
> *Stand up on the blue horizon*
> *And whose jewels, merge into sentiments*
> *To praise you, Maxcanú!*
> June 24, 1978, St. John's Day

original page on page 88

Haze over Pu'uc hills near Maxcanú with henequen plants in their final bloom in foreground.

In this poem Araceli reveres the beauty of the natural world in which Maxcanú lies. As many visitors to Yucatán note, the intensely blue skies of the peninsula, its dramatic cloud formations, and starkly white, low stone walls accented with bright flowers do make a memorable setting. So too, since much of the Yucatecan countryside is thickly vegetated, the songbirds of Araceli's poem flourish.

But Araceli refers to the unique setting of Maxcanú in her line, "The low hills with their distinct green." The Yucatecan peninsula is a flat plain—the view unimpeded from horizon to horizon. Yet bordering Maxcanú are the Pu'uc hills, the only rise in the plain for hundreds of miles. Located at the foot of the Pu'uc, the physical setting of Maxcanú is thus dramatic and distinct from other towns in Yucatán. Although the Pu'uc hills are only a few hundred feet high, their contrast with the surrounding level countryside defines their presence as the most notable feature of the natural world of Maxcanú. As no less an observer than John L. Stephens, the famous early nineteenth-century traveler to Yucatán, wrote when approaching Maxcanú:

[W]e came in sight of the sierra which traverses at that point
the whole peninsula of Yucatan from east to west. The sight of
hills was cheering, and with the reflection of the setting sun
upon them, they presented almost the first fine scenery I had
encountered in the country.[4]

The distinct green (*yax* in Yucatec Maya) that Araceli mentions in her
poem as the color of the Pu'uc hills is a fresh, vivid green that carpets the
countryside once the rainy season has begun.

Significantly, Araceli wrote this poem on June 24, St. John's Day. The
summer rainy season often begins before this date (hopefully on or shortly
after May 3, the Day of the Cross). If the rains do not come by June 24
(around the time of the summer solstice), however, it signals the likeli-
hood of a delayed rainy season or worse, drought. Thus St. John's Day is a
time of worried hope. No rain by this date means a likely drought that will
devastate the planting season so important for an agricultural town such
as Maxcanú.

In May 1976 the principal of the primary school in Maxcanú requested
that Araceli, as a former student in its adult education program, write a poem
about her town for the inauguration of a new wing to the school. Araceli
wrote the following longer poem in homage to her hometown, which she
read at the inauguration of the new wing.

MAXCANÚ
> *Maxcanú a little corner*
> *where the flamboyans grow*
>
> *aromas of the mayflowers*
> *the white film of the lemon trees*
> *Your common walls*
> *enlaced with cornflowers*
> *shine a divine mark*
> *below the blue of your sky.*
>
> *Your festivals and* vaquerías[5]
> *shine with your mestizas*[6]

and in the clothes that adorn them
sentiment is embroidered.
Sentiment of a past
that in the book of life
remains recorded . . . , and in history
will be the gift to your children

Land whose flat rocks
gave life to henequen
and your grand red earth
peanuts and jicamas also.
Cornfields, cultivated by your men
who work without ceasing

to make our land
the true land of the Maya.

The fruit of the old oak
and the flowers of the "jaabin,"[7]
are signs of good times
and a good harvest also.

Fragrant the subinché[8]
Yellow the tajonal[9]
if it blooms the dzidzilché[10]
also will have good honey.

So legendary is the ceiba
like the pheasant and the deer
legend of the petenes[11]
and their vast zapote *groves.*
this landscape is flowering
and in its musical background
the nightingale with its trills
cardinal plumage.

Your hill of the three crosses
is part of your great history,
and this is, everywhere
an impression in memory.
Your barrio called "Zaragoza"
populated by farmers
where a beautiful "Carmen"
is surrounded by flowers.
Of St. Patrick the corn grower
who awaits a good rain
looks for Isidro, the diviner,
in order to make the novenario.[12]
To have him content
he does the masses and rosaries,
and the cultivated lands, always good,
are fulfilled with his miracles.
From Tepeyac the venerated figure
in her chapel
with infinite tenderness
that ascends to the villa.
Of Guadalupe is this barrio
that in its December festivals

Lupita blesses the years
that come and go . . . always . . . always.

Maxcanú in these phrases
Is our heart
Our blood and our life
Shaped in emotion.
Beloved corner of the fatherland
That shelters our dreams,
Your love[13] . . . , sublime is Maxcanú!
That in this west, makes grand Yucatán!

Maxcanú, May 24, 1976

original pages on pages 89–91

In this longer poem, as in the previous two, Araceli begins by exalting the natural world of Maxcanú, mentioning especially the sky, the trees, and flowers. But in this homage to town life she introduces the human community first by honoring the women and then the men:

> *Your festivals and* vaquerías
> *shine with your mestizas*
> *and in the clothes that adorn them*
> *sentiment is embroidered.*
> *Sentiment of a past*
> *that in the book of life*
> *remains recorded . . . , and in history*
> *will be the gift to your children*

Important to Araceli's sense of community are the town festivals and especially the vaquerías. The vaquerías are lively festivals attended by crowds of people from the area in a celebration of rural town and ranch life. The vaquerías feature dances, regional foods, cattle roping, and bullfighting (in which the bull is not slain). Distinctive dances, songs, and humor (see the poem "Bomba" in this chapter) are part of these local celebrations.

In this stanza Araceli also notes the Maya women of her town and draws special attention to their clothing. She writes of how sentiment is sewn into the "*traje de la mestiza*" (see note 1). Araceli records here how the embroidery on women's huipils symbolically records the past so that it can become the inheritance of the coming generations.[14]

Araceli then honors the men of her community, acknowledging their persistent hard work as *Maya* farmers:

> *Land whose flat rocks*
> *gave life to henequen*
> *and your grand red earth*
> *peanuts and jicamas also.*
> *Cornfields, cultivated by your men*
> *who work without ceasing*
>
> *to make our land*
> *the true land of the Maya.*

Araceli continues writing about the plants common in Maxcanú as in other rural Yucatecan towns:

> *The fruit of the old oak*
> *and the flowers of the* "jaabin,"
> *are signs of good times*
> *and a good harvest also.*

> *Fragrant the* subinche
> *Yellow the* tajonal
> *if it blooms the* dzidzilche
> *also will have good honey.*

All four of the trees and shrubs Araceli mentions in her poem share the characteristic of attracting honeybees, important for pollenization and for the production of honey. Many rural people in Yucatán keep honeybees and produce their own honey. Since ancient times, honey production has been important throughout the Yucatán Peninsula. The jaabin in particular, however, is also a harbinger. If it has many flowers a good harvest will follow. Its purple flowers are distinctive and its fruits are said to rattle like maracas in the wind.

In the following stanza Araceli draws attention to elements of the natural world long associated with Yucatán:

> *So legendary is the ceiba*
> *like the pheasant and the deer*
> *legend of the* petenes
> *and their vast* zapote *groves.*
> *this landscape is flowering*
> *and in its musical background*
> *the nightingale with its trills*
> *cardinal plumage.*

The ceiba tree, the pheasant, and the deer are well-known references to Yucatán. All three are represented on the state shield. Yucatecans refer to their state as *la tierra del faisán y venado* (land of the pheasant and deer). While few wild pheasants or deer remain in Yucatán, they were once common. The ceiba tree (*Ceiba pentandra*) is the tallest, most majestic tree to grow in Yucatán, its spreading branches creating a top layer in the forest canopy. Its limbs host bromeliads and long vines that in turn create microniches for insects and frogs and aerial highways for monkeys.

The ancient Maya regarded the ceiba tree as the tree of life. According to an ancient Maya cosmovision the ceiba stood at the center of the earth connecting the layers of the underworld, earth, and heavens. Because the limbs of the ceiba grow perpendicular to its trunk the tree has a crosslike form. The ancient indigenous people of Yucatán used the cross as a sacred symbol long before the Spanish brought the Christian cross to the peninsula. Thus the Maya revered the stately ceiba in its cross form. Many Yucatecans continue to regard the ceiba tree as emblematic of their state admired for its soaring majesty above the flat terrain of Yucatán.

When Araceli was asked to compose this poem about Maxcanú she chose to write about the four barrios of Maxcanú: Zaragoza, Tres Cruces, San Patricio, and Guadalupe. Araceli links the natural and saintly worlds of Maxcanú with its barrios in the three following stanzas beginning with Barrio Zaragoza:

> *Your hill of the three crosses*
> *is part of your great history,*
> *and this is, everywhere*
> *an impression in memory.*
> *Your barrio called "Zaragoza"*
> *populated by farmers*
> *where a beautiful "Carmen"*
> *is surrounded by flowers.*

The hill to which Araceli refers in this stanza is part of the Pu'uc hills that border Maxcanú. On the crest of this hill is a small shrine with three crosses. Below the Hill of the Three Crosses lie the neighboring barrios of Zaragoza and Tres Cruces, where Araceli lives. Zaragoza has a more rural ambience as an outlying barrio of the town nearest the Hill of the Three Crosses. The families who live here are more likely to have larger house plots then their neighbors in the other three barrios. The Virgen del Carmen is the patron saint of Zaragoza; her statue graces the barrio chapel. In describing Zaragoza, Araceli uses a double image of "Carmen," referring to a common

*Araceli at house with three crosses in her neighborhood of
Barrio Tres Cruces.*

kind of tree in the barrio and also to the Virgen del Carmen, one of many local or regional symbolic variants of the Virgin Mary found throughout the Roman Catholic religious world. Although Araceli does not live in the barrio of Zaragoza, it is a favorite of hers and the home of several of her key supporters.

Araceli continues to honor the barrios of Maxcanú in the following:

> *Of St. Patrick the corn grower*
> *who awaits a good rain*
> *looks for Isidro, the diviner,*
> *in order to make the* novenario.
> *To have him content*
> *he does the masses and rosaries,*
> *and the cultivated lands, always good,*
> *are fulfilled with his miracles.*

In this stanza Araceli mentions two particular Roman Catholic saints, San Patricio and San Isidro, both of whom are linked to agricultural good fortune. Yet the barrio of San Patricio (Saint Patrick) has San Isidro not San Patricio as its patron saint. It is San Isidro's statue that lies in the barrio chapel of San Patricio. The seeming contradiction of the barrio name and representative saint originates in a vignette of Maxcanú territorial history.

San Isidro was an old barrio of Maxcanú that bordered a finca (farm, small ranch) whose owner was named Patricio (Patrick). He, in honor of his name, adopted Saint Patrick as his own patron. When Patricio died his name became associated with the locale even after the barrio and the finca were merged together. So the barrio became San Patricio but retained its original patron saint, San Isidro. In the early twentieth century the barrio was officially renamed after Manuel Gonzalez, an official of Governor Salvador Alvarado's administration.[15] No one in Maxcanú, however, refers to the barrio by its officially designated name; it remains San Patricio and San Isidro its patron saint.

Araceli continues her homage to the four barrios of Maxcanú by writing:

> *From Tepeyac the venerated figure*
> *in her chapel*
> *with infinite tenderness*

that ascends to the villa.
Of Guadalupe is this barrio
that in its December festivals

Lupita blesses the years
that come and go . . . always . . . always.

Araceli venerates the Virgin of Guadalupe as the patron saint of Mexico
and also of the Barrio Guadalupe in this stanza. December 12 is the Day of
the Virgin of Guadalupe. Araceli speaks of the Virgin as ascending from her
chapel on that day as a yearly blessing to the barrio named in her honor. She
uses a diminutive form, "Lupita," of the name "Guadalupe" to show an affec-
tionate respect for this important religious figure. The "Tepeyac" Araceli
mentions in her poem is the hill at whose feet the shrine to the Virgin of
Guadalupe was built in Mexico City. The Virgin Mary's miraculous appearance on this hillside to a peasant Nahua man during colonial times marked
the beginning of the legend of the Virgin of Guadalupe whose two shrines
(modern and colonial) are built near the hilltop locale of the shrine of the
Nahua goddess Tonanztin. Since colonial times the Virgin of Guadalupe
has become the most important religious symbol in Mexico and is revered
throughout Latin America.[16]
Araceli's last stanza of this poem pays homage to her beloved hometown as the center of its people's lives:

Maxcanú in these phrases
Is our heart
Our blood and our life
Shaped in emotion.
Beloved corner of the fatherland
That shelters our dreams,
Your love . . . , sublime is Maxcanú!
That in this west, makes grand Yucatán!

Araceli ends her poem joining Maxcanú townspeople to their town in
a metaphorically physical link. In her last two lines Araceli places Maxcanú
within the greater context of Yucatán state. She indicates that from Maxcanú's
locale in the west of Yucatán it glorifies its home state.

A Tribute to Humor

As a final tribute to the town life of Maxcanú Araceli wrote "Bombas" to honor a distinctively Yucatecan style of humor.[17] *Bombas* are an important part of community festivals and parties. As the gaiety progresses at local vaquerías, someone will suddenly yell "bomba!" The music stops and someone makes a rhymed joke, commenting upon life, politics, or whatever else may inspire her or him. Fellow partygoers applaud the bomba, judging its wit, rhyme, and cadence. Someone else may respond with a trenchant bomba of her or his own. When composing bombas Yucatecans may mix Yucatec Maya and Spanish to create a bilingual joke with layered meanings, one language playing off the other to make the bomba even more pointedly witty.

   What Araceli wrote here is not so much a bomba itself as an homage to bombas and to the festivals in which they are presented.

BOMBAS
> *From this beloved Yucatecan land comes the very pleasant rhythm*
> > *of the* jaranas *that shake to the beat of the drums with its twirls*
> > *and capricious silhouettes.*
>
> *A melody, . . . that when heard flows*
> *Harmonizes the spirit and the mind*
>
> *And these joyous airs shine in the pleasure and solace of our people.*
> > June 9, 1978
> > > > *original page on page 92*

   Araceli in this homage to the bomba also pays tribute to her distinctive Yucatecan homeland. The jaranas she mentions are the best known and most commonly performed dances of Yucatán. In her poem the bomba seems to refresh the very spirit of Araceli's fellow townspeople.

The Natural World of Yucatán

As is evident in Araceli's poems about Maxcanú, the natural world of Yucatán inspires her as a writer. In the following series of five poems, she makes the natural world itself the subject of her musings. In one of her most evocative poems Araceli describes the promise of a new day brought by the dawn.

Dawn

> When the soft air of the countryside
> refreshes the green body of the land
>
> clear is your gaze
> clean is your spirit
> and ideas flow from the crystalline spring
> that bathes the memory
> like a blue cascade
> of celestial effluvium
> because they have not yet been stained
> with the ash of daily routine.
>
> Wednesday, September 25, 1996
>
> *original page on page 93*

Daily sentiments are the essence of life.

In this lyrical and evocative poem about the experience of a dawning new day, Araceli honors the "everyday" in life as central to its meaning—even if daily routine is sometimes an ashy stain on a new day's promise. As she does on occasion, Araceli adds a postscript, "Daily sentiments are the essence of life," another tribute to the everyday.

The Rains

In late June 1998 Araceli wrote a series of four poems addressing the lagging start of the rainy season that year. May 3, the Day of the Cross, is traditionally seen as the time for the rains to commence. If the rainy season has not started by St. John's Day on June 24, however, then there is worry and concern. Newly planted crops will die. Townspeople will suffer the heat and humidity without the cool cleansing carried by the rains. Despite hopeful prayers the year 1998 brought only drought. The rains did not arrive until late July.

The first three poems particularly have a sense of waiting about them, of a paused passage of time. The final poem, "Reflections . . ." takes a prayerful tone as days go by without rain. Absent the late spring–early summer rains, farmers such as the townspeople of Maxcanú can do little but wait upon an unpredictable rainfall.

"The sky is repentant as though it wants to cry."

Araceli often portrays nature as a live actor in her poems. In this series rain walks, the sky sprinkles, clouds and wind make the decision to appear.

IT IS THE 18 OF JUNE AND NO RAIN . . . WHAT WILL WE DO?
What words, . . . the most fine cast
the most pure,

with the language only of the heart
that the sacred flows
from the sanctuary of our thoughts
and which the aureole of copal[18]
incense of an offering
rises up in the far distance.
Something that would be sublime
With the greatness of humility
That softens the winds
That caresses the clouds
so that the wide sky
would let fall its love
with a weeping benefactor
in the fresh drops of rain.
Two in the afternoon

July 18, 1998

original page on page 94

Four hours later, that same day, Araceli wrote the following poem.

REFLECTIONS . . .
It smells of rain
There is an aroma of refreshing humidity
some place . . . where? . . . Who knows!
But it feels like some rain fell here or there

The afternoon goes, almost calmly
In hope, . . . although slowly
Is there a day, . . . perhaps tomorrow

Some rain, walking, will visit us.
Same day, June 18, 1998, at 6:30 PM

original page on page 95

The next day Araceli wrote this poem.

It Seems That It Wants to Be Cloudy
The sky is repentant
as though it wants to cry
I am bold to ask
that it let go to sprinkle its flood of tears.

Amidst its dense clouds
the sky wants to relent
if there is a miracle, the drops of rain
that fall will not be lost.

If it is a good omen, the request
would be worthy of wonder
that the clouds and the wind have decided
at last, . . . to appear.
Friday, June 19, 1998

original page on page 96

Araceli ends the series of rain poems with a poem
she wrote the following day.

Reflections . . . (1998)
How grand human sentiments
ought be that reach to infinity
and there opening the heavens
can ask God
mercy and love for the world

How sublime ought to be
the words chosen
in prayer that could be sung

and that arriving to the clouds
would give us comfort in the rain

How pure has to be
our earthly heart
to convert it into a sanctuary
and in it, burn in perpetual flame,
charity, faith, and hope.
                    Thursday, June 20, 1998

                                    original page on page 97

   This last poem builds on prayer rather than mere hope. As the last in
the series of rain poems perhaps it reflects the disparateness Araceli and
her neighbors in Maxcanú come to feel when the rains are so delayed that it
seems they will never arrive.

Honoring Family and Friends

As Araceli writes homages to her town and to the natural world, she also
writes to honor family and friends. She composed the following four poems
for and about particular people in her life.

   The first is for Bertha, Araceli's daughter and oldest child. Bertha long
ago married and moved to Mérida, living in a barrio where most of the
other residents are also originally from Maxcanú. Bertha and her husband,
Carlos, have four children and six grandchildren. She works as an admin-
istrator in the Department of Public Education; her husband is an office
worker in the same department. One of their daughters, Zoila, is the author
of the short story, "Gossip," which appears in chapter 6, "Endings?" Another
daughter, Zazil, has been a steady participant in the ongoing conversations
with Araceli and me about women, politics, and the Maya (see "In Honor of
Zazil Espinosa Patrón," also in chapter 6).

To My Daughter, Bertha,
in Memory of Her Childhood
   As a little one
   as a fragile one
   you walked in the patio

in your first steps.

Like so with your little braids
like so with a lively nature
walking in your little steps
in pursuit of distraction.

Dolls you had none
not a single toy
well we were sparing
and we couldn't own [things].

You were walking in the patio
you were playing in the reeds
and as a little fragile one
you were looking for a place.

Like little ones
Like simple ones
These memories of mine
That I am going to leave you.

Monday, February 21, 1977

original page on page 98

This poignant poem underscores the fragility of a childhood lived in poverty. Araceli speaks as a mother only able to give her daughter simple memories rather than toys. She writes about the difficulty of finding one's place in life as someone young and vulnerable but yet who still searches. Although the poem is lovingly written, Araceli has never shown it to Bertha.

The following poem Araceli wrote to honor the marriage of two schoolteacher friends whom she met through her political activities. As Araceli tells the story Margarita and Manuel were very much in love but faced obstacles to their marriage. Margarita had once been unhappily married. So her mother did not wish her to remarry and take the chance of repeating the pain. Araceli was touched by the couple's devotion to each other, especially in overcoming the opposition of Margarita's mother. Araceli describes herself as an idealist in the way that she thinks about love. Thus she was moved by this struggle of two people in love to marry. In the final stanzas she mentions Eros, lending it an erotic air fitting for a poem dedicated to a newly married couple.

Araceli wrote this beautiful poem as her gift to Margarita and Manuel. She, however, never read this lovely piece at their wedding, thinking that there never was the right opportunity. She since has lost touch with Margarita and Manuel who live in Mérida.

For Margarita and Manuel
> *I have searched in my mind*
> *for what would be the right words*
> *and, that the moment that we are remembering*
> *remains recorded on a winged muse.*
> *Of the garden, to the sacred life*
> *there are roses perfuming the night*
> *and in honor of this memorable date*
> *we shower petals of love.*
>
> *The sentiment in worthy verse*
> *in the hours of friendship may*
> *the precious ones fill forever*
> *the beloved heart*
> *with these phrases eternally praised.*
>
> *Words that with love so sung*
> *we would dedicate to Eros*
> *and imprisoned in the arms of love*
> *they would remain these hours palpitating.*
> Mérida, Yucatan, Mexico, Saturday,
> February 9, 1980

original page on page 99

The remaining two poems Araceli wrote are dedicated to two foreign women anthropologists with whom she has worked, the Spanish folklorist Ascensión Amador Naranjo and me. Araceli wrote these poems in friendship. But perhaps she also wrote them because she considers us as intellectual companions who encouraged her efforts as a writer.

Often in this book I have placed Araceli's writings in the chronological order that she wrote them. In this case, however, since she wrote the poem to me as a greeting and the poem to Ascensión as a farewell, I have reversed the order, placing the poem to me before that written for Ascensión.

I Begin by Smiling to the Day
I begin by smiling to the day
a smile of life
to greet you, Kathleen
in complete harmony.

Even the cloudy sky
has something for you
soft air, delicate breezes
everything like colored jewels.

Even the sun hiding
behind the wings of clouds
opens them up to watch you walk.

Between the cornfields and cornflowers is your time to come

The month of June, of the rains
And the rain will cover your footsteps.
It is the spring of my land
foretelling the coming of summer
making the swallow return
every year.

With the fondness of Maxcanú
—Araceli
Maxcanú, Yucatán,
Saturday, June 15, 1996, 10 AM

original page on page 100

"I Begin by Smiling to the Day" is a poem of cordial welcome. In it Araceli uses the idea of recurring and sometimes coinciding cycles. She first mentions the annual June to October rainy season; second, my likely return to Yucatán during the summer months; and third, the annual return of the swallows. The line "Between the cornfields and cornflowers is your time to come" is also a reference to a repeating cycle. The time Araceli describes here occurs between the planting of the corn at the start of the rainy season and the blooming of the cornflowers later in the rainy season. This cycle of cornfields and cornflowers thus coincides with my usual June arrival and August departure.

Araceli constructs this poem with animated images of the natural world. The sun hiding behind the clouds and then opening them to watch one walk is one such image. The cloudy sky giving the gift of soft air and delicate breezes is another. She closes her poem by noting the fondness coming from Maxcanú, setting her town apart from the others I have visited in my yearly returns to Yucatán.

The second poem Araceli wrote as a farewell to Ascensión or, as she affectionately calls her with a nickname, "Choni." Araceli worked with Ascensión as part of a Spanish-Mexican scientific expedition that came to the nearby ancient Maya archaeological site of Oxkintok every summer for five years from 1986 to 1991. During this project Ascensión recorded Maya songs and stories from the townspeople of Maxcanú. Araceli gave Ascensión Yucatec Maya lessons and helped her collect Maya tales from older members of the Maxcanú community. Araceli also wrote two poems in Yucatec Maya, which Ascensión translated into Spanish for one of the project books. Once the study was completed, Ascensión gave Araceli copies of the books published from the project. They are among Araceli's most prized possessions. Ascensión occasionally returns to Yucatán and thus remained in contact with Araceli for some time. Unfortunately Ascensión and I have never met; my work with Araceli began two years after the Oxkintok expedition ended.

For Ascensión, Araceli wrote this beautiful poem of farewell:

FOR ASCENCIÓN [sic] AMADOR NARANJO
   Of the remembrances
   that you carry away from Yucatán
   do not forget the colorful message
   of the deer and pheasant.

   You carry away things engraved
   in the soul and heart

many songs so beautiful
always they will speak to you of love.

The distance is not important
The generous fragrances of my land
and its groves of palm trees
will move through the seven seas.

*And . . . as with "*la Peregrina*"*
You will return to our homes
And . . . on the wings of the swallows
You will come for new songs.
                    Maxcanu, September 1990

                                        original page on page 101

As in the poem Araceli wrote for me, her poem to Ascensión has the theme of a recurring cycle of arrival and departure. Araceli again uses the swallow as a symbol of cyclical journeys. "La peregrina" (the pilgrim or traveler) is also a reference to repeating cycles of travel and return. "La peregrina," however, has special significance in Yucatán. Felipe Carrillo Puerto, the famed governor of Yucatán (1922–24), commissioned the Yucatecan songwriter Ricardo Palmerin to write a song in honor of his love, Alma Reed, a North American journalist who met the governor while reporting on current events in Mexico. The result was the beautiful, haunting "La Peregrina." The celebrated love affair between Governor Felipe Carrillo Puerto and Alma Reed has become a romantic legend in Yucatán. Palmerin's beautiful song in homage to their love is still performed and revered in Yucatán today.

In her poem to Ascensión Araceli repeats the common symbols of the deer and the pheasant that reference Yucatán and appear on its state shield. Araceli closes her poem by using lyrical traveling images of the fragrances of Yucatán and its groves of palm trees as a means to transcend the distance between herself and Ascensión when she returns to Spain.

As part of our collaboration on this book, Araceli and I divided her writings into what we considered suitable chapters. For some chapters Araceli wrote introductions or endings or both. Although she wrote the following poem nineteen years ago, she chose it to end this chapter on place and community. Araceli wrote this poem bilingually. In it Araceli honors a sense of place and heritage by noting that traveling away from one's place does not erase one's heritage.

> TO REMEMBER/A MEMORY
>   *No matter how far your steps take you away*
>   *Do not forget the good roads of your land*
>   *Where they always call your* señorío[19]
>   *The desire of your land is*
>   *That you walk the beautiful roads*
>   *That there is health in your life*
>   *In your body, mind, and heart*
>   *Remember your origins in order to honor your name forever.*
>   November 4, 1983

original page on page 102

Conclusions

Araceli chooses poetry to express love for her community, her Yucatecan homeland, and some of the people important to her. Her attachment to her Yucatecan locale in Maxcanú and its surrounding natural world seems a fundamental part of her personal identity. She has lived here nearly all her life, most of it on the same half block of the same street. Her rootedness in this place seems to inspire her reflections on family and town life, friendship and love. Araceli's poetry demonstrates that the place of Maxcanú creates a wellspring of meaning for her. It inspires her writings in an expanding circle outward to include other events and people.[20]

Conversely, Araceli's symbolic construct of the natural world around Maxcanú described through her poetry endues it with a reality, alive and meaningful. Her locale of Maxcanú is both an inspiration and a subject for her poetry.

By composing the poems discussed in this chapter, Araceli locates herself firmly within her Maya community. Thus in a Gramscian sense she is positioned to represent a Maya worldview to others outside her Maya community. In her loyalty to the home place she underscores her identity as a Yucatec Maya representative, representing other Yucatec Maya. Araceli is rooted in her community and able through her writing to communicate its way of life to others.

Araceli has translated her loyalty to her community and her fellow townspeople not only through poetry but also by being politically active on their behalf for much of her adult life. The following chapter discusses her political activism, especially as a spokesperson for the Maya women of her Yucatecan community.

Junio 24 - 1978
Día de Sn. Juan

Canto a mi pueblo

Contemplo sin fin.... Tantos colores
que embellecen paso a paso Tus paisajes
aspirar el aroma de tus muchas flores,.
ver pájaros,... oir trines en tus hermosos ramajes.

Como fondo a tu gran pintura
Los cerros con su distinto verdor
alfombran con magia, con suave finura
tu historia hecha en leyendas, fama y canción.

Tus cerros que imágenes confunden
Se yerguen en el horizonte azul
y cual Joyas, en sentimientos se funden
para alabarte a ti ¡Maxcaní! .. ...

M A X C A N Ú

Maxcanú un rinconcito
donde existen los flamboyanes
aromas de flor de mayo
blancuras de limonaria·
Tus típicas albarradas
enlazadas de x-hailes
lucen un marco divino
bajo el azul de tu cielo.

Tus fiestas y vaquerías
se lucen con tus meztizas
Torno
y en el terreno que engalan
va bordado el sentimiento.
Sentimiento de un pasado
que en el libro de la vida
queda grabado..., y en historia
será el regalo a tus hijos

Tierra cuyos "tsek'eles"
dió la vida al henequen
y tus grandes "kankabales"
cacahuates y jícamas tambien.
Milpas, cultivo de tus hombres
que trabajan sin cesar
para hacer de nuestra tierra
el auténtico mayab.

El fruto del viejo roble
y las flores del "jaabin",
son señales de buén tiempo
y cosecha buena también.

Oloroso el subinché,
amarillo el tajonal,
si florece el "dzidzilché",
también habrá buena miel.

Tan legendario es el ceibo
como el faisán y el venado
leyenda de los "petenes"
y sus vastos zapotales.
Este paisaje es florido
y en su fondo musical
el ruiseñor con sus trinos
plumajes de cardenal.

Tu cerro de las "tres cruces"
parte es, de tu gran historia,
y esto es, a todas luces
un impacto en la memoria.
Tu barrio de "Zaragoza"
poblado de agricultores
donde una "Carmen" hermosa
está rodeada de flores.

De San Patricio el milpero
que espera una buena lluvia
busca a Isidro, cual agorero,
para hacerle el novenario.
Para tenerlo contento
le hace misas y rosarios,
y el labrados, siempre bueno,
le cumple con sus milagros.

Del Tepeyac la figura
venerada en su capilla
con la infinita ternura
que se eleve hasta la villa.
De Guadalupe es el barrio,
que en su fiesta decembrinas
Lupita bendice a los años
que vienen y van... siempre... siempre.

Maxcanú en estas frases
está nuestro corazón
nuestra sangre y nuestra vida
plasmados en la emoción.
Rinconcito de la patria
que cobija nuestros sueños,
tu cariño..., ¡sublime es Maxcanú!
que en este oeste..., ¡hace grande a Yucatán!

Maxcanú, mayo 24 - 1975.
Aracelly Cab Cumí.

Bombas.--

De esta tierra yucateca y cariñosa
es el ritmo de las muy gratas jaranas,
que al compás de los timbales se desgranan
con sus vueltas y figuras caprichosas.

Melodía,.. que, al oírlo que se viente
armonizan el espíritu y la mente
y estos aires de alegría que se esplenden
en el gozo y zolaz de nuestra gente.

Junio 9- 1978

ALBA...

Cuando el aire suave de los campos
refresca el verde cuerpo de la tierra
clara es tu mirada
albo es tu espíritu
y cual cristalino manantial
fluyen las ideas
que bañan la memoria
como cascada azul
de efluvio celestial
porque no se han manchado todavía
con el Tizne de la rutina diaria.

Araceli

miércoles 25 - Sep. 96

— Los sentimientos diarios
son los rubíos de la vida —

1998

Estamos a 18 de Junio y no llueve...¿que hacemos?
                                    ¡a 2 de la tarde

Que palabras,.. las mas castas
las más puras.
Con el idioma único del corazón
que sagradas pluyan
del santuario de nuestros pensamientos
y cual aureola de copal
inciencio de una ofrenda
se eleven al más allá.
Algo que sea sublime
con grandeza de homildad
que enternezcan a los vientos
que acaricien a las nubes
para que el cielo generoso
nos deje caer su amor
con un llanto bienhechor
en prescas gotas de lluvia.

                    A Cab

~~El mismo Junio 18 1998~~

El mismo Junio 18 - 1998 - como a la 6 30 P. M.

Reflexiones. - - - - ·

Huele a llovia
hay un aroma de humedad reconfortante
en alguna parte....¿donde..? ¡Quièn sabe!
pero se siente que cayó alguna llovia trashumante.

La tarde se va, casi colonada
en la esperanza,... aunque lentamente
habrá un día,.. tal vez mañana
nos visite alguna llovia caminante.

Viérnes 19 de Junio 1998.
   Parece que quiere nublarse.

El cielo está compungido
como que quiere llorar
a pedirle me he atrevido
que deje su llanto gotear.

En un nublado tupido
el cielo se quiere ablandar
si hay milagro no perdido
gotas de lluvia caeran.

Si es buen augurio el pedido
será digno de admirar
que nubes y viento han decidido
por fin,.. quererse aparear.

Junio 20 - 1998
Jueves

Reflexiones......

Cuán grandiosos deben ser
los sentimientos humanos
que lleguen al infinito
y allá abriendo los cielos
puedan pedir a Dios
piedad y amor para el mundo

Cuán sublimes deben ser
las palabras que escogidas
en oración sean cantadas
y que llegando a las nubes
nos den consuelo en la lluvia.

Cuán puro tiene que ser
nuestro corazón terreno
y convertirlo en santuario
y en él, arda en llama perenne
la caridad, la fé y la esperanza.

A mi hija Bertha. Recuerdo a su niñez.

Así de pequeñita
así de fragilita
andabas por el patio
ya en tus primeros pasos.

Así con tus trencitas
así, de genio vivo
andando en tus pasitos
en pos de distracción.

Muñecas no tenías
ningún juguete onas
pues éramos escasos
y no podía haber.

Andabas por el patio
jugabas en las bardas
y así de fragilita
buscabas vecindad.

Así de pequeñitos
así de sencillitos
estos recuerdos onios
que te voy a dejar

Lunes 21 de febrero de 1977.

Para Margarita y Manuel

He estado en mi mente rebuscando
que sean las palabras adecuadas
y, el momento que estamos recordando
quede impreso en una musa alada.

Del jardín, a la vida consagrada
hay rosas en la noche perfumando
y, en honor de esa fecha recordada
pétalos de amor vayan regando.

El sentimiento en verso valorado
en unas horas de amistad, preciadas
llenen para siempre el corazón amudo
con estas frases eternamente loadas.

Palabras que con amor así cantadas
a Eros vayamos dedicando
y en brazos del amor aprisionadas
queden, estas horas papitando.

Mérida Yucatán México — Sábado 9 de febrero — 1980

Sábado 10-AM.
291

NOTES Maxcanú Yuc. Junio 15-96

Empiezo a sonreirle al día
la sonrisa hacia la vida
para saludarte Kathleen
con un lujo de armonía.

Hasta el nublado del cielo
Tiene algo para ti
aire suave, brisa tenue
Todo fresco, con color.

Hasta este sol que se esconde
tras las alas de las nubes
pero que las entreabre
para ver tu caminar.

Entre milpas y x-hailes
es tu tiempo de venir
mes de junio, de las lluvias
Tus pasos van a cubrir.

Es el yax-Kin" de mi tierra
que agorera llama al verano
hasta ave de golondrina
~~para~~ y vuelve todos los años.

Con el afecto de Maxcaní
Araceli

Para Ascención Amador Naranjo
Antropóloga española., como despedida.

De los deseos soñados
que llevas do Yucatán
no olvides, el recado colorado
el venado y el paisan.

Grabadas llevas sus cosas
en el alma. y coragón
muchas canciones que hermosas
siempre te hablarán de amor.

No importando la distancia
surcaran los siete mares
las generosas fraganeias
de mi tierra y sus palmares.

Y... así con la Peregrina"
volverás a nuestros lares,
y....en alas de "Golondrinas"
vendrás por nuevos cantares.

Maxcanu Sep. de 1990

Para recordar noviembre 4 - 1985

Ompel Kaah-sahi

Kex buKaa u nachKunsKech
a ximbalé
ma a Tubsik u malo beilob a Kahal
Tuux baili Ku Tánal a siKbenil.

U Tsibol a Kahalé
Ka ximbana Kech Ti hatsuts beh
anak u toholali Tia Kuxtal
Ti a winKlil Ti a TuKul
Ti a puKsiK'al,.. he Toxa Ké
Kaasak a sihil
Kilich Kunta ak a K'abá
Tial baili.

Un Recuerdo

Por mucho que te alejen
Tus pasos
no olvides los buenos caminos
de tu Tierra
donde siempre llamarán
tu señorío.

El deseo de tu tierra es
que andes por bonitos caminos
que haya salud a tu vida
a tu cuerpo, a tu mente y corazón
recuerda tu nacimiento
para respetar tu nombre
para siempre.

I WOULD LIKE TO EXPRESS
> *I would like to express:*
> *Many things are said, so many words,*
> *that wish to propose everything, except a solution.*
> *Therefore there is no conclusion, for this*
> *great book called: Woman.*
> *There is no ending.*
> *It is . . . still . . . it is . . . yet . . .*

Inspired in the kitchen of my house
at 11:30 AM on March 8, 2002, as a remembrance
for the International Day of Women.

> —*Araceli Cab Cumí*

> *I am a woman . . . I searched*
> *I wished . . . I wish, I will wish . . .*

> *I am a woman . . . I searched but did not find,*
> *. . . but . . . I wished, . . . I wish . . . I will wish . . .*

—Araceli Cab Cumí, Tuesday, March 19, 2002

Quiero dexpresar:

Se dicen muchas cosas, tantas palabras,
que quieren decir todo, menos solución.
Por lo tanto no hay conclusión, para este
gran libro que se llama; Mujer.
No hay final.
Es.... todavía........es... aun...

Dado en la cocina de mi casa
siendo las 11.30 A.M. en el día 8
de marzo del 2002, como un recuerdo
para el día internacional de la mujer.

A Cab C

Soy mujer .... busqué
quise ... quiero, querré.....

CHAPTER THREE

On Behalf of Women

There is no conclusion, for this great book called: Woman.
—*Araceli Cab Cumí, March 2002*

A Career Begins

Araceli opens this chapter with two interconnected poems that she wrote to honor women on March 8, the International Day of Women. Her commemorative poems center upon a universal expression of women's aspirations and hopes. While not universally acknowledged, the International Day of Women is honored in Mexico and Araceli always celebrates the day.

As an activist on behalf of women's rights, Araceli is especially concerned with the Yucatec Maya women she represents. In the following poem Araceli expresses the often-unrealized human potential of Maya women such as herself. She especially underscores indigenous women's intellectual capacity.

THE WOMEN OF YUCATAN ... SPEAK
> *The women of Yucatan, . . . speak.*
> *These words are for ears that want to hear us, for eyes that want*
> *to see us, for all the razas¹ of all peoples.*
> *Women of the Mayab,² we are always searching.*
> *The moments, . . . the places, to attract all experience.*

Our spirit soars from the restlessness of our thoughts,
to realize the desire to broaden the paths of science and wisdom,
nurturing our born profession
of wanting to be truly wise and bearers of all lessons.

With the permission of all my fellow ciudadanas:
My name was registered in the town of Maxcanú, and in the
    Civil Registry, it is recorded as Araceli Angelica de J. Cab Cumí.
July 1997.

original page on page 133

The poem exemplifies Araceli's belief in women's potential—a belief that she has made a consistent theme in her writings and a center point of her political activities throughout her forty-three-year political career. As Araceli notes, while it is important that women speak, they also need to be heard. She calls for the ears of others to listen to the voices of Maya women. This book is Araceli speaking, the reader to listen.

Araceli began her political career forty-three years ago as a community activist in Maxcanú. As she wrote in one of her life narratives: "For this small family, I learned that my step had to be stronger to try to have a better life."[3]

Araceli started her engagement in politics with the desire to help her family. But she soon learned that her political engagement led to reflection and self-discovery. As she wrote a few sentences further on in this life narrative:

But at the same time I had to learn to know myself in order to know who I am and who I ought to be so that I could reach some goal. And so, little by little I learned that I could involve myself in political movements in my town.[4]

Araceli began her public service career by working with local self-help community groups and in the Maxcanú schools as a volunteer adult literacy teacher. From her base of support among those who knew her from these activities, Araceli was eventually elected to the town council of Maxcanú (regidora) in 1967. Several years later in 1971 she was elected to a regional post as secretary of the women's section of a campesino organization.

Araceli with her friend and political supporter Carmelita Dzul in front of the house altar in Carmelita's home in Maxcanú.

Many of the women who supported Araceli at the beginning of her political involvement have sustained her throughout her long career. They are her reference group and it is for them that she sees herself serving as a voice. They are her friends, neighbors, *comadres*, and relatives from her extended family.[5] These are the women who gather around her dining room table to talk among themselves and listen to Araceli.

Araceli closes her poem by acknowledging her women fellow citizens, ciudadanas. By using this specific form rather than the more generic *ciudadanos*, which would include both women and men, Araceli chose to emphasize women exclusively.

First Term in Congress: Exceptionality and Marginality

In 1973 an opportunity arose for Araceli that launched her political career at the statewide level. Local elections in Maxcanú sparked protests when a popular local candidate was defeated in the mayoralty race by a candidate whom many thought had less support. Voters in Maxcanú including Araceli questioned the validity of the election. In the congressional elections that followed soon after the electoral controversy in Maxcanú, a charismatic member of the PRI from Mérida, Carlos Jesus Capetillo Campos, was chosen by the PRI to run for the seat of the Fifth Congressional District in which Maxcanú is located. He chose Araceli as his suplente—a running mate who serves in office if the person at the head of the ticket cannot serve out the term of office to which she or he was elected. Some local schoolteachers in Maxcanú especially encouraged Araceli to accept the position as Capetillo Campos's running mate. Araceli did accept his offer.

Araceli is uncertain why she was chosen or even if she was the first choice as a running mate. There are some plausible reasons, however, why Capetillo Campos chose her. Araceli was politically prominent in Maxcanú and had been a leader in the protests over the disputed mayor's election. As a political strategy, Capetillo Campos as a loyal member of the PRI may have chosen Araceli as a means to smooth over the Maxcanú protest. Certainly local schoolteachers and those involved in cultural activities in Maxcanú also put forth Araceli's name as a potential candidate. Running on a PRI ticket Capetillo Campos, with Araceli as his suplente, won election as congressional representative from the Fifth Congressional District of Yucatán in 1973.

Most often the suplente on a winning election ticket never has to serve in office. Araceli, however, soon got the chance to take office as a congressional representative. Shortly after the election the governor of Yucatán, Carlos Loret de Mola, called upon Carlos Capetillo Campos to serve as head of the state police to help resolve a serious political crisis in Yucatán. In February 1974 a popular Yucatecan grassroots labor leader was tortured to death, his body dumped by a road in the neighboring state of Quintana Roo. Yucatecans were shocked by the crime and students especially protested, closing the local university for a time. Some suspected the state police of being implicated in the crime. Consequently the governor Loret de Mola chose Carlos Capetillo Campos to take over the directorship of the state police to deal with this crisis, especially as it concerned any questions about police involvement in the torture-murder. Araceli was then promoted to congressional representative and served out the remaining almost two years of Carlos Capetillo Campos's term.

Araceli thus became the first indigenous woman to serve as a representative in the Yucatecan Congress. Governor Loret de Mola welcomed

Araceli with her cousin and political supporter Dora Rodriguez at the doorway of the Yucatecan State Congress.

her, noting that it was good to have "una diputada mestiza" (a Maya woman as congressional representative). The governor did ask her, however, to not try to remove from office any of the elected officials from the fifth district—a likely reference to her opposition to the Maxcanú mayor who had taken office in a questionable election.

During her nearly two-year term of office Araceli sought to follow the political agenda set by Carlos Capetillo Campos as he had asked her to do. He was especially concerned with completing public works projects within the fifth district. He had also sought to have more state funds allocated to the municipalities—a chronic issue in Mexican politics because the central-ized control of funding at the federal level allows limited funds for local communities. Some critics accused Araceli of being only a figurehead with Carlos Capetillo Campos as the true power directing her agenda. She, how-ever, thought she had an obligation to her former running mate to follow a political agenda that she thought worthwhile and with which she basically agreed. Araceli reports that one of her proudest moments in her first term of office was getting funds to rebuild a fifth district school so deteriorated that it was in danger of collapse.

In her first term in Congress, Araceli was not only the sole Maya in the legislature but also the only woman. As such she found herself marginalized in the Congress as a double minority despite being a member of the domi-nant PRI political party. The difficulties she confronted, however, extended beyond the criticism of her supposed lack of independence from her former running mate.

During her term as representative Araceli faced obstacles to the politi-cal agenda closest to her heart—a platform concerned with women and the Maya. While serving her first congressional term, PRI officials kept her from delivering some policy statements that she had written particularly to present in Congress. As Araceli describes the party's opposition, they out-maneuvered her by such tactics as claiming that there was no time in the full legislative calendar for her to present her ideas. In 1974 she was unable to give the following speech about women:

WOMEN HAVE ALWAYS BEEN AN
EXAMPLE OF SELF-DENIAL . . . 1974
Women have always been an example of self-denial, of
self-sacrifice, and of being watchful over [others]—these

characteristics have formed an essential part of her being. In the past these characteristics were considered as subjugation, but in reality we know that it is nothing else but a combination of these sentiments that together make her a model of sacrifice and watchfulness for which she deserves to be understood by everyone.

All women from the time they are born into a life of ideas and feelings are being trained and oriented within an economic environment in which they evolve and in which their talents are being developed for the welfare of the family. Women also possess a great talent for managing household consumption economically. This shows her importance and power within the family, which is the base of society.

The times in which we live confront women with serious problems such as inflation, malnutrition, unemployment, and great demographic change. All of these problems goad women like motors of anxiety, like generators to act to our full capacity. Our ideas grant us a grand human sentiment as mothers, as wives, as collaborators with men. [These] ideas propel her to work together with him in the production of wealth. And by doing so they create a future for today's children and for young people for the good of the country.

original page on page 134

By today's standards of women's rights, this speech written twenty-nine years ago seems mild, even conservative in its argument on behalf of women's rights. Yet Araceli thinks that some PRI officials may have regarded this speech as divisive of their constituency because it singled out women as a distinct group. Consequently, party officials told Araceli that they were not able to find time in the legislative session to allow her to deliver her speech in Congress.

But the censorship by the PRI was not the only censorship Araceli experienced. Sometimes she silenced herself. As she says, as a "mestiza, *india*" with a grammar school education she felt herself inferior to her fellow legislators, many of whom were teachers or college educated. She sometimes felt as though she had nothing to say in congressional debate and feared ridicule from her fellow legislators. So she wrote and kept her ideas to herself.

The following policy paper is one such silent work, intended for a Congress of Indigenous Peoples that Araceli did not attend.

> ONE OF THE RIGHTS OF LAND OWNERSHIP . . . 1974
> One of the rights of land ownership, that is appropriated to us,
> as women, is in articles 103, 104, and 105 of the Federal Agrarian
> Reform Law, in articles that tell us that each *ejido*[6] ought to
> reserve for us a sufficient tillable area that ought to be developed
> and exploited collectively by women, who are duly organized to
> make a true alliance for production.
>
> This law has been fulfilled in reality but we want to declare
> that there are many obstacles that delay the process of legalizing
> the applications of many groups of *compañeras*.
>
> This delay, these obstacles, are due to our *compañeros*, the
> campesinos who are in large part in complicity with the Ejidal
> Commissions and Oversight Committees. They do not want to
> make room for an understanding of these [above] mentioned
> articles and they try to continue to marginate us as in the past.
>
> With the very best intention, with the desire to make them
> understand that what we want is authentic cooperation—in
> the effort, in the struggle to work the land, as real compañeras
> of our men of the countryside, we ask our agrarian authorities
> that the intent and understanding of the Laws, are fully explained
> to the men who have to carry the responsibilities of the ejido
> on their shoulders.
>
> We believe that each man, who by the majority vote, is
> elected to the Ejidal Commission or the Oversight Committee,
> ought to strive to understand each one of the chapters and articles
> of the Agrarian Law, so that in order to apply it without error and
> thus not serve, albeit many times without wanting to, harmful
> particular interests that weaken the authentic ideals of the ejido.
>
> Mexico calls us urgently to production and in our obligations;
> we men and women are responsible to obey the urgency of this
> call. If we have ourselves as women also the right to obtain credit,
> it is important to us to understand its significance and that [it is]
> within our rights to establish its legality.
>
> If we have the right to our allotment of land, if we have the

right to petition the necessary help, and to have recourse to get advice from these authorities in order to help us find sufficient human, technical, moral, social, and economic resources, that with their responsibility and our interest we could fight to overcome with our strengths the difficulties of each place, of each plot of land, we would apply the experience and technology relevant to each ecological situation.

My only remaining comments are to send greetings from my state to all the compañeras present in this Third Congress of Indigenous Peoples. If we have our allotment of lands, if we have legally the right to obtain credit, if we can rely upon assistance, training, and adequate technology, we can have Mexican women honor these rights, complying legally with our obligation "to work in order to produce."

We place in the struggle the most positive of our judgments, the judgment most firm and honest; that is and must be attributed from all women, and with respect to our male compañeros, we employ our equal status for the benefit of the nation.

PROPOSAL:
1. That the regional promoters employ the staff necessary to facilitate the process of the solicitations of organized women's groups. That they give the necessary attention to their needs and problems in order to implement in a positive way the Unity of Agriculture and Industry.
2. To prepare the ejidal authorities in all aspects of the Federal Law of Agrarian Reform, so that, with the necessary understanding of our rights, there will be a real collaboration with our fellow campesinos and so together we will build rural production on solid bases, and demonstrate the strength and authenticity of *indigenismo*.[7]

original pages on pages 135–37

In this policy paper Araceli seems to be trying to build alliances with her fellow congressional representatives while at the same time critiquing them. She wrote this speech to influence agrarian policy, a matter of great concern to the Maya campesinos she represents. The ejidal form of communal land ownership Araceli mentions in her paper is the economic and cultural base of many indigenous communities. Since the conquest, communal land ownership rights in indigenous communities have been steadily eroded as those more powerful have encroached on their lands. Using illegal means or subverting the legal system, the confiscation of lands held by indigenous peoples commonly has gone unsanctioned.

Ultimately changes were adopted in the Mexican Constitution that undermined communal land-holding rights. In particular changes in Article 27 of the Constitution, when eventually adopted, allowed for the sale of land previously owned by communities in perpetuity. Subsequently these changes to Article 27 had a negative impact on indigenous communities throughout Mexico.[8]

Some indigenous people motivated by extreme poverty sold their land and thus lost their livelihood while also divesting themselves of their greatest financial asset without any corresponding long-term gain. Many such people migrated away from their communities in search of work to cities where they lived as the most poor among the poor. Others became impoverished agricultural day laborers on the lands of those more wealthy. As land was sold as a commodity, wealth differences became more marked within indigenous communities, undermining community solidarity. Araceli always voted against changes in land tenure laws that dispossessed indigenous communities when she was in Congress.

In her first term in Congress, however, Araceli's exceptionality did not always lead to marginality. There were occasional efforts to recognize her indigenous heritage. In 1975 congressional leaders asked Araceli to write a speech in Yucatec Maya and Spanish to commemorate the anniversary of the assassination of the beloved former governor of Yucatán, Felipe Carrillo Puerto (the speech follows in chapter 4; see also endnote 14, "Introduction"). Her dissatisfaction with her ability to compose the speech in Yucatec Maya led her to remount efforts to learn to write the language of her childhood. In this case Araceli's exceptionality as the only Maya in the Yucatecan Congress received positive if ceremonial note.

Araceli's unique status in Congress sometimes led to recognition beyond the political realm. From photographs of Araceli during her first term in Congress she appears as a striking and vibrant forty-two-year-old Maya woman. The Yucatecan painter Francisco Castro Pacheco may have noticed her charismatic presence because he asked her to be a model for the Maya women whom he was painting in his murals commemorating the history of Yucatán. These murals are now permanently exhibited in the Governor's Palace in Mérida, the seat of the state government of Yucatán. Partly because of these murals the Governor's Palace is one of the most frequently visited tourist sites in Mérida.

Of the sixteen murals in the Governor's Palace, only three include women. One is a gaunt, stylized representation of a Maya woman with her equally starving family, the mural labeled *Drought, Pestilence and Hunger.* A second mural depicts a Maya woman whose name is lost to history. It was she who married Gonzalo Guerrero, one of two Spanish sailors shipwrecked off the coast of Yucatán in 1511. Both sailors, Gonzalo Guerrero and Gerónimo de Aguilar, made landfall in eastern Yucatán and lived with the Maya for several years. When a Spanish force appeared, giving them the chance of rescue, however, Guerrero refused. By that time he had integrated himself into Maya culture, married the Maya woman of unknown name, and had several children with her. According to some accounts, Guerrero fought with the Maya against the invading Spanish and likely died in battle. He is regarded as a hero in Yucatán because of his loyalty to the Maya and his embrace of their culture. The children of Guerrero and his Maya wife are referred to in the mural as "the first mestizos," that is, the first people in Yucatán (and maybe Mexico) to be of mixed indigenous and European heritage.[9] The other sailor, Gerónimo de Aguilar, chose rescue and became one of Cortés's principal translators, having learned some Yucatec Maya during his capture. As one of Cortés's translators, Gerónimo de Aguilar helped make possible the Spanish conquest of the Nahua (Aztecs), the most powerful indigenous state in sixteenth-century Mesoamerica.

Neither of these two murals by Francisco Castro Pacheco depicts a Maya woman who resembles Araceli. The third mural, however, shows a woman who has a resemblance to Araceli as she may have appeared in the earlier 1970s. This mural paints one of the saddest chapters in Yucatecan history—the sale of thousands of Maya children, women, and men as slaves to Cuban sugar producers in the mid-nineteenth century. While Araceli is not certain that she as a model was ultimately painted into this mural or any other, the woman in the central frame of the slavery mural resembles the younger Araceli.[10]

In summing up her first term in Congress, Araceli likens her reception as a political actor by other congressional representatives, even those from within her own political party, to that of *"un burro que toca la fluta"* (a donkey that plays the flute). As she explains her analogy of her fellow congress members' reaction to her presence in Congress, it was as though she were a burro who comes upon a flute and by sniffing around it accidentally blows into it in such a way that the flute produces a note. Thus those who characterized Araceli as un burro que toca la fluta saw her presence in Congress as accidental or freakish. It is denigrating to analogize a human with an animal, but that a burro is the animal referenced makes the phrase all the more significant and insulting. Referencing un burro, an animal associated with brutish stubbornness and an unwillingness to work or submit to commands, cloaks the expression with racism.[11]

Second Term in Congress: Turbulence and Alliance

After her term of office in the Yucatecan State Congress ended in 1975, Araceli continued to serve in various women's and campesino organizations within the PRI. While circulating through these offices, she also helped in PRI election campaigns including the presidential campaign of Miguel de La Madrid, the PRI candidate who won the Mexican presidency in 1982. Yet despite her dedication to the party and her obvious political talents, Araceli seemed to have no future within the PRI. After her term in the Yucatecan Congress, PRI leaders proposed no higher office for her. Ultimately after many years as a party loyalist, Araceli left the PRI in 1987 because of her distaste with what she viewed as the manipulative style of the party and the practiced self-interest of party members. Araceli reports that party officials seemed stunned by her decision. Even her ladino godparents who had never visited her before came to her home trying to convince her not to leave the PRI.

In 1990 Araceli again served in Congress, this time for a full three-year term. By the time of her second term in office, however, she had changed her political party affiliation to serve as a representative of the Partido del Frente Cardenista para la Reconstrucción Nacional (the Party of the Cardenista Front for the National Reconstruction). The PFCRN was originally formed as the Socialist Workers' Party in 1975. It adopted its new name in 1988 when joining a coalition of leftist parties that sought to challenge the long dominant PRI.

Some political observers noted that the PFCRN was disingenuously associating itself with the Cárdenas name in order to win elections. Lázaro Cárdenas was a reform-minded president of Mexico (1934–40) long remembered as a national hero for his efforts to help the poorest of his nation. The same mantle of reform is worn by his son Cuauhtémoc Cárdenas who has served in a variety of governmental posts, including governor of Michoacán state and mayor of Mexico City. Cuauhtémoc Cárdenas was instrumental in forming the major left-of-center political party in Mexico, the PRD (Partido de la Revolución Democrática, Party of the Democratic Revolution). The PFCRN, however, was not affiliated with the PRD or with Cuauhtémoc Cárdenas.

In Yucatán a dissident member of the PRI who was a leader of the henequen workers, Jose Maria "Pepe" Escamilla, left the PRI and organized a local affiliate of the PFCRN, more popularly known as the Frente Cardenista. He came to Maxcanú to invite Araceli to join the Frente, which she did. Araceli was then elected as a member from the Frente Cardenista under the Mexican electoral system whereby minority parties are allocated seats in Congress depending upon the percentage of the total vote the party had won in state elections.

Yet her tenure with the Frente Cardenista was short. Araceli quickly became disenchanted with the inaction of the Frente and resigned from the party in May 1991 amid her congressional term. For a time the local press referred to Araceli as "*la diputada sin partido*" (the congressional representative with no political party). By that time a new left-of-center political party, the PT (Partido del Trabajo, Workers' Party), had established itself in Yucatán. The PT is one of the political parties arising from Mexico's transformation from a single party to a multiparty democracy. Some observers maintain that the PT was formed as a leftist party to siphon leftist votes from the PRI and thus weaken the party in its ability to elect candidates. Such a maneuver also could split and thus diminish the power of the leftist vote. In Yucatán, a region with its own distinct politics often at odds with those of central Mexico, the PT was the only leftist party in the state for much of the 1990s. The leader of the PT in Yucatán, Eric Villanueva Mokul, invited Araceli to join the PT. She accepted, resigning from the PFCRN and joining the PT to become a congressional representative of that party in June 1991. Araceli's party change gave the PT a ready-made legislative representative.

In her second congressional term there were several Maya and two other women in the Yucatecan Congress. Araceli, however, remained the only *Maya woman* in Congress. In addition to her status as a double minority, she, as a representative of a new dissident party, was limited in her

POR LA AUTONOMIA MUNICIPAL

POR UN DESARROLLO RURAL
INTEGRAL

ORGANIZATE EN EL PARTIDO DEL TRABAJO
CALLE 66 # 500 B, ENTRE 59 Y 61
TEL. 28-38-36.

ARACELI CAB CUMI
CANDIDATA DEL PARTIDO DEL TRABAJO PARA EL SENADO
DE LA REPUBLICA POR EL ESTADO DE YUCATAN

POR LA AUTONOMIA MUNICIPAL

POR UN DESARROLLO RURAL
INTEGRAL

ORGANIZATE EN EL PARTIDO DEL TRABAJO
CALLE 66 # 500 B, ENTRE 59 Y 61
TEL. 28-38-36.

*Araceli's campaign poster as a PT (Partido del Trabajo)
candidate for the Mexican Senate.*

political space to maneuver. Consequently Araceli's legislative agenda was again curtailed in her second term of office as it had been in her first, if not quite for the same reasons.

Araceli wrote the following policy paper just prior to serving her second term in Congress. This policy statement addresses women's rights vis-à-vis agrarian issues.

Rights

It is not to say which or what is the number of the article, for it is well-known that the Mexican Agrarian Law grants the women of the campo access to their rights.

A right born of their ancestral *solar*,[12] rights strengthened by the support and sustenance of the Independence, Reform, and Revolution.

Compañera woman, messenger in the conspiration against colonialism, in the struggle for independence. Compañera woman, in the carriage where Juarez sustained and guarded the sovereignty of Mexico against foreign intervention. Campesina soldier who carried in her skirt food and arms, fearlessly crossing the lines of fire, and whose shawl wrapped the wounded and dying revolutionaries dead in the battles of the revolution. Woman who defended the abandoned trench firing the canon of the revolution decisively.

These are their heirs, those who now strive to realize their rights in the fields of production, who seek accessible credit for their aspirations that could be agriculture, pig, poultry, and bee farming, etc. Because Yucatecan campesinas have always excelled in crafts production. But the sad truth is to realize that all or at least most of the time, this only seems a dream because real agricultural and cattle-raising projects for women are rarely seen.

How beautiful it would be to be able to speak of an agroindustry project of women! There would be farmland, animal husbandry, and the establishment of programs and internal regulations, purely female ejidal authorities, day care centers to educate children, *nixtamal*[13] mills, and places or equipment for processing the products of the campo.

Financing exists, and the law protects it, but it is also manipulated to determine what groups receive programs and are announced. And these can also disappear without a logical explanation to those involved. If there is "debt" or bankruptcy, the campo is at fault, never the program leadership, the oversight system, or the medical personnel or who knows what other things and causes.

Women leaders most of the time are shut out of acknowledging [these facts] because of the pressures of personal interest or they are [thought of being] manipulated like little sheep. For example, if "so and so" has a lot of power to do or undo things, it is because he has the support of the "system," etc. This seems very vulgar or rude, doesn't it? But from these petty things the gigantic failures of the programs grow—bad for men, worse for women in the campo.

In the political arena, women in general terms, despite their capacity for participation, their intelligence, and gift to serve their community [are not selected], but always in elections, those who are selected [as candidates] are those who represent best the predominant party interests never because of [their] strong leadership among women's groups.

The complement of creation is the couple, never can one speak of completeness in the singular, because it is not only one but we are two: man and woman.

Araceli Cab Cumí,
Maxcanu, Yucatan,
August 1, 1990

original pages on pages 138–39

In this speech Araceli notes the rights of women to participate in the agricultural production of the countryside. She emphasizes that Yucatecan women have always been skilled craftswomen. She also makes the case that campesina women should have the resources to widen their economic possibilities to include animal husbandry and raising crops. She also maintains that women should have control over their production and have work structured to meet their needs, in particular to accommodate to their child-care responsibilities. In her speech she uses the terms "compañera women," literally "companion women." Araceli's employment of this phrase represents an enhanced emphasis on her solidarity with other women.

Although during her second term in Congress Araceli was again a minority of minorities as the only indigenous woman in Congress and a representative of a small political party, she did gain some political voice by forming an alliance with another woman legislator, Diputada Blanca Estrada of the PRI. Together Blanca Estrada and Araceli attempted to promote discussion of women's issues, especially pertaining to women's labor. In particular they were concerned about the effects of the end of the henequen subsidies on Yucatecan campesinas. Araceli and Blanca also campaigned to have the legislature sponsor a conference on women in recognition of International Women's Day. Neither Blanca's PRI nor Araceli's PT, however, were supportive of their alliance or their legislative initiatives. Although their efforts were not successful, they nevertheless overcame party opposition and different ethnic backgrounds to work together.

Araceli also notes that Blanca Estrada, although from the PRI as was the governor of Yucatán at that time, Dulce Maria Sauri de Riancho, was not in the governor's faction of the party. Araceli thinks that conflicting factional loyalties may have limited Blanca's ability to move their political agenda through the Congress since many of the congressional representatives were from the governor's faction. Thus party factionalism worked against the legislative alliance of Blanca Estrada and Araceli on behalf of women.

Araceli wrote the following speech to deliver to a special meeting of the Federation of Insurgent Women held in Mexico City. She wrote the speech to commemorate the seventy-fifth anniversary of the First Feminist Congress held in Mérida, Yucatán, in 1916. Once again, however, Araceli went unheard since the lack of funds prevented her from attending the special meeting. Later she discovered that as a Yucatecan state congresswoman she could have had funds from the Congress available to her. No one, however, had told her about such funds and Araceli had not asked. Such a circumstance underscored Araceli's isolation in Congress. Apparently congressional officials never explained to her the resources or benefits available to her as a congressional representative. Araceli never used the health benefits available to her either because she was unaware that she was entitled to them. Despite not being able to attend the conference, Araceli was, however, able to deliver this speech in the Yucatecan Congress.

Araceli was still a member of the Frente Cardenista when she wrote the following speech, so the PFCRN that appears with her signature is the

acronym for Partido del Frente Cardenista para la Reconstrucción Nacional.
A local journalist who had either heard her give this speech in Congress or
read a copy of it criticized Araceli for her poetic mode of expression, especially
the opening paragraph. He thought that her use of metaphor to describe the
essence of Maya life as linked to common features of the Yucatecan countryside ridiculous, labeling it "*cantinflastesco*" after the famous Mexican comic
Cantinflas who often played a buffoon in his films.

SPEECH TO THE FEDERATION OF INSURGENT WOMEN
From the crystalline flow of the cenotes, from the dark-eyed gaze
of the deer, from the beautiful colored plume of the pheasant that
form the scenery of the henequen landscape, the life of the Maya
people arises.

And from the Kankabales, from the Tsk'eles, from the
Chultunes, from the Haltunes, from the Aktunes,[14] from the
summit of the Puucs the image of the Maya woman arises. She
who as [in] the beginning and as maiden, with the circumstance,
of the time of submission, will accept the sacrifice offering her life
to the guardian gods, to benefit her people.

From then, through history as life in the Yucatecan peninsula
was evolving, time was forming the destiny of the campesina
woman. Coming up to our present time, she is yet recognized
as an important part from [being] the gear of the family to her
arduous agricultural tasks. The campesina still fights against
countless obstacles in order to realize her aspirations. [She] is an
active participant in the struggle to produce and considering her
good intentions in work balances the benefits to her family, her
people in order to win continuing social peace as an important
part of national sovereignty.

Through this capacity of sacrifice and self-abnegation,
our campesina voice raises its murmur and in this tribunal of
the state legislature bands together in the insurgency [in] the
opposition protests for the actions not honored. We make our
presence known, participating in the event, that from Sunday,
January 13, 1991, has been designated to commemorate the
seventy-fifth Anniversary of the First Feminist Congress. And
with the best of our efforts, we hope to conclude this celebration

with the guarantee of land tenure, rights, salaries, credits, judicial redress, and the benefits of emancipation, retirement, promotion by merit, and the general defense of women.
We wish to protect the respect, which we deserve in order to secure the linkage of harmony and fraternity for the present and future of Yucatecan woman.

Merida, Yucatan, January 15, 1991
Federation of Insurgent Women
P.F.C.R.N.
C. Aracelly Cab Cumí[15]

original page on page 140

In this speech Araceli employs many Yucatecan symbols to underscore her central theme that campesina women should be respected for all their hard work and granted benefits that would help them and their families.

Araceli uses another important event in Yucatecan political history to emphasize her point. In 1916 Yucatán hosted two feminist congresses, the first such meetings in Mexico and the second in Latin America (the first was in Buenos Aires in 1910). Organized by Salvador Alvarado, the military governor of Yucatán, the two congresses brought mostly middle-class Latina women, many of whom were schoolteachers, together to discuss women's rights issues in January 1916 and again in November of that year. Despite their ethnic and socioeconomic homogeneity, however, the delegates sharply divided on suffrage, women's sexuality, roles in society, and equality with men. The exclusion of indigenous and lower income women, who constituted by far the largest percentage of women in the population of Yucatán at the time, narrowed the scope of the congresses and limited their impact. Nonetheless, they did serve to bring debate about women's issues into the open and place Yucatán at the center of the women's movement in Mexico at least for a time.[16]

In 1992 Araceli attended a Mexican women legislators conference at Ixtapan de la Sal in the state of Mexico. She reports that she was the only indigenous woman legislator at this conference. During the conference the news came that Rigoberta Menchú, the Guatemalan Maya activist, had won the Nobel Prize for Peace. Encouraged by her friend and fellow congresswoman Blanca Estrada and joined by the only other female Yucatecan congressional representative, Beatriz Peralta Chacon, Araceli wrote the following letter to her fellow state legislators to deliver upon her

return from the women legislators conference. She, Blanca Estrada, and
Beatriz Peralta Chacon jointly presented this letter of resolution to the
Yucatecan Congress.

LETTER TO THE YUCATECAN CONGRESS
CONCERNING RIGOBERTA MENCHÚ
Honorable Executive Board:
Fellow Members of Congress:
Community that looks to us and listens to us, I come today
October 21 in the Second Working Session and also in the Third
Period of the Regular Legislative Session of the 52nd Congress
to declare: That in accord with the Invitation received in this
Honorable Legislature, I attended the First National Meeting
of Women Legislators. The Meeting was held in Ixtapan de la
Sal, State of Mexico, the 16, 17, and 18 of the current month.
It was a beneficial experience for moving forward our social
struggle. I am honored to mention the solidarity of my two fellow
Congresswomen with whom I attended these National Meetings,
Beatriz Peralta Chacon and Blanca G. Estrada Mora.

As an attachment to my presentation, I seek the approval of
this Honorable Legislature to deliver a Proclamation of Recognition
and Congratulations to the Defender of Human and Social Rights
of the Maya people of Guatemala, Rigoberta Menchu.

This great woman by the authenticity of her struggle has been
[deemed] worthy of receiving global recognition with the Nobel
Prize for Peace. I present my request in the form officially required.

Attentively,
Diputada Araceli Cab Cumí

Copy: President, Commission of Indigenous Affairs,
Congress of the State of Yucatan

original page on page 141

Despite the proposal, however, the Yucatecan Congress ignored this
resolution to honor Rigoberta Menchú. The deliberate inattention of the
Yucatecan Congress was especially hurtful to Araceli because she regards
Rigoberta Menchú as a personal hero and a great Maya leader. Araceli has

read both of Rigoberta Menchú's books, *Me llamo Rigoberta Menchú y así me nació la conciencia* (translated into an English title as *I, Rigoberta Menchú: An Indian Woman in Guatemala*) and *Rigoberta, La nieta de los Mayas* (in English as *Crossing Borders*).[17] Although Araceli knew of Ms. Menchú as an internationally acclaimed indigenous leader, reading her autobiography moved Araceli to honor Rigoberta Menchú because of all she had been caused to suffer by her activism on behalf of the Maya.

Once Araceli saw Rigoberta Menchú on the Miami-based television show *Cristina*.[18] Araceli was impressed at how well she spoke, especially in the company of some quite notable Latina activists. Because she admires Ms. Menchú's dedication and bravery, the congressional inattention to the resolution to honor her as a Nobel Prize winner was doubly insulting to Araceli as a woman and as a Maya.

Rinconada and Revival: Going Forward

In 1993 Araceli ran as a PT candidate for the Mexican Senate representing Yucatán, albeit unsuccessfully. Araceli's last term of office as an elected official ended with the inauguration of the new congressional representatives in January 1994. Once Araceli left office, she continued for a time serving as a member of the state governing board of the PT.

Later in 1994, however, the PT in Yucatán split and a majority of its members left to join the PRD (Partido de la Revolución Democrática, Party of the Democratic Revolution). The PRD is the major left-of-center party in Mexico and it quickly supplanted the PT in Yucatán as the principal leftist party. Despite the majority defection from the PT to the PRD, Araceli remained loyal to the weakened PT. A year after the PT split, however, Araceli left the PT in a dispute with the party's national leadership over regional versus national-level decision-making authority. In Mexican politics disputes that pit regional political leaders and interests against national ones continue to occur as Mexico wrestles with a highly centralized state within a strongly regional nation—no more so than in Yucatán.

After Araceli left the PT her political participation diminished for the first time in four decades. She said she felt "rinconada" (put in the corner, marginated). At age seventy-five Araceli appears to be closing her political career. She seems to be concluding her political life as she began it—as a community activist in her hometown of Maxcanú focusing on the issues of indigenous women. Her long career has left her disenchanted with political parties, however. She now seeks only informal links to such parties, preferring instead to work directly with the women of her town. Because of her disillusionment with political parties in general, Araceli affiliates only informally with some local partisans of the PRD.

But Araceli's period of being rinconada may not last. In the May 2001 elections the local PRD divided over the issue of an alliance with the PAN, Mexico's principal right-of-center party and the victor in the 2000 and 2006 presidential elections. Such alliances between political parties of the left and right, despite their ideological differences, have become common as the parties seek to move their agenda forward while limiting the power of the once dominant PRI. The majority of PRD members favored the alliance. Araceli, however, joined the other faction within the PRD, called Nueva Izquierda (New Left). In the March 2002 local party elections in Maxcanú Araceli ran for president of the local PRD committee as a member of the minority Nueva Izquierda but lost to a PRD member of the majority faction. Nonetheless Araceli plans to continue to work within the Nueva Izquierda faction of the PRD.

Araceli continues to work organizing the women of her town in the NGO (nongovernmental organization) she started long ago, Kaxan-Alabolal (Searching for Hope). Because of her husband Pablo's illness the past several years, she has had to curtail greatly her activities with Kaxan-Alabolal. After a long illness Pablo died in June 2002. Now alone with fewer familial responsibilities, Araceli may revive her political career at least at the local level in Maxcanú.

An essay Araceli wrote recently demonstrates that she has not ended her activism on behalf of women regardless of her future in partisan politics. Araceli composed the following essay in honor of the International Day of Women, March 8, 2002. In this essay perhaps more than in any other she claims the rights of women as individuals to be central actors in their own lives.

WOMEN AT THE SUMMIT OF THE PRESENT TIME
She has diverse ways of being, of looking, of acting about that
which she thinks, feels, proposes, disposes, and does.
        She can speak without believing, see without accepting,
propose without deciding.

The situation of women in politics, in the social and the economic, is perverse, and that in spite of the voices that raise themselves from distinct angles, in favor of equality and gender, I could personally say, there are steps, improvements, but there continue to be lags.

I will always say that there is a first level for those that by birth, a social scale, they progress and they are successful. We have examples from the national, state, and even municipal [level] that they get, those that we know in their political trajectory, representation at international levels but that their representation is only for those of the upper class.

Many average women are consistent in getting a place that is worthy of their capacity for struggle with the force of their accomplishments in education and they are well prepared.

Very many, [have] survive[d] confronting the economic crisis with their household production or their domestic service, with much disadvantage. Yet their necessities have not been legislated with honesty. But they are going to create for their families what they consider in their clear minds, a dignified life.

Among all these diverse ways of acting women are still beaten by misunderstanding, marginalization, and ingratitude. That is to say, there is no development for women, a real recognition of their worth, be it as a politician, professional, housewife, campesina, or indigenous woman, the legitimate right to be simply a woman: with desires, with talents, with virtues, or faults but with hopes, with intelligence in service to her family and community.

There is also an obstacle in the path of women that limits their complete development and that is fanaticism.

Still the perseverance of machismo or conservatism makes women subordinate to a mistaken obedience, toward many reasons that they make of their conduct and attitude, a mistaken labor that minimizes their femininity, their judgment of life, their intellect, the stability of their spirit and that has them appear as only a shadow of the home, of the countryside, of a profession.

How many of us are there that don't get to realize our born

creativity because we have a heart heavy with the stone of doubt, an uncertainty and an insecurity because it has made us feel that we are measured with a cup of devaluation by that which depending on what the circumstances are, we don't know what to do, in the kitchen or in the bed. The effects of race, of customs, of time, of husbands, of children, of society, etc. . . .

But . . . , how many [of us] are there who distort the true cause of things, as the interest for the family, the problem of our town, our state, our country in its politics, social and economic development, to which we give little importance because our vanity, our fickleness, our inconsistency or our temperament may be much stronger.[19] Our real everyday life is an important part of politics. We know that in the arena of debate, that we do not dare to expound freely and congruently a broad and reasonable judgment about free love, divorce, abortion, sexual preferences, prostitution, addictions, and single mothers as themes that we ought to consider very important for their controversy or contradiction.

Nevertheless there is a history: from the past toward the limit of our horizon and there is reflection, to acknowledge our faults and errors in both successes and failures.

And in spite of all that we don't want to give room to negative things and we ought to elevate the sentiments of forgiveness, of goodness of our service as the Universe demands: with humanity.

original pages on pages 142–46

Araceli begins by noting the complexity of women's individual characters. She mentions that while there are improvements in women's lives, there are many issues still to be resolved. She comments that elite and middle-class women benefit more from the advances of modernization than do the poor. Araceli particularly notes that religious conservatism and male privilege and dominance (machismo) are obstacles for women. She also mentions that any issues of women's sexuality are absolutely not discussed. Araceli has grown with the consciousness of the times. In this essay she mentions for the first time issues such as sexual preference and substance addiction. She closes by calling for women's self-reflection and activism to continue to press for women's rights as a human rights issue.

Conclusions

Araceli defines herself as an intellectual, cherishing the life of the mind and its expression through her writings and political engagement. Her position as an intellectual is rooted in her lived experience as a Maya woman. She is embedded in her Maya community and, through her writings and political participation, able to express its life and worldview. Araceli as an organic intellectual has found her greatest opportunity to articulate the worldview of her community as a political party partisan and elected representative. Araceli remains the only indigenous woman to have served in the Yucatecan state legislature to date.

Araceli wrote the poems, speeches, and policy papers included in this chapter as expressions of her activist agenda for women and in particular the Maya women she views herself as representing. She notes three issues in particular. First, she maintains that women have great human potential and aspirations, especially an untapped or unrecognized intellectual capacity. Second, she proposes that women's roles within the family as wives and mothers are important and should be recognized. But more importantly, women's roles should be expanded given women's talents and desires as people. Third, women have an appropriate role in agricultural production that ought to be supported and recognized. Araceli understands the position of Maya women and the society of which they are a part. In her writings included in this chapter she is critical of the position of Maya women in society as those most likely to experience poverty, discrimination, and exclusion.

Araceli has mediated her representation of Maya women and the wider Yucatecan society of which they are a part through her participation in politics. As the only Maya woman ever to be elected to the Yucatecan State Congress, she was in a pivotal position to express the worldview of her community, make a critique of the state policies toward it, and move an activist agenda forward to better the lives of those she represents.

Despite political party infighting, the politics of exclusion, and prejudice against women and indigenous people, politicians from four political parties (the PRI, PRD, PT and Frente Cardenista) have recognized Araceli's talents and included her in their party organizations to some degree for more than thirty years. Her experience within the four parties, however, has varied. Araceli has had a muted success with her mediated representation of her community.

The PRI provided her with an opening to be involved in politics and

*A victorious Araceli standing in author's front
yard in Miami.*

allocated her some party and state positions for over a decade. Yet the PRI never proposed her for more responsible, powerful positions within the party or supported her for higher political office after her congressional term ended. The PRI often delegated her to the margins of the party and silenced her voice, seemingly wishing her presence as a Maya woman leader but not her participation as a Maya woman leader.

Although elected to Congress for a second term under the banner of the Frente Cardenista, Araceli's tenure in this party was very brief. She shortly changed allegiances to become a member of the PT. Of the four political parties with which Araceli has affiliated, the PT seemed to have offered her the best opportunities to represent Maya women and move forward her agenda for them. In the PT Araceli had a clear leadership role in the organization of the party and a more central voice in the policy-making decision process than with any of the other three parties. The PT was the only party ever to support her candidacy for national office when the party nominated her as its candidate for the Senate in 1993.

Araceli's political future became intertwined with that of the PT. The loss of power of the PT to the PRD led to its near demise as a politically significant party in Yucatán. Finally the conflict between the local leaders of the PT and those from the national party organization hastened Araceli's withdrawal from partisan party politics.

Araceli's future within the party with which she now loosely associates, the PRD, is indeterminate. As an affiliate with the Nueva Izquierda faction of the PRD, she has become politically active again after a time on the political sidelines. Yet membership in a minority faction within a minority party will limit Araceli's participation in the partisan politics of Yucatán.

Araceli closes this chapter with the following essay, one of the four diarylike essays she wrote over the period of a year from 1995 to 1996.

AND . . . WELL . . . WHAT CAN I SAY ABOUT MYSELF?
And . . . well . . . what can I say about myself? . . . It is important for what . . . or for whom, something perhaps so brief, as my biography?

My biography could be as brief as those of all of the women of my race. Our poverty, from birth, could not be insignificant, we form part of the universal richness of material and trivial deficiencies.

And . . . our greatness is visible, because we are great in
generosity We knew how to give everything to time and destiny:
faithful love, nobility, sacrifices, abnegation, in total service,
without fear of the consequences, nor asking for anything in
exchange.

If there is the audacity to say that we accept being oppressed
or compromised, we don't take it as an insult, affront, or
humiliation.

Our ancestral race, that gives us life, gave us with a perpetual,
incommensurable light, with a great spiritual strength, enabling
us to resist the yoke of circumstances, of the worldly road that we
must walk in this physical life.

A richness to love and give all.

A greatness to hate and to recover from it all.

The facets of our personality are exposed to the expression
of human hardness. But we always overcome the falls, raising
ourselves with the force of our aspirations. Many times, [we are]
left behind by the marginalization of a mistaken social context in
the false formula of racial etiquette: all riches good for those with
white skin, oblivion and poverty for those without.

July 6, 1995

original page on page 147

In this poem Araceli continues to explore the themes of the human
worth of Maya women and the importance of the tradition of the rich Maya
past to the Maya present. She also, especially in her closing lines, analyzes
the disadvantaged position of indigenous people vis-à-vis nonindigenous
people, paving the way for the following chapter about her activism on
behalf of her fellow Maya.

Julio 1997

La mujer de Yucatan,.. dice
Estas palabras, son para los oídos que
quieran escucharnos, para los ojos que quieran
vernos, para todas las razas de todos
los pueblos.....

Las mujeres del mayab, estamos buscando
siempre,..... los momentos,...el lugar, para atraer
todas las experiencias, y para eso, tenemos
levantado el ánimo en la inquietud de nuestras
ideas, realizar el deseo de engrandecer los ca_
minos de la ciencia y la sabiduría, alimentando
nuestra nata profecionalidad, al querer ser
verdaderas sabedoras y promotoras de todas
las enseñanzas.

Con el permiso de todas mis con ciudadanas:

Mi nombre fue registrado en el pueblo de
Maxcanú, y en un acta de Registro Civil,
consta como Araceli Angelica de J.
Cab Cumi.

CONGRESO DEL ESTADO
CORRESPONDENCIA
PARTICULAR
DE LOS
CIUDADANOS DIPUTADOS
MERIDA, YUCATAN.

ARACELLY CAB DE PATRON.
Dip. por el 5o. Distrito Electoral.

1974 (no pude presentar)

La mujer siempre ha sido ejemplo de abnegación, de sacrificio, de desvelos, algo que forma parte esencial de su ser, que en los tiempos pasados fue calificado como sojuzgamiento, pero que en la actualidad sentimos y sabemos que no es otra cosa que un conjunto de sentimientos que la hacen ser valiente en casos urgentes, que la hacen ser modelo de sacrificio y de desvelo, por lo cual merece ser comprendida por la colectividad.

Toda mujer, desde que nace a la vida de las ideas y de los sentimientos, se va capacitando y orientando dentro del medio ambiente económico en que se desenvuelve y va desarrolando sus facultades en bien de la familia.

La mujer posee también un gran ingenio para administrar económicamente los bienes de consumo en el hogar, lo que pone de mayor relieve su presencia y su acción en la familia que es la base de la sociedad.

Los tiempos que nos han tocado vivir nos enfrentan a las mujeres a graves problemas como son la carestía, la subalimentación, el desempleo y el enorme desarrollo demografico, problemas todos ellos que sirven a la mujer como acicate, como motores de nuestra inquietud, como generadores de toda capacidad de nuestra acción y de nuestras ideas que permitan con un gran sentido humano a la mujer madre, a la mujer esposa, ser la mejer colaboradora del hombre y la impulsan a trabajar junto con él en la producción de las riquezas y así elaborar un futuro para la niñez y para la juventud de hoy en bien del pais.

PONENCIA

1974 no pude presentar)

Uno de los derecho para la tenencia de la tierra,
está adjudicado a nosotras, las mujeres, en los artículos
103- 104- y 105 de la Ley Federal de Reforma Agraria, -
artículos que nos dicen que en cada ejido debe reservárse
nos una superficie buena, laborable que debe ser fomenta-
da y explotada colectivamente por mujeres, que organizadas
debidamente hagan una verdadera alianza para la producción.

Esta Ley se ha venido cumpliendo en verdad, pero que
remos aclarar que hay muchos obstáculos que hacen largo el
proceso de legalización de las solicitudes de muchos gru -
pos de compañeras.

Esta tardanza, estos obstáculos, se deben a que todavía nuestros compañeros los campesinos, en la mayoría con-
la investidura de Comisariados Ejidales y Consejos de Vigi
lancia, no quieren dar cabida al entendimiento de estos artículos mencionados y tratan de seguir marginándonos a las
épocas pasadas.

Con la mas sana intención, con el deseo de hacer com
prender que lo que queremos es una auténtica cooperación -
en el esfuerzo, en la lucha por trabajar la tierra, como -
auténticas compañeras de nuestros hombres del campo, pedimos a nuestras autoridades agrarias que la orientación, ca
pacitación y conocimiento de las Leyes, lleguen amplias a-
la mente de los hombres que tengan que llevar a cuestas la
responsabilidad del ejido.

##

Cada hombre, que por mayoría de votos, llega al -
Comisariado Ejidal o Consejo de Vigilancia, creemos debe-
capacitarse para conocer, cada uno de los capítulos y artículos de la Ley Agraria, para que al aplicarla, sea sin
equivocación y así no servir, muchas veces sin querer, -
intereses nocivos, particulares, que desvirtuan el auténtico ᴏ- ideal del ejido.

México nos llama urgentemente a la producción y en
nuestras obligaciones, hombres y mujeres somos responsables de cumplir con la urgencia de este llamado. Si tene_
mos nosotras las mujeres derecho también al crédito, nos-
es importante comprender lo que significa el mismo, y que
dentro de nuestros derechos se estabilice su legalidad.

Sí tenemos derecho a nuestra dotación de tierra, -
tenemos derecho a solicitar la asesoría necesaria, y que,
al acudir a las dependencias autorizadas para asesorarnos
encontremos el suficiente material humano, técnico, moral
social y económico, que con su responsabilidad y nuestro-
interes luchemos por vencer con nuestros esfuerzos la pro_
blemática de cada lugar, de cada tierra, pongamos la expe_
riencia y la tecnología correspondiente de acuerdo a su -
situación ecológica.

Sólo me resta decir como saludo de mi estado a todas las compañeras presentes en este 3er. Congreso de Pue_
blos Indigenas, que si tenemos nuestra dotación de tierras,
si tenemos legalmente derecho a los créditos, sí contamos-
con la asesoría, capacitación y tecnología adecuada, haga-
mos las mujeres mexicanas honor a estos derechos, cumplien
do lealmente con nuestra obligación"trabajar para producir"

                                                    ###

- 3 -

Pongámos en la lucha lo mas positivo de nuestros criterios, el criterio más firme y honesto; que es y - debe de ser atributo de toda mujer, y con el respeto hacia nuestros compañeros varones, utilicemos nuestro - estatus de igualdad, en beneficio del país.

PROPUESTA:

1o. Que en las promotorías de zona, se insta len el personal necesario para agilizar- el proceso, en los trámites de solicitud a los grupos organizados de mujeres. Dar la atención debida a sus necesidades y - problemas para realizar en forma positiva la Unidad Agrícola e Industrial.

2o. Capacitar a las autoridades ejidales en - todos los conocimientos de la Ley Federal de la Reforma Agraria, para que, con la - comprensión debida de nuestros derechos, tener una auténtica colaboración de nuestros compañeros campesinos y asi juntos - construír sobre bases sólidas, la produc- ción del campo, y demostrar la fuerza y - autenticidad del indigenísmo.

DERECHOS

NO HAY QUE DECIR, TAL O CUAL NUMERO ES EL ARTICULO, SE SABE AMPLIA
MENTE QUE LA LEY AGRARIA DE MEXICO, CONCEDE A LA MUJER DEL CAMPO ,
LA APERTURA A SUS DERECHOS.

DERECHO NATO DESDE EL SOLAR ANCESTRAL, DERECHO FORTALECIDO CON
LAS VITAMINAS EN EL ALIMENTO DE LA INDEPENDENCIA, LA REFORMA Y LA
REVOLUCION.

COMPAÑERA MUJER, MENSAJERA EN LA CONSPIRACION CONTRA EL COLONIA
JE EN LA LUCHA DE INDEPENDENCIA. COMPAÑERA MUJER, EN LOS CARRUA--
JES DONDE JUAREZ SOSTUVO Y GUARDO LA SOBERANIA DE MEXICO CONTRA LA
INTERVENCION EXTRAJERA. CAMPESINA SOLDADERA EN CUYAS FALDAS LLEVA-
BA ALIMENTOS Y ARMAS, CRUZANDO TEMERARIA LAS LINEAS DE FUEGO, Y EN
CUYO REBOZO VENDO A LOS HERIDOS O AMORTAJO A LOS REVOLUCIONARIOS -
MUERTOS EN LAS BATALLAS DE LA REVOLUCION. MUJER QUE DEFENDIO LA --
TRINCHERA ABANDONADA DISPARANDO CON DECISION EL CAÑON DEFENSOR DE
LA REVOLUCION.

HEREDERA SON, LAS QUE AHORA, ASPIRAN LA REALIZACION DE SUS DERE
CHOS EN LOS CAMPOS DE LA PRODUCCION,LOS CREDITOS ABIERTOS PARA SUS
ASPIRACIONES QUE PUEDEN SER LA PORCICULTURA, AVICULTURA, AGRICULTU
RA, APICULTURA, ETC., PORQUE EN LO ARTESANAL,ES PROPIO EN TODAS --
LAS CAMPESINAS YUCATECAS. PERO CON VERDADERA LASTIMA, HAY QUE RE
CONOCER QUE TODO, O LA MAYOR PARTE DE LAS VECES, ESTO SOLO PARECE
SER UN SUEÑO, PORQUE LA REALIZACION DE AUTENTICAS UNIDADES AGROPE-
CUARIAS DE LA MUJER NO SON VISIBLES.

¡ QUE BONITO SERIA PODER HABLAR DE UNA UNIDAD AGROINDUSTRIAL DE
LA MUJER ! ESTARIAN AREAS DE CULTIVO CRIANSAS DE ANIMALES, PROGRA-
MAS Y REGLAMENTACION INTERNA, AUTORIDADES EJIDALES NETAMENTE FEME-
NINAS, ESTANCIAS INFANTILES CON ATENCION EDUCATIVA PARA LOS NIÑOS

MOLINOS DE NIXTAMAL, Y LUGARES O COSAS PROPIAS PARA LA INDUSTRIA-
LIZACION DE LOS PRODUCTOS DEL CAMPO.

LOS CREDITOS LOS HAY,LA LEY LOS AMPARA,PERO TAMBIEN SON MANIPU-
LADOS PARA DETERMINAR LOS GRUPOS QUE SE PROGRAMAN Y SE PUBLICAN,PE
RO QUE TAMBIEN DESAPARESEN SIN EXPLICACION LOGICA PARA LAS INTERE
SADAS. SI HAY "DEUDA", SI HAY QUIEBRA,LA CULPA ES DEL CAMPO, JAMAS
LA TIENEN LA JEFATURA DE PROGRAMA, LA INSPECCION, O PERSONAL MEDI-
CO O QUIEN SABE QUE COSAS Y CAUSAS.

LAS LIDERESAS,EN LA MAYOR DE LAS VECES SE LES VETA EL CONOCIMIEN
TO POR PRESIONES DE INTERES PERSONAL,O MANIPULACIONES COMO LAS QUE
CONOCEMOS POR BORREGUITOS,COMO POR EJEMPLO QUE SI "FULANITO O SOTA-
NITO TIENE MUCHO ,PODER PARA HACER O DESACER PORQUE TIENE EL APOYO
DEL SISTEMA ETC., PARECE MUY VULGAR O RUDO ¿ VERDAD ? PERO DE ES=
TAS PEQUEÑECES SE AGIGANTA EL FRACASO DE LOS PROGRAMAS TANTO PARA
EL HOMBRE,PEOR PARA LA MUJER DEL CAMPO.

EN EL CAMPO DE LA POLITICA,LA MUJER EN TERMINOS GENERALES, CON
SU CAPACIDAD DE PARTICIPACION, SU INTELIGENCIA Y SU DON DE CRITE--
RIOS EN EL SERVICO AL PUEBLO, SIEMPRE EN LA ELECCION,SE SEÑALA A
LA QUE CUBRE EL INTERES DEL DEDO PREPOTENTE, NUNCA POR UNA UNIDAD
FUERTE DE RECONOCIDO CONGLOMERADO FEMENINO.

EL COMPLEMENTO DE LA CREACION ES LA PAREJA, JAMAS PUEDE HABLAR
SE DE UN COMPLETO EN SINGULAR, PORQUE NO SOLO ES UNO SINO SOMOS -
DOS: HOMBRE Y MUJER.

MAXCANU, YUC., 1 DE AGOSTO DE 1990.
POR : ARACELLY CAB DE B.

DESDE LAS EMANACIONES CRISTALINAS DE LOS CENOTES, DESDE LA MIRADA
DE LOS OBSCUROS OJOS DEL VENADO, DESDE LA BELLEZA COLORIDA DEL PLUMA
JE DEL FAISAN QUE HACEN EL FONDO DEL PAISAJE HENEQUENERO, SURGE LA -
VIDA DEL MAYAB.

Y DE LOS KANKABALES DE LOS TSK'ELES, DE LOS CHULTUNES, DE LOS HAL
TUNES, DE LOS AKTUNES, DE LAS CIMAS DE LOS PUUKES SURGE LA IMAGEN DE
LA MUJER MAYA, AQUELLA QUE, COMO PRINCIPIO Y COMO DONCELLA, CON LA -
CIRCUNSTANCIA, DE LA EPOCA DE SUMISION, ACEPTARA EL SACRIFICIO, OFREN
DANDO SU VIDA A LOS DIOCES TUTELARES, EN BENEFICIO DE SU PUEBLO.

DESDE ENTONCES, A TRAVES DE LOS HISTORICOS EPISODIOS QUE FUERON -
EVOLUCIONANDO LA VIDA DE LA PENINSULA DE YUCATAN, EL TIEMPO FUE FOR-
JANDO EL DESTINO DE LA MUJER CAMPESINA. LLEGAR A NUESTRO TIEMPO, --
AUN RECONOCIDA COMO PARTE IMPORTANTE, DESDE EL ENGRANAJE FAMILIAR, -
HASTA LAS ARDUAS TAREAS DEL CAMPO DE LA PRODUCCION, TODAVIA, TIENE -
LA CAMPESINA, QUE SORTEAR INNUMERABLES OBSTACULOS PARA REALIZAR SUS
ASPIRACIONES, COMO PARTICIPANTE ACTIVA EN LA LUCHA, POR PRODUCIR, --
CONSIDERANDO QUE CON SU BUENA INTENCION EN EL TRABAJO, EQUILIBRA EL
BENEFICIO HACIA SU FAMILIA, SU PUEBLO, PARA LOGRAR LA CONSERVACION -
DE LA PAZ SOCIAL COMO PARTE IMPORTANTE DE LA SOBERANIA DEL PAIS.

POR ESA CAPACIDAD DE SACRIFICIO Y ABNEGACION, NUESTRA VOZ CAMPESI
NA, ELEVA SU RUMOR, Y EN LA TRIBUNA DE ESTE PALACIO LEGISLATIVO Y A
BANDERADAS EN LA INSURGENCIA, ~~PARTIDO REVOLUCIONARIO DE LA INSTITUCIONAL FUERZA EN FEDERA~~
~~CION NACIONAL,~~ HACEMOS NOTAR NUESTRA PRESENCIA, PARTICIPANDO EN LOS -
TRABAJOS, QUE DESDE EL DOMINGO 13 DE ESTE MES DE ENERO DE 1991, SE -
HAN ABIERTO PARA CONMEMORAR EL 75 ANIVERSARIO DEL PRIMER CONGRESO FE
MINISTA Y QUE PONIENDO LO MEJOR DE NUESTRO ESFUERZO, ESPERAMOS, AL -
CONCLUIR ESTOS TRABAJOS DEJAR LA GARANTIA DE TERRENOS FIRMES, EN DE-
RECHOS, SALARIOS, CREDITOS, FORMAS JURIDICAS Y MEJORES PARA LA ENMAN
CIPACON, JUBILACION, PREMIO A SUS MERITOS, Y EN DEFENSA GENERAL DE -
LA MUJER, QUE SE HAGA VALER EL RESPETO A QUE SOMOS ACREEDORAS PARA -
ASEGURAR EL ESLABON DE CONCORDIA Y FRATERNIDAD EN EL PRESENTE Y FUTU
RO DE LA MUJER YUCATECA.

MERIDA, YUCATAN, A 15 DE ENERO DE 1991.
FEDERACION DE MUJERES INSURGENTES
P.F.C.R.N.

H. CONGRESO
DEL
ESTADO

Correspondencia Particular de los C. C. Diputados
de la L I I Legislatura del Estado de Yucatán
Mérida, Yuc., a 21 de Octubre de 1992.

HONORABLE MESA DIRECTIVA :

COMPAÑEROS DIPUTADOS :

     Pueblo que nos mira y nos escucha, tomo el día de-
Hoy 21 de Octubre en la Segunda Sesión de Trabajo, y tam --
bién en el Tercer Período Ordinario de Trabajos, Legislati-
vos de esta LII Legislatura para manifestar : Que de acuer-
do a la Invitación recibida en esta Honorable Camára Local,
acudí al Primer Encuentro Nacional de Mujeres Legislativas,
Encuentro que se verificó en Ixtapan de la Sal, Estado de -
México, días 16, 17 y 18 del Mes en Curso; el cual fué de -
Una experiencia beneficiosa para seguir adelante en nuestra
Lucha Social. Me es honroso mencionar la Solidaridad de mis
dos Compañeras Diputadas, ya que fuimos las Tres a estos --
Trabajos Nacionales, BEATRIZ PERALTA CHACON Y BLANCA G. ES-
TRADA MORA.

     Como complemento a mi intervención Solicito la ---
Aprobación de esta H. Legislatura, hacer llegar Un Documen-
to de Reconocimiento y Felicitación a la Defensora de los -
Derechos Humanos y Sociales de la Gran Etnia de las Raíces
Mayas del Pueblo de Guatemala, RIGOBERTA MENCHU.

     Esta Gran Mujer que por la autenticidad de su Lu -
cha ha sido digna de recibir el Reconocimiento Mundial con-
el Premio Nobel de la Paz, hago llegar mi Solicitud en la -
forma Oficial requerida.

A t e n t a m e n t e,

DIP. ARACELI CAB CUMI

c.c.p. PRESIDENCIA DE LA COMISION DE ASUNTOS INDIGENAS DE-
ESTA HONORABLE LEGISLATURA.

Marzo-Viernes 8-2002

La mujer a la altura de
esta actualidad.

Tiene diversas formas de estar, de mirar
de actuar sobre lo que piensa, siente,
propone, dispone y hace.

Puede decir sin creer, puede ver sin
aceptar, puede proponer sin concluir.

La situación de la mujer en la política
en lo social y en lo económico, esta por
verse, y a pesar de las voces que se alzan
desde sus distintos ángulos, en pró de la
equidad y género, podría yo en lo personal
decir, hay escalas, hay aumento, pero
sigue habiendo rezagos.

Siempre diré que hay un primer plano
para aquellas que por nacimiento, escala
social, progresan y son exitosas, y tenemos
ejemplos, desde lo nacional, estatal y hasta
municipal, que logran, las que conocemos
en su trayectoria política, representaciones

de niveles internacionales, pero que su
representación solo es para lucro a las
de su clase alta.

Muchas mujeres del término medio, son
constantes, para obtener el lugar que
merecen por su capacidad de luchar con
la fuerza de sus logros en la educación
y que llegan a una buena preparación.

Un montón, que sobreviven encarando
la crisis económica, con su producción
casera, o su servicio doméstico, con
mucha desventaja, ya que estos menesteres no han sido legislados, con menos
tidad, pero que van sacando a su familia
a lo que consideran en su mente limpia
una vida digna.

Entre todas estas diversidades de conducta, la mujer es aun golpeada por
la incomprensión, la marginación,
y la ingratitud.
Es decir, no se ha desarrollado, para

la mujer, el auténtico reconocimiento a
su valor, ya sea como política, como
profesionista, ama de casa, campesina
o indígena, el legítimo derecho de ser
sencillamente una mujer: con deseos, con
aptitudes con virtudes o con fallas, pero
con aspiraciones, con la inteligencia en el
servicio, a su familia y a su comunidad.

También hay el obstáculo en el camino
de la mujer, que limita su desarrollo
íntegro y es el fanatismo.

Todavía la permanencia del machismo
o el conservadurismo, hacen que la mujer
esté supeditada a una equivocada
obediencia, hacia muchas causas que
hacen de su conducta y actitud, una
labor errónea que minimisa, su femi-
neidad, su criterio de la vida, su intelec-
to, la firmesa de su espíritu y que la
hace aparecer, solo como una sombra
del hogar, del campo, de la profesión.

Cuántas habemos que no logramos realizar nuestra nata creatividad, porque tenemos, el corazon oprimido por la piedra de la. duda, la incerti dumbre y la inseguridad, porque se nos ha hecho sentir, que somos medidas con la tasa de la devaluación, por lo que, según sean las sircunstancias, no sabemos hacer, en la cocina o en la cama. Efectos de las raices, costumbres, el tiempo, el marido, los hijos, la sociedad etc......,

Pero ....., cuantas, habemos que desvir—. tuamos el verdadero. cause de las cosas, como lo intereses por la familia, la problemática de nuestro pueblo, de nuestro ~~por~~ estado, de nuestro país, en su poli- tica y desarrollo social y ~~economico~~. económico, a los cuales damos poca importancia porque puede ser más fuerte nuestra vanidad, nuestra. veleidad, nuestra inconstancia o nuestro temperamento.

Nuestra vida cotidiana actual, es parte
importante en la política.
Tenemos presente, que en la mesa de
los debates, no nos atrevemos a exponer
con libertad y congruencia, un criterio
amplio y razonado sobre el amor libre,
el divorcio, el aborto, las preferencias
sexuales, la prostitución y las adicciones,
las madres solteras, como temas que
debemos considerar muy importantes, por
su controversia o contradicción.

Sin embargo hay un recorrido: del pasado hacia el límite de nuestro horizonte y hay reflexión, reconocer nuestras
fallas y herrores, tanto en el éxito como
en el fracaso.

Y a pesar de todo no queremos darle
cabida a las cosas negativas, y debemos enarbolar los sentimientos del
perdón, la bondad en nuestro servicio,
como lo demanda el Universo:
Con humanidad.

Marcaná Oax. a 6 de Julio – 1995

Y... pues... ¿qué puedo decir de mí?... ¿es importante para qué... o para quién algo tan quizá pequeño, como mi biografía?

Mi biografía puede ser tan pequeña como la de todas las mujeres de mi raza.

La pobreza nuestra, de cuna, no puede ser insignificante, formamos parte de la universal riqueza de carencias materiales y triviales.

Y... nuestra grandeza es visible, porque somos grandes en generosidad.

Supimos darle al tiempo y al destino todo: amor leal, nobleza, sacrificios, abnegación, en un servicio total, sin medir consecuencias, ni pedir nada a cambio.

Si hay el atrevimiento de decir que aceptamos estar supeditadas o condicionadas, no lo tomamos como insulto afrenta o humillación.

Nuestra raíz ancestral, al darnos vida, nos la dió con una luz perenne, incomensurable, con una gran fortaleza de espíritu, capacitándonos para resistir el yugo de las circunstancias, del camino mundanal que nos toca caminar en la vida física.

Riqueza para amar y darlo todo.

Grandeza para odiar y cobrarlo todo.

Las facetas de nuestra personalidad, están expuestas a la expresión de la dureza humana, pero siempre nos sobreponemos a las caídas, levantándonos con la fuerza de nuestras aspiraciones; muchas veces rezagadas por la marginación de un contexto social equivocado en el formulismo falso de una etiqueta racial; todos los bienes para los de piel blanca, el olvido y la pobreza para los que no la tienen.

I AM ALSO OF CORN

I am also of corn
My house is an ear of corn
In the beans is my spirit
And in fountain of the wells
You would find, the wise words that
To my questions are the answers . . .
—Araceli Cab Cumí, Hotel San Juan,
Monday, March 18, 2002

Yo también soy de maíz
mi casa es la mazorca
en el frijol está mi espíritu
y en la fuente de los pozos
quisiera hallar, a mis preguntas
las sabias palabras que eran de las
respuestas . . . . .

Yo también soy de maíz
y mi casa es la mazorca, . . .
mi espíritu es el frijol
y en la fuente de los pozos
quisiera, hallar, a mis preguntas
las sabias palabras de las
respuestas . . . . . .

Lunes 18 de marzo - 2002
Hotel "Sn. Juan"

Araceli Cab C.

CHAPTER FOUR

An Agenda for the Maya

I am also of corn.
—*Araceli Cab Cumí, March 2002*

Honoring the Maya

Araceli composed the preceding poem especially to open this chapter about her political work with and on behalf of her fellow Yucatec Maya. In it she links her identity as a Maya to the natural world, particularly to the basic foodstuff crops, corn and beans, of the Maya campesinos for many millennia. Corn is especially important since its cycle of clearing fields, planting, caretaking of the growing crop, and ultimately its harvesting structure the campesinos' days and set a rhythm to the rituals attendant to the various stages of crop production. Corn is also the base of the campesino garden. Crops such as yams and jicamas grow among its roots. Squashes and watermelons flourish in the cornstalks' protective shade. Cornstalks support the climbing pole beans. Corn has been important and central to the Maya as a crop and as a symbol since ancient times. Consequently, it is understandable why Araceli places corn symbolically at the center of her self-definition as a Maya.

Araceli also finds poetic resolution of her identity as a Maya in the symbolic imagery of water, a reflective surface that appears to ask and answer questions simultaneously as an image rebounds back and forth. In her opening poem she references the garden wells where campesinos retrieve water and perhaps also the natural wells, the cenotes, that puncture the landscape in parts of the Yucatán Peninsula.

Araceli wrote the following poem on New Year's Day 1986 as a hopeful message for the coming year:

IDEAL
The dawn begins to open her gate
to let the light of the day to enter
people wake up to their daily routine
to their constant labor of struggle and work.
The whispering of voices and the murmuring of steps . . . ,
words that are heard in the pursuit of hope
of a better day, in the new year.
Of what will be! of the good and the bad
The year really could be new
when the light of the sun of justice
levels the scales of the poor
their rights of beneficial equality would stand out
Not sickness, nor hunger, nor misery!
Neither a child barefoot nor starving!
Neither an old person sunk in oblivion!
For all . . . the sun . . . the moon and the stars!

January 1, 1986
Thinking of better days for campesinos.
Araceli Cab Cumí

original page on page 178

In this poem Araceli writes of a better time for the Maya campesinos who are her neighbors and constituents. Although Araceli rarely speaks directly about the inspirations for her poetry, she says she wrote this poem at her home in Maxcanú after listening to the sounds of the campesinos going to work early one morning. The imagery and lyricism of the poem underscore its hopeful, almost prayerful message. It seems part prayer and part Araceli's activist agenda as a Maya leader. As with other of her poems she portrays the natural world as an active force such as in the opening phrase, "The dawn begins to open her gate." On March 21, 1994, Araceli

Araceli with friend and political supporter José Tec at his refreshment stand in the Maxcanú market.

recited the following poem to an audience of faculty and students at Florida International University. She had written it to commemorate her first visit to the campus and indeed her first visit to the United States. In this poem she demonstrates her pride as a Maya and presents the Maya as people not only with a past and present but also a future. She insists in her poem on the humanity of the Maya, their deep roots in the Yucatecan homeland, and their strong links to a Maya past. She begins by asking to be heard:

I HAVE HERE
(My ruins speak)
> *Stop, . . . and listen to me*
> *I want you to relive*
> *our passionate history*
> *and . . . while you listen to my voice*
> *telling our life, make*

echoes in your memory,
relive it with me
with a common remembrance
I am . . . the voice of your memory!

My legend . . . you will find, . . .
you will glimpse my shadow, . . .
my silhouettes appear, . . . and I am here
in each rusty corner
in each stoop collapsed
by this oxide called time.
Look at me! . . . I am here
where I have always been
Waiting for your following call.

See me and listen to me, the whisper
in a soft murmuring of the ceibas
my image see . . . like a reflected light
in the dark eyes of a deer
You can mirror in my gracefulness
Where my image you can admire
And make shine your sentiments
And my beauty, . . . you will see, . . . is without equal,
In the colorful plumage of the pheasant . . .

I am the Maya that laughs and sings
And that also suffers and cries . . .
That I was, . . . I am . . . I will be great
Corn, tree, flower, and fruit
The life of this land, that is the mother
of the cinnamon skin of my Maya children, . . .
people of yesterday, . . . today . . . people forever.
Caminante![1] *Have you heard well what I have told you?*
Have you seen me? Have you sensed me?

I am Oxkintok, I am Entsil[2]
And in X-pukil-Tun[3] *is my echo*

*Araceli by a ceiba
tree in Maxcanú.*

*I am X-Kan-Maya, Chuyub-balam
X-Ulmil[4] that with Uklan[5] make romance
and in X-la-pak[6] guard their loves
that Chak-xix and Chakal always envied
and Aktun Kopo and Aktun On[7] never forgot.
To sing the songs, very honorable
in the voices of Román, Isamuel, and of Donato.*
                    March 10, 1994

                              original pages on pages 179–80

*Araceli at the base
of a ceiba tree in
Maxcanú.*

In her poem Araceli claims recognition of the Maya as a living people
with an ongoing culture. She draws attention to history and locates the sentiments of her poem by referencing common symbols of Yucatán, that is,
the ceiba tree, the deer, and the pheasant. The soaring, stately ceiba tree
(*Ceiba pentandra*) lies at the heart of the Maya forest, as the cornstalk lies
at the center of a Maya garden. Named *yaxche* or "first tree," the ceiba is
considered the tree of life. As the tallest tree in the tropical canopy the ceiba
harbors a rich microenvironment of aerial plants, birds, insects, and small
animals. Frogs reproduce in the pools of the bromeliad cups growing on

its trunk and branches. Monkeys travel its limbs as an aerial passage away from the dangers of the ground. The ancient people of Yucatán believed that a great ceiba grew at the center of the world, connecting the realms of a layered cosmos: its roots in the underworld, its trunk extending through the middle layers of earth, and its branches reaching into heaven.

The deer and the pheasant are animals commonly associated with Yucatán. They appear on the official state shield; Yucatán state is referred to as la tierra de faisán y venado, "the land of the pheasant and deer." More common before they were overhunted and their habitat altered, deer and wild pheasants were once a source of meat protein for the Yucatecan campesinos. Some consider deer as allies, guardians of children or forest-dwelling alter egos of individuals.[8] Several pheasant varieties, such as chachalacas, guans, and curassows of the Cracidae family, inhabit the peninsula. Also less commonly found is the oscillated turkey, long prized for its colorful feathers. Regardless of the relative scarcity of deer and some of the pheasant species, Yucatán remains symbolically "the land of the pheasant and deer."

In this poem Araceli writes of echoes, reflections, and mirrors. She uses the symbolism of the duality of the mirror, the reflection back and forth, of time echoing back from past and present to recall the ancient Maya and their significance to the contemporary times.

Araceli draws her symbolism from the natural world of Yucatán, referencing the deer, the pheasant, and the ceiba. But she also calls forth the image of the caminante. The word can be translated as "traveler" or "walker" but neither of these words captures what "caminante" means for many Yucatecans. "El Caminante" is a well-known, beloved, and certainly the most nostalgic song about Yucatán. It invokes a traveler on the ancient byways of the Maya. The song is slow paced and solemn as though the singers were walking in a procession. It was composed in 1931, the music by Augusto "Guty" Alberto Cárdenas Pinelosta and the lyrics by Antonio Mediz Bolio, both famous sons of Yucatán. Araceli uses "caminante" here and in other poems as another reference point to Yucatán.

At the end of her poem Araceli highlights both features of the natural world around Maxcanú and the settlement sites of the ancient Maya near her hometown, linking the contemporary Maya to nature and to the past. Oxkintok is a large ancient Maya site that lies in a dramatic setting of a hilltop plateau in the Pu'uc hills near Maxcanú. Entsil is the name given the largest pyramid within Oxkintok. X-pukil-Tun is a cave near Maxcanú.

X-Kan-Maya, Chuyub-balam, and X-Ulmil are small ancient Maya sites also near Maxcanú. According to Araceli's description, Uklan, the only nonplace name in Araceli's poem, is an Atlas-like mythical Maya ancestor. X-la-pak is an ancient Maya site located in the same Pu'uc region as Maxcanú. It is one of the three sites long opened to tourists in southwestern Yucatán along with Labna and Sayil as *la ruta Pu'uc* (Pu'uc route). All three are relatively close to the largest and most famous ancient Maya site in the region, Uxmal.

Chak-xix, Chakal, Aktun Kopo, and Aktun On are caves near Maxcanú. These four cave sites Araceli mentions in her poem are significant as named places because caves are considered entrances to the underworld according to Maya tradition. Caves are dark and damp, inhabited by bats and vultures—reminders of the death associated with the underworld. Caves are also inhibited by snakes—animals considered special as those who travel the edge between the earth and the underworld.

The three men, Román, Isamuel, and Donato, whom Araceli mentions in the last line of the poem, were revered in Maxcanú for their knowledge of the Maya and their storytelling abilities. They worked along with Araceli on the joint Spanish-Mexican archaeology project that came to Maxcanú each summer from 1986 to 1991. The three men worked with Spanish folklorist Ascensión Amador Naranjo, recording the rich tales of Maxcanú as they remembered them. The men are now all deceased. Araceli chose to honor Román, Isamuel, and Donato in her poem.

In capsule form "I Have Here" underscores some of the major themes of Araceli's political career: the continuity of Maya people as *Maya*, the importance of Yucatán as a Maya homeland, and the pride and humanity of the Maya as indigenous people.

An Awakening through Language

In 1974 as a new congressional representative and the only Maya in Congress, Araceli was asked to write a commemorative essay in Yucatec Maya for the annual January 3 anniversary of the assassination of the long-venerated former governor of Yucatán, Felipe Carrillo Puerto. Araceli was an appropriate choice as a speaker at the graveside ceremony of the former governor since he is remembered as an advocate on behalf of the Maya and also a proponent of women's rights.

Dissatisfied with her efforts to write the commemorative speech in

Maya, Araceli began to intensify her private study of the language. By concentrating on her few Yucatec Maya books and consulting a bilingual Yucatec Maya–Spanish dictionary, Araceli taught herself to read and write her first spoken language. Her speech follows.

SPEECH IN HONOR OF FELIPE CARRILLO PUERTO
Mr. Governor, Carlos Loret de Mola
Mr. Chief Justice
Commander of the 32nd Military Zone
Mr. Melchor Zozaya Raz, President of the
    Socialist Party of the Southeast
Mr. Efrain Ceballos Gutierrez, Mayor of Merida
Ladies and Gentlemen:
To exalt the memory of Felipe Carrillo Puerto is the daily task of every Yucatecan completely identified with the history of social struggle in Yucatán. We all know about the struggle for a better Mexico from the socialist trenches of Yucatán.

Carrillo Puerto was born in Motul in 1874 and was assassinated in Mérida by the antirevolutionary hordes on the third of January 1924.

He was a humble man; he was "the driver of Motul" as a poet has called him.[9] His humility emerged from a body arrogantly tall of stature. His humility also flowed from his smooth but energetic gaze: the gaze from his green eyes fixed always on the destiny of the humble people of Yucatán, of Mexico, and the entire world. A humility of hope, of faith, of social justice because he was a fair man, a just man, an admirable man from whatever point of view in which his indelible image is contemplated in our heart[s] and for all the ways in which one must help the disinherited of fortune.[10]

Before receiving the venomous shots of the reaction[aries] in his distinguished chest, he pronounced the last message of his prodigal and prodigious life which continues to be a message of strength and tenderness: "Don't abandon my Indians!" Yes, this really was his ultimate message, a message from a man of international stature that has converted in a message the most vital and pure of our America.

Mr. Governor, Ladies and Gentlemen:

Those who have faith in what our destiny will be from a greatness comparable with the inheritance that our Maya ancestors have left us; we must gaze with a lifted countenance, strengthened by our anxieties of the struggle. We must build channels always, not in the tranquil mold of indifference. [We must not] wait for others to come to resolve for us the problems that we ourselves ought to resolve. Besides our faith in our future is based on an indefatigable struggle from the present with an honest participation of ideas, of principles in which personal egos are put aside. We must acknowledge that it is not important who does things but what is important to us is that the problems are resolved. That the wants disappear and that peace and work be the daily routine of our Yucatán life. That with a socialist spirit based in the strength and sacrifice of the Proletarian Martyr constitutes in an illustrious example that serves not only as admiration but also as a guide to those disoriented by the circumstances of the time in which we live or by that found in the ideological pressures that they receive. They look for peace. But they have not found the road. They wish to better themselves but they don't value the struggle that they must undertake in order to obtain it.

If yesterday Carrillo Puerto was someone who believed in a struggle that fully satisfied the anxieties of the Yucatecan people, today we ought not to look for a single foreign product, in a single imported idea that we the governing preach daily with an example of absolute dedication and work. Today we want to say on this luminous morning in front of the generations of yesterday, of today, and of tomorrow that Carrillo Puerto has not died while a single Yucatecan lives in whom dwells the spirit of social justice and the desire to serve others.

Mérida, Yucatán, January 2, 1975
Congresswoman Araceli Cab de Patrón
original pages on pages 181–85

In this very regional speech Araceli evokes Yucatecan pride and recalls Felipe Carrillo Puerto's history as an activist, placing it within the context of Yucatán's own early twentieth-century variant of socialism. Perhaps because she wrote this speech early in her career it seems to contain more political rhetoric than the speeches she wrote later when her political analysis became more nuanced, more clearly and originally expressed.

Felipe Carrillo Puerto is Yucatán's most revered political figure. He was governor of the state from February 1922 until his assassination on January 3, 1924. Known as a socialist reformer he sought to bring change to a monocrop (henequen) wealthy, but socially retrograde Yucatán. Felipe Carrillo Puerto is remembered as taking a special interest in improving the lives of women and the Maya. In his reform efforts he was aided by various members of his family including his sister Elvia Carrillo Puerto—one of the people to whom Araceli dedicated this book. He was a charismatic man who lived an eventful and unconventional life. Today he is one of the most revered figures in Yucatecan history, subject of song, poetry, and legend. Every January 3 his death is commemorated at a special ceremony at the cemetery in Mérida where he is buried. It was for this ceremony that Araceli was asked to write the speech. The request to deliver the speech in Yucatec Maya was likely intended as a compliment honoring Felipe Carrillo Puerto who, although not Maya, spoke fluent Yucatec Maya himself.

Felipe Carrillo Puerto had an atypical physical appearance for a person from Yucatán because of his height and light eyes. Yet Araceli draws attention to his tall stature and green eyes as underscoring his humility rather than setting him apart as privileged. She also refers to him as having lived a prodigal and prodigious life. "Prodigal" likely refers to his rebellion against the status quo and social convention. "Prodigious" likely references his ambitious reforms for Yucatán especially on behalf of the poor, the Maya, and women. In this poem his becomes an elevated image—Felipe Carrillo Puerto installed as a Yucatecan icon.

Araceli's speech derives historical precedence from a most revered figure in Yucatecan history for today's struggle for rights of indigenous peoples. She states that Felipe Carrillo Puerto lives on in the spirit of Yucatecans, making the very regional, prideful claim that Yucatecans can resolve their own problems and do not need outside help. As arguably the most regionally distinct area in Mexico, Yucatecans often emphasize their distinctiveness not only historically but also culturally and politically from the rest of the republic.

At the conclusion of this speech Araceli signs her surname as "Patrón," her husband Pablo's paternal surname, which Araceli adopted at marriage.

Early in her political career, however, she reverted to her birth family names, "Cab Cumí." As she explains it, she did so "because I don't have a patron." Pablo's surname translates as "patrón" or "patron" in Spanish and English, respectively, carrying for Araceli a burden of patronage and obedience that she obviously does not feel.

Patrón is a common Spanish surname in Yucatán. Araceli's birth family surnames, Cab Cumí, however, are Maya. Given her preference for Maya names this too may have been a factor in her name change. Apparently Pablo never objected to Araceli reverting to her family surnames.

In Defense of the Maya

The following three pieces Araceli wrote as public policy addresses about issues affecting the Yucatec Maya. They are given chronologically from the earliest (1989) to the latest (1991). The first address was published in the *Diario del Sudeste*, a local newspaper subsidized by the state government. Araceli wrote this essay in response to an invitation to a human rights symposium that her friend and fellow congressional representative Blanca Estrada had extended to her. It is one of her most passionate and angry.

PANEL OF THE WOMEN'S DELEGATION FROM THE MUNICIPALITY OF MAXCANU, PRESENTED FOR THE MEXICAN LEAGUE FOR THE DEFENSE OF HUMAN RIGHTS FORUM, DECEMBER 9–11, 1989. Henequen was one of the seeds that put in a furrow, and fruitful for life, from which the Yucatán Peninsula was born in time and destiny.[11] Henequen, therefore, in the annals of time and history, is the greatest human right of the Yucatecan people.

But, . . . henequen until the moment of attending this forum (that is useless) for exposing its tragic odyssey, through periods of political priorities, is culminating its extinction. It [the extinction of henequen production] was planned to go away by the agreement of important personal interests of powerful people into order to satisfy their own egos and ambitions of power. They have used dishonest means with attitudes that have broken the back of the henequen industry and therefore, have shattered the faith, hope, and humanity of the campesino.

The dishonesty with which the henequen situation has

been manipulated has licensed corruption to the point of dehumanizing the campesino leaders. Far from protecting the dignity that agave signifies, [the campesino leaders] still possess their sell-out and servile attitude to the supposed grand personages. They use them [the campesino leaders] in order to fill their pockets with goods to live well and represent themselves before the world, if possible, as brilliant omnipotents, figures of high political preponderance.

Meanwhile, however, the henequen countryside agonizes and the campesinos have fallen in the lethargy of ignominy, exchanging their deception, their despair, and their loss of faith for vices fostered by the power of the bourgeois and the pretense of political power whose ultimate goal seems not only to finish off henequen but also to disappear the Maya people.

We feel that this system, despite the high sounding names of programs, logotypes, or campaign slogans, only attempts to distract the intelligence of the people, but in reality opens arms to protect capitalism.

If we are invited to use our right to speak, this forum will receive the denunciations of those who have been witnesses with their fatigue in the arduous labor of the henequen plantings. Today many of them, worthy Yucatecan citizens, appear in the list of pensioners or are widows that receive only a token sum on which to subsist for the rest of their days, lamenting in the pain of ridicule and mockery that the death of henequen signifies.

In the defense of liberty, equality, and justice stated in the universal declaration of human rights, proclaimed and accepted by the United Nations in 1948, we ask, in justice, for the right of the Yucatecan campesinos the recovery of our henequen as a social base from where the work of our people cleaves better pathways in the life of the indigenous Maya.

Maxcanú, Yucatán, Mexico, December 1989
Ciudadana Aracelly Cab Cumi[12]
original pages on pages 186–87

Henequen is the *Agave fourcroydes* Lem., a variety of bromeliad that grows well in the thin stony soil in the northwest part of the Yucatán

Peninsula. The Maya of Yucatán have grown henequen for centuries. Most commonly its dried leaves are separated into fibers that are twined together to make a coarse rope. In the early twentieth century henequen found its largest market as the binder twine used in mechanical reapers. It became the major cash crop of Yucatán as its use in the reapers opened a large commercial market for its fibers especially in the United States. To put henequen into commercial production a monocrop plantation economy developed in Yucatán. Under these economic circumstances, many Maya campesinos worked in slavery-like conditions as debt peons on henequen plantations.

Henequen, called the "green gold" of Yucatán, infused the state with wealth for the plantation class and at times enhanced the state treasury. By the 1930s, however, the crop began to be replaced by cheaper plant fibers grown elsewhere and eventually by synthetic fibers. Almost simultaneously with its demise federally mandated land reforms during the 1930s turned much henequen production over to small producers, in many cases Maya campesinos. With almost no global market for henequen, however, the Mexican government subsidized its production and thus exercised considerable political control over the campesinos who produced henequen. In the early 1990s the federal government began to withdraw its costly subsidies to henequen production causing much economic dislocation among the campesinos in Yucatán who had depended on the subsidies for their livelihood.

Araceli's speech addresses this economic crisis. In her speech she makes the interesting argument that henequen production is tied to Maya indigenous identity and to their human rights as campesinos. She considers the campo as agricultural land and that the campesinos by cultivating their crops bring this land to life. Despite its better-known history as a monocrop grown on plantations with thousands of Maya working as debt peons, henequen is now mostly grown by small campesino producers. For many Maya campesinos raising this crop is their principal way of earning a cash income.

Araceli witnessed the disruption of her constituents' lives as the federal government withdrew henequen subsidies. For many families the indemnification payments allotted them when they ceased to grow henequen were insufficient to carry them over into new economic activities. Having been lifelong henequen farmers, many campesinos were ill equipped to turn to other means of earning income. Also the areas of Yucatán where henequen is produced have a thin, stony soil ideal for henequen but difficult for other crops, making new kinds of agriculture problematic.

A field of henequen.

Workers unloading cut henequen leaves.

Pressing process to rid henequen of moisture.

Workers drying henequen fibers.

Henequen waste byproduct, sometimes used as fertilizer.

Old henequen processing plant at ex-hacienda Yaxcopoil.

Former Mérida home of henequen plantation owners, now a bank.

Araceli, as she expresses her ideas in this speech, considers henequen production as a symbol of indigenous identity and claims its production as a critical human right. By so doing she is underscoring the important point that the campesinos should be represented in policy-making decisions that gravely affect them, such as the end of the state henequen subsidies. She is critical not only of the indemnification that occurred but also of the process by which it occurred. Araceli observes that campesino leaders were undermined and, in some cases, corrupted by being placed as middlemen between their fellow campesinos and the state policy makers who ordered the end of subsidies and structured the indemnification.

As are the deer and the pheasant, henequen is symbolically associated with Yucatán. Unlike the two animals on the state shield, however, henequen has a more painful and ambiguous association as a Yucatecan symbol. It references great wealth for a few but for many campesinos it symbolizes nearly a century of, first, debt peonage, followed by state dominance through crop subsidies, and now an imposed economic change disrupting their lives and livelihoods.

Perhaps because Araceli witnessed the suffering of the campesinos herself, she wrote this especially passionate speech. It is more harsh and bitter than her usual political statements. More often Araceli writes speeches that are hopeful and empowering, often drawing upon the grandeur of ancient Maya culture and the relevance of Maya cultural traditions to the present.

During her second congressional period as a former PRI member and former elected official of the party, the PRI tried to win Araceli again to their side, especially on the critical issue of the dismantling of the henequen industry. Many of the people in her district were former henequen producers whose subsidies ended and who received one-time indemnity payments. She resisted these efforts to court her support because she saw herself as representing and defending the campesinos most affected by the demise of state support for the henequen industry. Araceli persisted in presenting her view that the dismantling of the henequen industry was devastating to Yucatecan campesinos.

Araceli criticized the governor of Yucatán, Dulce Maria Sauri de Riancho, who had the onerous responsibility to institute the indemnification of the henequen industry. By dismantling the henequen industry Araceli considered the governor to have not fulfilled her promises to the campesinos.

During congressional hearings concerning henequen-related issues in 1993, a young PRI party member chastised Araceli for her critique of the governor. As Araceli recalls the incident, his comments seemed to deny her the right to an opinion, particularly one adverse to his own and that of his political party. The chair of the hearings, however, defended Araceli's right to speak on this issue as she chose.

The following presentation Araceli wrote to open the congressional session in 1991 when she began her second term in office. But she did not present it at the opening of the congressional session. Araceli says she felt outnumbered since she was elected as a representative of a small minority party, the PFCRN (popularly the Frente Cardenista). Upon reflection years later, Araceli sees her inaction as cowardly. She partly blames her ignorance of political workings at the time for silencing herself. Araceli must have felt very alone since she considered no one to be her political mentor, no one consistently to be an ally in the political arena until she began to work with fellow congressional representative Blanca Estrada.

Honorable Presidium

With the following statement, if I am permitted to give good tidings to those, taking into account the collaboration of this [public] servant, from this day of January 1, 1991, the 52nd Legislature of the state of Yucatan.

My cordial greetings to all my fellow Congressmen.

So now as a whole, I send to all the people of Yucatan a fraternal greeting of the new year to say: our presence here as part of the 52nd Legislature is in collaboration and in which our judgment, our opinion, our protests will be with the best intentions of searching for a dialogue of compromise. It could be within that is an adequate, possible, or probable solution to the difficulties of time and the circumstances in which people live.

The people, comprised of men, women, and young people who labor in the fields, many perhaps a little, hope that in this year with the experiences of the past, everything will move along more surely to achieve greater productivity.

With this we wish to say that we hope that the governmental agencies will make good on their promises: call them credits, welfare programs, the global food program, F.I.R.A., F.I.R.C.O.,[13] the S.R.H.,[14] PRONASOL,[15] etc., etc. in total all that is contemplated as a mark of the federal and state governments and which [they] ought to guarantee the public in a true solidarity.

But the reality of all this is that to see and feel that the people exercise the right of social security, that they have the right to ask for better education, that they have the right to safeguard their health, that they have the right to just and adequate salaries, that they have the right to hope for dignity and honor in order to live better.[16]

That the people, in their freedom of expression, would analyze, in order to find in this expression, the true essence of their motives and could channel their attitude in the benefit that their will hopes.[17]

To have the right for equal justice, for a justice that is sustained with truth and reason; not a justice that is

obscured with garrote and jail, falsely supported by pride or
social discrimination.

In the countryside, the campesinos have an enormous desire
to channel the paths of work toward a better production. Of
course the countryside is the best guaranty of social security
because in the countryside the roots of the people's social status
is planted, cared for, and fertilized for the sake of the state for the
benefit of the country.

We say this with all respect for the laws that govern this
beloved epical and great state of Yucatan.

Merida, Yucatan, January 7, 1991

Respectfully,
"For a government of workers, in order that the land and its
products would [be] for the campesinos."[18]

C. Dip. Aracelly Cab Cumi

P.F.C.R.N.

original pages on pages 188–89

In this never delivered speech Araceli asks for basic aid for campesinos
and that state agencies fulfill the promises of their programs. It is a hopeful address attempting to rally support to help the people of Yucatán as a
new legislative session began. The four state agencies that she mentions in
particular, the FIRA, FIRCO, SRH, and the PRONASOL, all aid small agricultural producers in some way either by providing small subsidies, water
management, or funds to foster economic development.

The next speech of these three that Araceli wrote addressing problems
of the Yucatecan campesinos was not delivered in congress but at a special
conference at Ixtapan de la Sal. It was subsequently published in the archive
of the conference. By the time she wrote this speech she had switched her
political party affiliation to the PT (Partido de Trabajo, Workers' Party).
At the time she says that she was annoyed that the party leader who had
recruited her for the PT did not help her with the composition of this
speech. In his defense he may have thought that as a congressional representative she did not need help writing a policy speech. Araceli's friend
and fellow congresswoman Blanca Estrada seems to have understood her
better—knowing that Araceli might like some support and encouragement.
Blanca also arranged to have Araceli's speech typed.

THE SOLIDARITY OF INDIGENOUS PEOPLE
The solidarity of indigenous people was by tradition and it
was seen as mutual aid enabling people to do productive
work. There was no sense of paying or cost; everything was
an exchange of products between each village, town, region,
or human settlement. Everything was sharing, the good
and the bad.

This practice of solidarity was utilized during the time
of the haciendas like the *fajina*[19] or obligatory work in
benefit to the straw bosses and at the same time as work to
improve and conserve the feudal landlords. By this means
the dignity and marvelous culture of indigenous people were
crushed and auctioned by the white men with premeditation,
treachery, and venality. And [this] made them feel ridiculed
and without value.

Social solidarity ought to be realized retaking the traditional
roots with the respect due ethnic pluralism in the intent of
complementing the legal precepts embedded in the Constitution
and so to witness the advancement of social development in
modern times.

Congressional Speech 1992
original pages on pages 190–91

In this speech Araceli draws upon Maya traditions of cooperation and
community, of reciprocity and sharing. She notes how the Spanish employed
these traditions to their advantage and thus subjugated the Maya by using
their own cultural practices against them. In particular she mentions the
fajina, a form of collective labor in which the people of a community work
together on projects for the common good. The conquering Spanish, however, used this form of community cooperation as a form of corvée or forced
labor on projects of their own choosing. Araceli draws upon the indigenous
cultural tradition of the fajina as a reprise of what could be useful and relevant from the Maya past to build a better society today.

Araceli refers to ethnic pluralism as the reality in contemporary times
and calls for a Mexican democracy based on such pluralism and Constitution
law. In her speech Araceli claims respect for the Maya as *indigenous* peoples
and their rightful participation within the Mexican state.

In Honor of the Not So Honorable

Araceli wrote the following acrostic, a form she uses occasionally, for a left-ist political movement, the Frente Liberal Mexicano (Mexican Liberal Front) that seems to have originated in central Mexico.[20] In 1997 some leaders of the Frente came to Yucatán seeking supporters. A local Maxcanú political associate of Araceli's asked her to write something supporting the Frente to be published in a Yucatecan newspaper. Her associate, however, never retrieved her work and so it was never published. Araceli knows little about the Frente, which seemed to have faded away from Yucatán as mysteriously as it arrived. Despite her patriotic and laudatory words, Araceli thought that the Frente was not what it appeared. She retains a suspicious memory of them. This acrostic represents a very fleeting acquaintance with this political current.

As Araceli wrote this acrostic, the first letters of each line spelled "FRENTE LIBERAL MEXICANO" down the left-hand margin. I have retained her form here to give an idea of how her original acrostic appears in Spanish.

ACROSTIC TO . . .

F   *Unswerving all, now we demand*
R   *Reviving our strong patriotic desire*
E   *We enter this century . . . Mexicans!*
N   *The rising sun, . . . that which we present the world*
T   *Taken by the hand, always brothers*[21]
E   *Bad past buried with honor.*

L   *We will cultivate hope in our land*
I   *Beginning our new stage in our history,*
B   *Good for all, . . . in a new era*
E   *Expressed as a fruit of victory*
R   *Reasoning ideas that generate*
A   *Great privileges that give glory*
L   *Liberty, . . . Democracy, . . . beneficent justice.*

M   *Mexicans! . . . united, we embrace this strong desire*
E   *Among all, . . . we crown peace in the world*
X   *Cornflowers, . . . garlands of this earth*
I   *Impeccable our idea and very profound*
C   *With the boldness of the eagle in its flight*

A   *We drown in its mud the unclean evil*
N   *New revolutions of the subsoil are born*[22]
O   *Offering of the nopal,*[23] *... green, ... serene.*

Maxcanú, Yucatán, Mexico, 1997

original page on page 192

In her acrostic Araceli references a common Yucatecan plant, the corn-flower, as well as such pan-Mexican symbols as the nopal cactus and the eagle, which appear in the center of the Mexican national flag. Her rallying call to her fellow citizens draws upon agricultural analogies such as cultivating hope, drowning evil in its mud, and new revolutions arising from the subsoil. Araceli's analogies no doubt spring from her life experience in a rural, agricultural town. But they are also appropriate for a political statement about a nation whose economy has been agriculturally based for much of its history.

A Mural Inspires a Poem

In February 1999 Araceli and I walked around downtown Mérida deciding what photographs to take to recall best her life in Mérida as a congressional representative. We paused at the Governor's Palace, the grand building on the central plaza (Plaza Mayor) of Mérida that is the seat of state government. We stood looking out the second-floor ballroom windows to the tree-filled plaza below. Around the walls of this ballroom are twenty-seven murals depicting the history of Yucatán painted by Francisco Castro Pacheco during the 1970s. As Araceli turned from the plaza view to face the murals she suddenly frowned, her face hardening. When I asked her what was wrong, she simply pointed to the mural in front of us.

The mural we faced was the one depicting the sale of Maya into slavery under Cuban sugar producers during the mid-nineteenth century (*La venta de Indios*). Araceli and I were silent for several minutes. Later that day I said to her, "You seemed very affected by that mural. Maybe you should write something about it?" That night she wrote the following poem.

REFLECTION . . .
   Instantly, my eyes alighted
   And I saw, the past arrested in a mural
   My mind agitated, . . . and . . . the memories burst forth

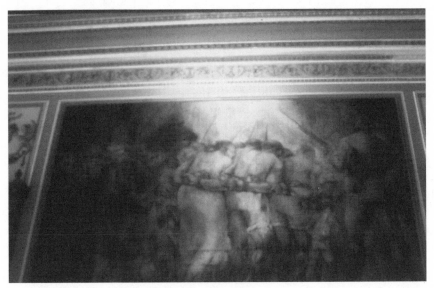

Slavery mural in Governor's Palace in Mérida, painted by Francisco Castro Pacheco.

I relived the pain of that ancestral time.

I thought . . . if through the fault of destiny slavery and
        shame were shackled about my
race
as an evil,
Nevermore, . . . with chains did they succeed in extinguishing
        our great spiritual flame.

White skin, . . . whip that fed on brown backs
And with pride and arrogance to erase the blessed ritual,
But never from my powerful raza did voices lament
Because our casta[24] is of blood without equal.

The past and its sorrows inspired me
and from this frame of the mural, the pain I want to make verses,
and from that time set the tears in pearls,

to offer, in these lines, a most beautiful necklace.
Mérida, Yucatán, February 9, 1999
original page on page 193

Slavery was officially abolished in Mexico in 1821 with the nation's independence from Spain. Slavery continued for the Maya, however, well into the early twentieth century. During the Yucatec Maya rebellion known as the Caste War of Yucatán (1846–55) the Yucatecan state government under Governor Miguel Barbachano sold Maya people to Cuba as slave labor for the island's sugar plantations.[25] The majority of Maya included in this sale, however, were not the rebel Maya but those Maya from western Yucatán who by in large were not so directly involved in the War of the Castes. The selling of the Maya into slavery in Cuba continued until 1855 when Yucatecan governor Santiago Mendez temporarily ended it. Governor Pantaleón Barrera revived the Maya slave trade a short time later in 1857. The slave trade finally ended by federal decree in 1861. President Benito Juárez, the only indigenous individual ever to serve as president of the Republic of Mexico, issued the decree. Despite President Juárez's ruling, however, some Maya were sent to Veracruz state on the Gulf Coast of Mexico to work on plantations under the direction of General Jose Maria de la Vega in the early days of the twentieth century.

Once the "export slavery" of the Maya ended, however, it was replaced by the slavery of debt peonage. With the destruction of Yucatecan sugar plantations in the Caste War, a new crop, henequen, emerged as the peninsula's main agricultural product. Used as cordage in shipyards and then as binder twine for mechanical reapers, the blond fibers of *Agave fourcroydes* Lem. enriched elite Yucatecan plantation owners and enslaved the Maya workers who tended and processed the crop. Poorly paid and unable to meet basic expenses without loans from the plantation owners, Maya henequen workers remained bound by their debts to the plantations where they labored under strict factory-like discipline. General Salvador Alvarado who had been sent to Yucatán by the Mexican federal government to curb the troublesome regional disputes of Yucatán finally abolished debt peonage in 1915.

In her poem Araceli turns around a painful Maya past to pay homage to an enduring Maya spirit. But for her slavery is not an abstract, a long ago event painful only upon reflection. Araceli's connection to Maya slavery is as close as her grandparents. They, along with her husband's grandparents, worked on henequen plantations bound by debt peonage. With the

1915 abolition of this all-but-in-name form of slavery her grandparents and Pablo's moved to Maxcanú to begin an emancipated life, if one not yet free from poverty. As discussed in chapter 3, Araceli may have been one of the models from whom the artist Francisco Castro Pacheco drew his figures of the Maya slaves. This even more personal tie to the murals and what they represent perhaps heated Araceli's anger and inspired her poem.

In July 2000 my husband and I combined a trip to Yucatán to visit Araceli with a vacation to the west coast of the peninsula. One of our stops was the coastal town of Sisal. Neither of us had ever been to this isolated fishing village—once a major shipping port for the peninsula's henequen crop. Years ago a coast road linked Sisal north to Progreso and south to Celestún. But the road had been "eaten by the jungle" as local people say, meaning that traffic was so little on this one-lane road that the jungle vegetation eventually overgrew it. In 1988 Hurricane Gilbert completed Sisal's isolation by reconfiguring the coastline, taking out sections of the road and its jungle cover entirely. Now only an east-west road links the town to the rest of the peninsula. So apart has Sisal become that people living on the coast refer to it as an island.

It was precisely Sisal's isolation that drew my husband and I. The drive on the almost traffic-less road to the town left us feeling as though time had slowed. While in Sisal we enjoyed its calm isolation and vacant beaches. Every evening we spent some time on the old pier watching the low waves of the Gulf wash in from the horizon. We sat on the pier and watched the fishermen try their luck, small gas lamps lighting their efforts. Sisal seemed eternally peaceful, revealing nothing of its past.

But Sisal has a sad history. Only after returning from our trip and reading the new edition of Reed's *The Caste War of Yucatán* was I reminded that Sisal was one of the ports from which the thousands of Maya were shipped out, sold in slavery to Cuba. Recalling our peaceful evenings on the old pier, I thought how different the experience of Sisal must have been for the captive Maya. Loaded on ships as so much cargo, watching the flat jungle of their Yucatecan homeland disappear into the Gulf forever. I imagined their sadness sailing away to slavery and death, away from Yucatán.

Conclusions: A *Maya* Woman Still

The following essay is one of four that Araceli has written in a diarylike format. Again she centers upon the endurance of the Maya and the inspiration of a

Maya past. She also writes of the loneliness of indigenous people, especially the loneliness of their social exclusion.

AND WELL . . . WHAT CAN I THINK?
Maxcanú, Thursday, September 8, 1994, 10:30 AM
And well . . . , what can I think? . . . a piece of my humble biography is important for whom . . . , as important as the humble biographies of the women of my raza.

Our poverty, of birthplace, cannot be insignificant; we
form part of the universal richness of material scarcity and travails.
But . . . , our greatness is humble.
We are great in generosity.
We know how to give all to time and destiny, love, loyalty,
nobility, sacrifices, self-denial, service . . . , surrendering all . . . ,
neither judging nor asking anything in return.

If someone says that we accept being oppressed or imposed upon, we do not take it as an insult, affront, or humiliation.

Our ancestral race, that gives us life, gave life to us with an aureole of a perpetual light, immeasurable as spiritual greatness, enabling us to accept the yoke of circumstances of this worldly time that inspires us to walk in this physical existence.

original page on page 194

Throughout her political career Araceli has sought inclusion, equity, and political rights for her fellow Yucatec Maya and by extension for the other fifty-five officially recognized indigenous peoples of Mexico. She has also claimed Maya collective cultural practices as relevant to contemporary life for both Maya and non-Maya peoples.[26]

Araceli outlines her own policy platform based upon socioeconomic equity, recognition of the humanity and wisdom of the Maya, and their inclusion as *indigenous peoples* in all aspects of the life of Mexico as a nation and a culture. As basic rights for the Maya she calls for socioeconomic equity and a role for the Maya in public policy decision making.

Through the poems, essays, and speeches of this chapter, and the previous one, Araceli strongly roots her position in a Gramscian sense within her Maya community of campesinos. From this position she is able to express their worldview to others and able to undertake an activist agenda to build better lives for her fellow townspeople and constituents.

Araceli as an indigenous Maya woman has an identity as a political activist through her long career in politics. But she also has an identity as a producer of knowledge through her writing. In the following chapter Araceli demonstrates her talent as a poet exploring the complicated themes of human emotion from her perspective as a Maya woman.

Enero - 1,986 - Pensando en
Mejores días para los campesinos

IDEAL

La aurora empieza a abrir su puerta
para dejar pasar la luz del día
despierta el pueblo a su rutina diaria
a su labor constante de lucha y de trabajo.
Murmullo de voces y rumor de pasos.....,
palabras que se escuchan en pos de la esperanza
de un día mejor, un año nuevo...
¡de que serán! de buenas o de malas

El año deveras sería nuevo
cuando la luz del sol de la justicia
nivele la balanza de los pobres
resalten sus derechos de igualdad propicia
¡ni enfermedad, ni hambre, ni miseria!
¡ningun niño descalzo o desnutrido!
¡ningun anciano hundido en el olvido!
¡para Todos...el sol...la luna y las estrellas!

Heme.. aquí

Detente,... y escúchame
que quiero que revivas
nuestra historia ardiente
y.... al escuchar mi voz,
contando nuestra vida
has eco en tu memoria,
revívela conmigo.
con un común acuerdo
¡ Soy.. la voz de tu recuerdo!

Mi leyenda encontrarás,...
vislumbrarás mis sombras,....
mis silvetas surgirán,... y heme aquí
en cada rincón enmohecido
en cada escalinata derrumbada
por ese óxido lle nado tiempo.
¡mírame!...estoy aquí
donde he estado siempre
esperando tu llamado consecuente.

Veme y escúchame el susurro,
en el suave murmullo de mis ceibas
mi imagen vé....como trasluce
en los obscuros ojos del venado.
Te puedes espejar en mi donaire.
donde mi imagen puedes tu mirar
y hacer brillar tus sentimientos
y mi belleza ,..verás ,..que es sin igual,
en el plumaje colorido del faisán...

Heme aquí
(Hablan mis ruinas)

Soy el mayab, que ríe y canta
y que también sufre y que llora...
que fuí,.. que soy... seré grandeza
raíz, árbol, flor y fruto
la vida de esta tierra, que es la madre
de piel canela de mis hijos mayas,...
pueblos de ayer,.. de hoy... pueblos de siempre.
¡Caminante! ¿Has oído bien lo que te digo?
¿Me has visto? ¿Me has sentido?

Soy Oxkintok, soy Entsil
    en X-pukil. Tun está mi eco
'soy X-Kah-maya, CHuyub-balam
X-Ulmil que con UKlan hacen romance
y en X-La-pak' guardaron sus amores
que CHak-xix, y CHakalhaas siempre envidiaron
y Aktun Kopo y Aktun On nunca olvidaron.
Cantar de los cantares,.. muy honrados
en las voces de Román, Isamael y de Donato.

Ah-belnalil wa'nti belankil k-kahal
Yom Karlos Loret Molá·a
Yom ah-chontán u Kanal Kochil Tibil
Yom h-mek'-tantah oxlahun Kapel holkanil
Yom Melchor Zozaya R, ah-chontán muckbalil
Yom Efrain Ceballos Q. ah-chontánil t molayil
Koleleex winikeex:

U tial Kanalkonsik u Káhali Felipe Kamillo
Puerto-é, u meyahi sansamal Tolakal h-mayac
óhup u Káholi yetel u Kahlayi u yaltamba
molayi. Tolakloneex k-hohé bix batenahik
tiolal empiel Méxiko lalail, ixtak ti u tulomi
molayil ti Yukatán.
Karrillo Puerto-é, sihnal Motul ti u habí 1,874,
h-kinsaá FHó tumen u K'asiloo Yakali
Yaltamba, ti u oxpiel Kin u yax makil 1,924.

Winik ah-chintal, tu batá h-Karretanal-i Motul
hebix tänik tomen untol h.ik'tanil.
U ah-chintalé', hók' ti u wimbali Kawal, h-Kara
bakal. U ah-chintalé, beyxan Ku mamananka
ti u tsutsuki pakat, balé chich-ol,
U yax pakat yichobé, etsan bailí ti u Kintahi
winikoo ah-chintaloo, ti Yukatán, ti Mexiko yetel
ti u tolisí Yok'okab.

Ump'el chintalí ti alabolal, CK-ol, yutsil molay.
Tumen latí-é winik tibilí, winik, malé ol
winik ch'aantsil, ixtak hé balak u tuni Rakat
Tuux Ka ilak u malo winbalí ti K-puKSIKál
yetel tulakal beob tuux yan K-antik hé max
otsil tumen mixaán u pack-taK'in.

Mali u K'am ti u Kilich tsem u yol u tsonoo
le K'asiloo' tu mum chitá u tsok u Kúben tán
Ti u Kuxtal ah-sat, maKtsil, Ku belbesik
u mak' u tán yetel u mum-olal:
¡ Maá pàtikeex in masewaloo!
Bey u habilé lelá u tsok u Kúben tán
huntol winik, Ku sasilKantik yetel le tána
Tulaka yoK'o Kab tumen tsok u sotKuba
u Kuxaní u Kúben tána, Ti asab
x maxihul ti K-Amérika.

Yum Halach, Koleleex, winiKeex :

Maxoo yantoón, oK-ol, ti he Kintahé hawalí
ti ump'el nohochil Ket yetel le pàtate tu
pàtatoon K-ohilaKabi mayao, yan K-ilik
yetel u Kanlí K-tanilé, yetel xot-olé, yetel
K-tsibola le yaltamba, yan K-belbesik

③

baili, maa yetel u hetsli Kap'el oli, Ka
K-paaté Ka talak hepelbi, K-mok-yailoo
Tumen u nah hepe'lik, tumen yantoon u
ok-oli u talel Kinoo, u chun ompel yaltamba
x-má Kanani, ti K-mol siil, yetel yotsil et-
mal tukuloo, ti chun pahiloo tuux K-tsik
tseli Kabal tsutiloo, ichil K-batsil, anaktoon
tanile', baax Kahti max Kun betik baloo
baax K-Kate', tulakal mok-yayle', hepul taak
Ka xuluk le ominaniloo, hebe le hetsli meyahe'
u nukul u ximbal tulaka mayao, yetel u
pixani malayiloo,.. nukbesak yetel u muk'il
u chohan-Kibi u mum yail otsiloo bé, Ka a
waku nah bey esah sasile', Ka a meyah nak
ma chen u tial hak'oli,... bey xan bey pay
u tial maxoo, ma u Kaxto' bei, tumen
u sutukoo le Kitioo, Kuxli Konoo wa tumen
hulan u tukuloo tsantioo, tan u Kaxkoo
hets-oli, ma u Kaxtoo bei, u K'at u Kanoo
u yaltamba nahu betkeo u tiaa u tialinkoo.
Wa holhé Karrillo Poerto tu si is-sa ompel
yaltamba tu chupá u iKil-ik u Kahil
Yokatané, baklae ma u nah Kaxtik mix
bal helani, mix umpel helan tukul, Tumen
yantoon u esah Khalachoo gKu Kuhikhtoon

④

u meyahoo.
Behlae K.Hat alé, ti le sasil hats.Kabilá
Tu tan K.chila Kabiloo holheé, behlá yetel
samalé, hebé Karrillo Puertaé, ma kimení
Kitak yan umpʼel maya Ku Kʼuin-t
ti u pixané u yotsil onolay yetel u
tsibolah u meyah u tial u laKʼoo.

Merida Yucatán Enero 3-1975

Araceli Colr S

SR. GOBERNADOR CONSTITUCIONAL DEL ESTADO.
DON CARLOS LOPEZ DE MOLA.
SR. PRESIDENTE DEL TRIBUNAL SUPERIOR DE JUSTICIA.
SR. CMDTE. DE LA 32a. ZONA MILITAR.
SR. MELCHOR ZOZAYA BAZ, PRESIDENTE DEL PARTIDO SOCIALISTA DEL
SURESTE.
SR. EFRAIN CEBALLOS GUTIERREZ, PRESIDENTE MUNICIPAL DE MERIDA.
SEÑORAS Y SEÑORES:

Honrar la memoria de Felipe Carrillo Puerto es tarea diaria
de todo yucateco plenamente identificado con la historia de la lucha social de Yucatán. Todos sabemos como luchó por un México mejor desde su trinchera socialista de Yucatán.

Carrillo Puerto nació en Motul en 1874 y fué asesinado en Mérida por las hordas antirrevolucionarias el 3 de enero de 1924.

Fué un hombre humilde, fué " el carretero de Motul " como le
llamó un poeta... su humildad aunque era un hombre arrogante alto
de estatura. Su humildad también le fluía de su mirada suave pero
... mirada de que ... estaba fijos siempre en el destino ... de Yucatán, de México y del mundo ente
... justicia social porque...
... justiciero, hombre cabal, hombre admirable desde
cualquier punto de vista en que se contemple su imagen indeleble
en nuestro corazón y por todos los caminos en que haya que soco-
rrer a un desheredado ...

Ahora ... ... las balas envenenadas -
de la traición ... ... su vida pródiga y
próvida ... siendo ... ... y de ternura! -
... mis indios ! Si, ... fué su último -
... hombre de proyección internacional que se ha
... en ... más vivo y más puro de nuestra América.

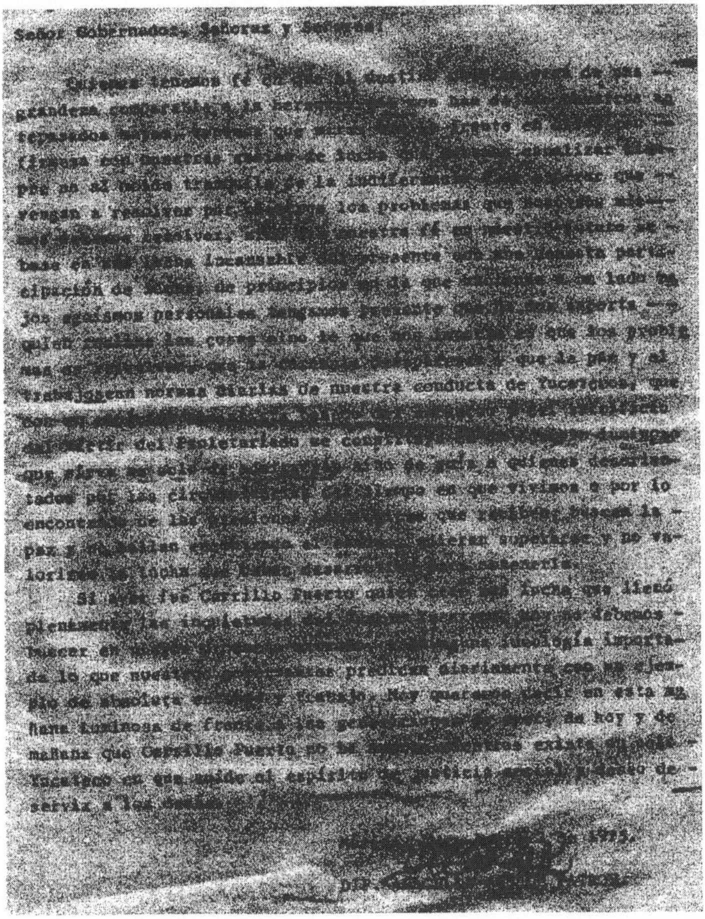

Señor Gobernador, Señoras y Señores:

Quienes tenemos fé en que el destino [illegible] de una [illegible] grandeza comparable a la [illegible] nos [illegible] repasados mayas, [illegible] que [illegible] frente a [illegible] firmeza con [illegible] de lucha [illegible] realizar [illegible] pie en el [illegible] tranquila de la indiferencia [illegible] que vengan a resolver [illegible] los problemas que [illegible] resolver, [illegible] nuestra fé en [illegible] base en [illegible] lucha incansable [illegible] participación de [illegible] de principios [illegible] que [illegible] a un lado los egoismos personales [illegible] importa quien [illegible] las cosas sino lo que [illegible] que los problemas [illegible] que la paz y el trabajo sean normas diarias de nuestra conducta de Yucatecos, que [illegible] del Proletariado se [illegible] que sirva [illegible] de guía a quienes [illegible] tados por las [illegible] tiempo en que vivimos y por lo [illegible] de las [illegible] que [illegible] la paz y [illegible] superarse y no valorizar la lucha que [illegible].

Si [illegible] fue Carrillo Puerto quien [illegible] lucha que llenó plenamente las [illegible] no debemos buscar en [illegible] ideología importada lo que nuestros [illegible] practican diariamente con un ejemplo de absoluta [illegible] y trabajo. Hoy queremos decir en esta mañana luminosa de [illegible] las [illegible] de hoy y de mañana que Carrillo Puerto no ha [illegible] existe [illegible] Yucateco en que anide el espíritu de justicia [illegible] deseo de servir a los [illegible].

PONENCIA DE LA REPRESENTACION FEMENIL DEL MUNICIPIO DE MAXCANU,
QUE PRESENTA LA LIGA MEXICANA POR LA DEFENSA DE LOS DERECHOS HUMA
NOS EN EL FORO QUE TENDRA LUGAR, LOS DIAS 9, 10 Y 11 DE DICIEM
BRE DE 1989.

El henequén, fué una de las simientes que puesta en el surco, y
fecundada por la vida, en el tiempo y el destino del los cuáles na
ció la Península de Yucatán.

Es el henequén, por lo tanto, en los anales del tiempo y de la
historia, el más grande derecho humano del pueblo yucateco.

Pero, ... el henequén hasta el momento de venir a este Foro
(que no sirva) para exponer su trágica odisea, que a través de pe-
ríodos de prioridades políticas, está culminando su extinción.que
se ha ido programando de acuredo a la importancia de los intereses
de los personajes, que para satisfacción de su ego personal, ambición de poder, han utilizado manejos deshonestos con actitudes que
han descuartizado al campo henequenero y por lo tanto, han hecho -
añicos, la fé, la esperanza y la humanidad del campesino.

La deshonestidad con que se ha manejado la situación henequenera,
fortaleció la corrupción, al grado de maliar a los líderes campesi
nos que lejos de proteger la dignidad que significa el agave, po--
nen todavía su actitud vendida y servil a los supuestos grandes --
personajes, que los utilizan para llenarse los bolsillos con bie--
nes materiales para su buen vivir y representar ante el mundo, si
es posible, sus personas con brillantés omnipotente, figuras de al
ta preponderancia política.

Mientras tanto, el campo henequenero agoniza, y los campesinos
han caído en el letargo de la ignominia, trocando su decepción, su
desesperanza y la pérdida de la fé, en vicios también propiciados
por el poder de la burguesía y la prepotencia del poder político
cuya finalidad, al parecer es, no sólo acabar con el henequén sino,
desaparecer a la raza Maya.

Sentimos que este sistema a pesar de nombres rimbombantes de --

programas, logotipos o frases de campaña, sólo trata de distraer - la inteligencia del pueblo, pero que en realidad abre los brazos - para proteger el capitalismo.

Si estamos invitados para utilizar nuestro derecho de hablar, - recibe este Foro la denuncia de aquellos que habiendo sido los testigos, con su fatiga en la labor ardua que efectuaron en los planteles heneQueneros, y que actualmente, muchos de ellos dignos ciudadanos yucatecos, figuran en la lista de los jubilados o son viudas que reciben una exigua cantidad para subsistir el resto de sus días, lamentandose en el dolor de la burla y el escarnio que significa la muerte del henequén.

En defensa de la libertad, igualdad y justicia enunciados en la declaración universal de los derechos humanos, proclamada y aceptada por la Organización de las Naciones Unidas en 1948, pedimos - en justicia por el derecho de los campesinos yucatecos la reivindicación de nuestro henequén, como base social de donde parte el - trabajo de nuestra raíz étnica, hacia mejores caminos en la vida - del indígena maya.

Maxcanú, Yuc., Méx., Diciembre de   1989.

C. ARACELLY CAB CUMI.

Lo que debí decir.
No hubo oportunidad

HONORABLE PRESIDIUM:

CON LA VENIA CORRESPONDIENTE, ME PERMITO, DAR LOS BUENOS DESEOS, A LOS QUE, CONTANDO CON LA COLABORACION DE ESTA SERVIDORA, FORMAN - DESDE EL PRIMERO DE ENERO DE MIL NOVECIENTOS NOVENTA Y UNO, LAS LII_ LEGISLATURA DEL ESTADO DE YUCATAN.

MIS CORDIALES SALUDOS A TODOS LOS COMPAÑEROS DIPUTADOS.

AHORA BIEN, EN CONJUNTO, ENVIO A TODO EL PUEBLO DE YUCATAN EL SA_ LUDO FRATERNAL DE AÑO NUEVO, PARA DECIR: NUESTRA PRESENCIA AQUI CO_ MO PARTE DE ESTA LII LEGISLATURA, ES DE COLABORACION Y QUE NUESTRO_ CRITERIO, NUESTRA OPINION, NUESTRAS PROTESTAS, SERAN CON LA MEJOR - INTENCION DE BUSCAR EL DIALOGO PARA LA CONCERTACION, QUE SEAN DEN-- TRO DE LO ADECUADO, LO POSIBLE O PROBABLE SOLUCION DE LA PROBLEMATI_ CA DEL TIEMPO Y LAS CIRCUNSTANCIAS QUE VIVE EL PUEBLO.

EL PUEBLO, QUE COMPUESTO POR HOMBRES, MUJERES Y JOVENES QUE LABO_ RAN EL CAMPO, MUCHOS QUIZA EN PEQUEÑO, ESPERAN QUE EN ESTE AÑO CON_ LAS EXPERIENCIAS DEL PASADO CAMINEN MAS ACERTADAMENTE TODAS LAS CO- SAS PARA LOGRAR UNA MEJOR PRODUCTIVIDAD.

CON ESTO QUEREMOS DECIR QUE ESPERAMOS QUE LAS DEPENDENCIAS GUBER_ NAMENTALES CUMPLAM SU COMETIDO, LLAMESE CREDITOS, PROGRAMAS DE BIE- NESTAR, PROGRAMA MUNDIAL DE ALIMENTOS, F.I.R.A., F.I.R.C.O., REFOR- MA AGRARIA, LA S.R.H., PROMASOL, ETC., ETC., EN FIN TODO AQUELLO -- QUE SE CONTEMPLA COMO UN MARCO DEL GOBIERNO FEDERAL Y ESTATAL Y QUE DEBE ACREDITARSE CON EL PUEBLO EN UNA VERDADERA SOLIDARIDAD.

PERO PARA LA REALIDAD DE TODO ESTO, HAY QUE VER Y SENTIR QUE EL_ PUEBLO EJERCE EL DERECHO DE LA SEGURIDAD SOCIAL, QUE TENGA DERECHO_

A PEDIR MEJOR EDUCACION, QUE TENGA DERECHO A VELAR SU SALUD, QUE --
TENGA DERCHO A SALARIOS DIGNOS Y ADECUADOS, QUE TENGA DERECHO A AS-
PIRAR ASI, COMO A LA ESCUELA DIGNA, A UN TECHO HONROSO PARA VIVIR ME
JOR.

QUE EL PUEBLO, EN SU LIBERTAD DE EXPRESION, SEA ANALIZADO, PARA
ENCONTRAR EN ESA EXPRESION, LA VERDADERA ESENCIA DE SUS MOTIVOS, Y
PODER ENCAUSAR SU ACTITUD EN EL BENEFICIO QUE SU VOLUNTAD ASPIRA.

TENER DERECHO A LA JUSTICIA POR IGUALDAD, A LA JUSTICIA QUE SE -
SUSTENTA CON LA VERDAD Y LA RAZON, NO A LA JUSTICIA QUE SE OSCURECE
CON EL GARROTE Y LA CERCEL, ALIMENTADA FALSAMENTE POR LA PREPOTEN-
CIA O LA DESCRIMINACION SOCIAL.

EN EL CAMPO, LOS CAMPESINOS TIENEN EL ENORME DESEO DE ENCAUSAR --
LOS CAMINOS DEL TRABAJO HACIA UNA MEJOR PRODUCCION, POR LO TANTO ES
EL CAMPO EL MEJOR ACREEDOR DE LA SEGURIDAD SOCIAL, PORQUE EN EL CAM-
PO SE SIEMBRA, SE CUIDA, SE FERTILIZAN LAS RAICES DEL STATUS SOCIAL
DEL PUEBLO EN BIEN DEL ESTADO PARA BENEFICIO DEL PAIS.

DECIMOS ESTO CON TODO EL RESPETO A LAS LEYES QUE RIGEN ESTE QUE-
RIDO EPOPEYICO Y GRANDE ESTADO DE YUCATAN.

MERIDA, YUC., A 7 DE ENERO DE 1991

A T E N T A M E N T E

"POR UN GOBIERNO DE LOS TRABAJADORES. PARA
QUE LA TIERRA Y SUS PRODUCTOS SEAN PARA -
LOS CAMPSINOS".

C. DIP. ARACELLY CAB CUMI
P. F. C. R. N.

La solidaridad de los pueblos
indígenas era por tradición
y, así se veía cómo ~~como~~ la
ayuda mutua hacía prosperar
los trabajos productivos.
No había el conocimiento del pago,
o cobro, todo era un intercabio
entre los productos, de cada pueblo,
región o asentamiento humano,
Todo era compartir los bienes y
los males.

Este comportamiento de solida
ridad, fué utilizado en tiem
po de las haciendas, como
"fajina", o trabajo obligatorio
en beneficio de los amos y al
mismo tiempo como ~~obra~~ traba
Jo gratuito para mejorar y conser-
var los feudos hacendarios; y es
esta aplicación se fueron sobajand
la dignidad de los indígenas y
su maravillosa cultura, fué puesta en
subasta por los hombres blancos; con la
Proselitación, elevosía y ventaja, de h
los sentirse sin valor y hasta ridicu...
ridiculizá...

La solidaridad social, debe
realizarse retomando las
raices tradicionales, con el
respeto que merecen las
pluralidades étnicas, en el
intento de cumplimentar los preceptos
legales plasmados en la constitución
y así ver ... dar el ...
social en la modernidad.

H. CONGRESO
DEL
ESTADO

YUCATAN

LII

Acróstico a......

Firmes todos, ahora demandamos
Reviviendo nuestro anhelo ciudadano
Entremos a este siglo...¡mexicanos!
Naciente el sol,... que, al mundo presentamos
Tomados de la mano,... siem hermanos
Enterrando con honor,..males pasados.

Labraremos la esperanza en nuestras tierras
Iniciando nueva etapa en nuestra historia,
Bien a todos,...en una nueva era
Expresada como fruto de victoria
Razonando las ideas que generan
Altos privilegios que den gloria
Libertad,... Democracia,... justicia bienhechora.

Mexicanos!...unidos, enlacemos este anhelo
Entre todos,...la paz coronemos en el mundo
X-hailes",... las guirnaldas de este suelo
Impecable nuestro ideal y muy profundo
Con el temple del águila en su vuelo
Ahogaremos en su lodo al mal inmundo
Naceran las nuevas gestas del sub-suelo
Ofrenda del nopal,...verde,...sereno.

Maxcanu Yucatán Mexico - Año 1997

Araceli A. de J. Cab E.

REFLEXION . . . . .

Instantes fueron,... en que mis ojos se posaron
y vi, el pasado plasmado en un mural
se agitó mi mente,.. y... los recuerdos afloraron
reviví el dolor, de aquella época ancestral.

Pensé... si a la culpa de un destino se esposaron
la esclavitud y el oprobio hacia mi raza, como un mal,
pero nunca jamás,... con cadenas se lograron
apagar nuestra gran llama espiritual.

Piel blanca,... látigo que en espaldas morenas se cebaron
y con orgullo y con soberbia, borrar gloria ritual,
pero nunca de mi raza fuerte las voces se quejaron
porque nuestra casta, es de sangre sin igual.

El pasado y sus tristezas, me inspiraron
y de ese cuadro del mural, el dolor quiero rimar,
y de aquel tiempo, las lágrimas en perlas se engarzaron,
para ofrecer, en estas líneas, el mas bello collar.

Maxcanú jueves septiembre 8 1994   10:30 AM.

*Y pues..., ¿que puedo pensar?... es importante para quien un -
pedazo de mi pequeña biografía..., tan importante es como las pe-
queñas biografías de las mujeres de mi raza.*
     *La pobreza nuestra, de cuna, no puede ser insignificante; - -
formamos parte de lariqueza universal de carencias materiales y
triviales.*

Pero..., nuestra grandeza es humilde.
Somos grandes en generosidad.
     *Sabemos dar al tiempo y al destino todo, amor, lealtad, nobleza, sacrificios, abnegación, servicio..., entrega total..., sin medir ni
pedir nada a cambio.*

     *Si alguien dice que aceptamos estar supeditados o condicio-
nados, no lo tomamos como insulto, afrenta o humillación.*

     *Nuestra raíz ancestral, al darnos la vida, nos la dió con la   -
aureola de una luz perenne, incomensurable como lo es la grandeza espiritual, capacitandonos para aceptar el yugo de las sircunstancias del periodo mundanal que nos toca caminar en la vida fisica.*

ANOTHER PHASE

Like all the humans in creation, I also have a heart in which there is
a little corner where laid the secret, the mystery, called love.
Love for my town, for my people.
Love for man and woman, passionate sentiments that exalt the
generosity of forgiveness, understanding the incomprehensible
Love that forgives the oblivion and the humiliation.
Love that is hidden in the shadow so that he who is loved can be
happy.
Love that lasts an eternity although it is of a minute
How wonderful love ought to be!
How fortunate are those who love and know how to inspire love.
I have here what I guarded.
Now it is no longer a mystery, neither is it secret.

—Araceli Cab Cumí, Summer 2000

otra face

Como todos los seres de la creación, yo también tengo un
corazón en el cual, hay un rinconcito donde estaba el secreto,
el misterio, llamado amor.
Amor a mi pueblo, a mi gente.
Amor de hombre y mujer, sentimientos apasionados que subliman
la generosidad del perdón, comprendiendo la incomprensión.
Amor que perdona el olvido y la humillación.
Amor que se esconde, en la sombra, para que el ser amado sea feliz.
Amor que vale una eternidad, aun que sea de un minuto.
Que maravilloso debe ser el amor!
Que afortunados los que aman y saben inspirar amor.
He aquí lo que yo guardaba,
Ya no es ningún misterio, ya no es ningún secreto

CHAPTER FIVE

Poetry

"Because I Have a Heart"

Love that lasts an eternity although it is of a minute.
—*Araceli Cab Cumí, Summer 2000*

Discarded Pages and a Fallen Leaf

Beginning in May 1976 and continuing off and on until June 1999, Araceli wrote a series of thirteen love poems interconnected by themes of intimacy, longing, and solitude. As she explains in the opening poem, which she composed especially for this chapter, she wrote these poems "because I have a heart" (*porque tengo un corazón*).

The opening and closing poems of this twenty-three-year series have the same title, "Hoja suelta." As I explained in the introduction, I have translated the plural of this complex phrase, "hojas sueltas," as "discarded pages." When Araceli suggested "hojas sueltas" as the title for this book, it was the only occasion in which she used this phrase as a plural—in this case as a reference both to her earliest writings that she had thrown away as well as to the scattered pages of her work that she conserved.

But the phrase "hoja(s) suelta(s)" has more meaning to Araceli, however, than a book title she selected for its pointed and poignant humor. Araceli invokes this phrase in its singular as a title to introduce and then conclude her series of poems.

Araceli seated in a tú y yo *(you and I) park bench whose curved style allows two people to converse face to face easily.*

What then does "hoja suelta" mean to Araceli? As I explained in the introduction, "hoja" can be translated from Spanish to English as "page," "leaf," or "sheet of paper" depending on the context. "Suelta" from the verb "soltar" can be translated variously as "to unfasten, loosen," "to throw away, discard," or "to fall, drop." "Hoja suelta" thus becomes a complex phrase because of the interplay of its two words, each having a variety of possible meanings and consequently many possible translations.

Araceli plays with these variant meanings when she employs "hoja suelta" in her writings. In 1999 she wrote a poem, "A una pregunta—Porqué 'hoja suelta'?" (To a Question—Why "Discarded Pages"?), in response to my asking her about her use of the phrase. Araceli uses "hoja suelta" in this poem, and also in the acknowledgments of this book, as a reference to life's vagaries and chances—a consistent leitmotif of her writings. In answer to my question about her repeated use of this symbolic phrase, Araceli wrote in 1999:

To a Question—Why "Discarded Pages"?

Feelings, scenes of
all of life and
perhaps beyond life itself
Fluent of an ideal, of an illusion
Of desires, of hope, and of faith.
Drops of love, whispers, and sighs
in the blossomed corner of our intimacy.

Seeds fertile by the weeping of the soul that searches . . . that wants
to germinate
In the tree of life that radiates light
And of the fruits that illuminate the truth,
The best intentions, a great humanity . . .
Then a falling leaf
That was loosened by a soft breeze
Could have fallen by chance in a flower garden
or trine¹ of aromas and flowers.

But my falling leaf could also
have been carried off by a harsh wind
of a wicked storm,
that could carry it away to inhospitable places
to arid deserts or to dark rocks hidden under the sea
whose evil jags could destroy it,
and so my dear falling leaf could be ripped
and in so many pieces, would turn to dust
would turn to nothing . . .

For this my sentiment, molded
in words, many times
cannot find a title, a name
that could be read or touched
it could only be or wish to be
a fallen leaf . . .

Thursday, February 4, 1999

original pages on pages 210–11

In the stanzas beginning as "Seeds fertile by the weeping of the soul that searches" and "But my falling leaf could also," Araceli lyrically describes the vagaries of life chances. One could find oneself in a flower garden or just as easily in a desert or under the sea. Her life, where her fallen leaf landed, however, has led her to poetry. The closing stanza of her poem seems to give a sense of potential waiting to blossom coupled with a humble sense of self-acceptance.

The poems that follow in Araceli's series resonate with the common human experience of abandonment, betrayal, longing, and also of intimacy, lost or never held. Her style of expression is direct and elegant. Araceli alone knows the muse for her poetry. She has cloaked the inspiration for her poems in a privacy I respect. It is possible that human sentiment itself is the muse of Araceli's poetry as it may have been for other poets.[2] She writes her emotions and thoughts through her poems. In her life as a Maya woman and an exceptional individual Araceli has had few channels of expression open to her. Her intelligence and forceful personality may have distanced her from others in the context of her life as a Maya woman in a small town. Araceli has sometimes remarked that her family doesn't understand her. It also seems that she has not encountered very many kindred spirits or people who at least understood her talents and valued her as an intellectual capable of producing fine poetry. The women of Maxcanú who have supported her throughout her long political career admire her intellectual abilities and political achievements but none have read her poetry.

Araceli's poems are transcendent of a single life or culture. Nonetheless some of the symbolism and references she uses in her poems are rooted in her regional milieu. She references the natural world, especially the pheasant, deer, and the ceiba tree of Yucatán, in her poems as she does in her essays and political writings.

Araceli's series of thirteen poems follows in the chronological order that she wrote them. I have chosen to present her poems without commentary beyond this opening and a concluding statement. Araceli's poems stand on their own as time- and place-transcendent expressions of deep human emotion.

In these poems she addresses a love lost, never realized, or never returned, sometimes referencing physical expressions of love. Others of this series portray her gift of love to another or the passage of time in remembrance of love. Her haunting poems transform pain into beauty. She begins her poetic series in 1976 with the first "Hoja suelta" poem, addressing a loneliness that becomes a companionate solitude:

HOJA SUELTA (1976)
(*Discarded Page/Fallen Leaf [1976]*)
> *When I realize*
> *that to look for love, isn't worth it*
> *because it isn't possible*
> *to find affection that could be real;*
> *I feel the presence of a great companion,*
> *one that understands me and that does not defraud me*
> *one that always listens and that does not deceive me:*
> *It is my solitude.*
>
> *It with its silence*
> *gives answer to many and many questions,*
> *that of longing*
> *that never found its normal channel*
> *and, of course, never overflowed*
> *because never was there another soul equal,*
> *where the sentiments of love and friendship could make a nest*
> *I realize*
> *that too much time has passed,*
> *over my longing, I see*
> *that the sky has spread out its gray mantle*
> *is when I feel most that always I had it*
> *in my long hours of meditation*
> *it always is my great companion:*
>
> *My great solitude.*

May 24, 1976, A. Cab Cumí

original page on page 212

In the following twelve poems Araceli continues writing her thoughts about love. The poems are presented in the order they were written, each expressing Araceli's nuanced views of themes of human love.

FOR . . .

> *The memory of a tear fallen*
> *from your eyes, like a pure feeling,*
> *like a flower shed from your life*
> *and which as it falls . . . was the love of this moment.*
> *The enchantment of this tear . . . overpowered.*
> *An oath gushed out of my soul*
> *If by this enchantment I felt overcome*
> *Believing myself in your life . . . the complement[3]*
> *If the memory of these hours so dear*
> *Erased the torments from your life*
> *Like a beautiful flowering rain*
> *whose drops are these thoughts.*

August 15, 1979

original page on page 213

FOR A NIGHT

> *And . . . so as you came*
> *you want to move away*
> *You never offered me anything*
> *You have to go away*
>
> *You scent my night*
> *those kisses that you left me*
> *squandered stars*
> *palpitating caresses*
>
> *You leave here in my body*
> *All your heat of the night*
> *You leave me in [my] mouth*
> *All your aroma . . . night*
>
> *You leave in my soul*
> *A stamp of freshness*
> *Your soul . . . night . . .*
> *An eternity of tenderness*

Monday, August 20, 1979

original page on page 214

To Say

> I don't know if I can write some prose
> Or perhaps it could be a sonnet
> I only want that the perfume of my roses
> To perfume for you this moment.
> From my garden, the scented flowers
> in a perfume, delicate and very discrete,
> envelop you and tell you many things
> among them, my greatest secret.
>
> All this with the greatest respect
> To God, . . . who knows about my things
> I ask that you analyze all this,
>
> And, . . . if you find that these loving phrases
> embellish your life this moment
> Take them all, . . . because they are my roses.
>   September 11, 1979

original page on page 215

To a Letter

> That humble letter that sheltered
> the most pure and beautiful sentiments
> that paper in which it spoke
> although uncertain and distant the hope.
>
> That letter that said with sadness
> "when you left, you told me that you would return"
> and I believed you, I kept on hoping for your return
> because I wanted to believe that you had not lied to me.
>
> "Nonetheless, I predicted in your silence
> that you have forgotten me
> that some other love, from me has torn you
> another love that perhaps you have erased me."
>
> This is the sadness that confined

that letter that never was read,
by that one,[4] that for your forgetfulness was written
with a love that could not be returned

That letter has inspired me
to transform in verse the sadness
to make of that fruitless wait, a poem
and a delusion in song converted.

February 1980

original page on page 216

How . . .
   How are you going to stop loving me
   If you never loved me?
   How are you going to forget me
   if I never was in [with] you?
   I am going to stay very sad
   if I never see you again
   Because I, . . . did love you
   Because [for][5] me, I was with you.

   How to note my absence
   if I were never present
   in your memory never
   a trace remained
   My sentiment
   That you never understood
   I cannot break the wall
   of another love

October 26, 1983

original page on page 217

THINKING IN THE NIGHT[6]
   The scattered clouds
   the clouds, . . . like little bits
   of cotton
   in the warped window frame

the steel blue of the skies.
It is the sleep of this day
whose eyelids in dreams
fall into a night lullaby,
of the birds.
In the stirring of the winds
Softly swing the scents
They are the ladies, . . . the gentlemen
The lemon groves and the jasmines . . . of the province[7]
that wait, . . . to cover
the grand cloak of the night.

The night of Monday, October 30, 1984

original page on page 218

SEARCHING

I search and I search.
And in searching, so went my time.
On the road I find you.
But I meet you out of time

That something went wrong
in the turn of my destiny
that nothing can remedy
because the passing of the years falls upon me.

1985

original page on page 219

FOR A MEMORY

In the silence of the night
I awake with the murmur
of a distant song . . .
My thoughts return to you
love that you denied me
the shelter of your arms
and closed to me your heart.

The so distant voice that was singing
a song that of love

a night of serenade . . . remembered
a romantic voice that touched
and . . . to feel. how far you were
my heart shuddered
and in sorrow my dream grieved.

Your absence is something that envelopes me
in an oblivion sad and slow
yet so, . . . I encourage myself
to speak, of you, the lost one
my memory of love, soft, serene.
my heart therefore, . . . has kept a promise to you.

1986

original page on page 220

I Don't Know

I never wanted you to go
You only said that you were going
I did not even tell that to come
so you drew near me.

I never wanted you to forget me
And yet you forgot me, I know it
But neither did I demand that you follow me
You are free to go, also I know.

I don't know in what I failed
what I did wrong, . . . so that I lost you
but I believe that I loved you
and I will pass time to forget you.

November 1988

original page on page 221

Chimera

I would like to have you, . . . to reach with my hands
to touch your body, . . . to fill it with caresses
but I can only touch your image with my eyes

through memories.
I would like . . . with my lips on yours
to feel your soul blended with my kisses
But I can only kiss you with my soul
because you as always are very far away.
I would like . . . with my body united with yours
to make you feel an ardent fire,
but . . . in my heart . . . alone . . . the fire consumes me
in the infinite desire to have you.
If you could listen to my voice, I could tell you
that I loved you, . . . love you . . . and will love you . . .
that you were, you are, and you will be
my past, . . . my present . . . and . . . future.

November 14, 1989

original page on page 222

FRAGMENTS

I will never return to see you,
beautiful illusion of my soul.
I will never return to look at you
to see in your eyes harmony,
but . . . I am going to remember you
with your last words of that day
and so . . . then . . . I am not going to forget you
because you will always be the joy of my life.

Tears, . . . pearls of life
murmuring songstresses that flow
when there is happiness.
Tears, . . . sublime messengers
That overflow all your tenderness
Forming a flowing crystalline of the eye.
Tears, . . . cool and sweet
When something inspires them
As part of an ideal.

Sunday, January 21, 1990

original page on page 223

The last poem in the series, also entitled "Hoja suelta" as is the opening poem, Araceli wrote originally in 1980 and substantially revised in 1996.[8] This poem addresses a love that seems to have never completed its bright promise. It concludes the thirteen-poem series of love themes: gifts of love, abandonment, betrayal, longing, and also of intimacy, lost or never held.

HOJA SUELTA (1996)
(Discarded Page/Fallen Leaf [1996])

My ears are full of joy
if the things you told are true
if the night of this day is real
with the beautiful words that you loved me.

In the heavens total harmony sounded
the brilliant stars that you saw
courted with smooth melodies
the ideal that between the two exist.

In the light of your eyes I saw that there was
A feeling that in words you transformed
And took the lethargy out of my soul
In an infinite longing to feel you.

I thought, . . .
If it would be possible still
That the rosebush of my life that is sad
Would bloom for you, my love
With the love that in words you gave me.

I don't know if what I wrote are quatrains
Or if they can be called redondillas[9]
I don't know either if they could be sonnets
I only know that for you, . . . it is poetry.

Night of Monday, February 4, 1980;
redrafted June 1996

original page on page 224

Conclusions

Poetry is a written form of expression intended to be read; but it is also a performance waiting to be experienced. Poetry readings by authors are important because they give life to the poems not evident in print. The Yucatec Maya have a long tradition of oral expression that emphasizes performance as integral to the telling of stories.[10] Since Araceli has written part of her story as a woman in her poems, perhaps she will have the occasion to perform her poetry and give it expression beyond the pages of this book.

As perhaps in no other chapter, Araceli demonstrates here her humanity as a Maya woman, and by extension that of other Maya women, who as individuals have a fully fleshed emotional life and the ability to express their emotions through poetry. Araceli's poems are expressions of her creativity and intellect, one more venue in which she compellingly presents the worldview of a Maya woman to those foreign to her culture. While her poetry has no overt political agenda, Araceli's poems underscore her credentials as an organic intellectual representing the worldview of a Maya woman, particularly her intimate emotional life as a woman, to others.

Now in her seventies, Araceli reflects upon her life and considers her future in the next chapter, "Endings?"

a una pregunta — — — — —
Porqué hojas sueltas?

Jueves
Febrero 4 - 99

Sentimientos, esencias de
lo Todo de la vida y
quizá mas allá de la vida misma.
Fluidos del ideal, de la ilusión
de los deseos, de la esperanza y de la fé.
Gotas de amor, susurros y suspiros
en el rincón florido de nuestra intimidad.
Semilla fecundada por los lloros
del alma que busca,... que quiere germinar;
en el arbol de vida que irradie luz.
y dé los frutos que dominen la verdad,
las buenas intensiones, una gran humanidad....
Entonces alguna hoja suelta
que fuese desprendida, por una suave brisa
~~podría~~ pudiese caer, acaso en un vergel
de jardines, y trinos , de aromas y de flor.

Mas tambien pudiese mi hoja suelta,
arrebatada, ser por bruscos vientos
de ráfagas malvadas
que puedan arrastrarla a parajes inhospitos
hacia desiertos áridos, o hacia oscuros abrojos
cuyas malas espinas la puedan destrozar,
asi mi amada hoja suelta, será rota
y ya en tantos de pedazos, se volvería polvo
se volvería nada...

Por eso mi sentimiento, plasmado
en palabras, no pueden muchas veces
encontrar un titulo, un nombre
que se pueda leer o se pueda tocar,
pues solo puede o quiera ser,...
hoja suelta...

Hoja Suelta

Cuando me doy cuenta
que buscar cariños, no vale la pena,
porque no es posible
encontrar afectos que sean verdad;
siento la presencia de gran compañera,
la que me comprende, y no me defrauda
la que siempre escucha y no me engaña:
es mi soledad.

Ella que con su silencio
da respuesta a tantas y tantas preguntas,
la de los anhelos
que nunca encontraron su cauce normal
y por lo tanto no se desbordaron
porque nunca hubo otra alma igual,
donde hagan el nido muchos sentimientos
de amor y amistad.

Me estoy dando cuenta,
que ha pasado demasiado el tiempo,
sobre mis anhelos veo,
que el ocaso tiende ya su manto gris.
es cuando mas siento que siempre la tuve
y..en mis horas largas de meditaciones
ella siempre es mi gran compañera:
mi gran soledad.

Mayo 24-1976

A. Cab.

NOTES Agosto 15-1979

POR ...

El reeverdo de una lágrima caída
de tus ojos, como puro sentimiento
como flor que deshojada de tu vida
y que al caer... fué amor de ese momento.
Al encanto de esa lágrima... vencida
brotó de mi alma un juramento
si a ese encanto me sentí rendida
creyéndome en tu vida... el complemento
Si el reeverdo de esas horas tan queridas
de tu vida borraron los tormentos
como hermosa lluvia florecida
cuyas gotas son estos pensamientos.

TU MEN

Ti u Káh-sahil u yal a wich lubane'
Ti a wichoo bey x-mayihuli a-bahoob
bebix nik-té p'ep-leetaan Ti-a Kuxtale
ix Ka h-bané, tu yabilah-le sotaKo.
Ti u ah-esil le yal ich-tsoy sabené
Ti le in pixán top'é ump'el hach-tán
wa ti-e' ah-esil, tin wuyhimba Kubimbaé
uoKsahil tin hool in Ketil a Kuxtal
Wa ti u Káhsahil le sotaK ichimobó
Ti a Kuxtal Tu Tubesah, oumsa-tu-ya obé
bey xKichpan chaK Ku lolanKil
ah-té chuhoo letiobé, le tuKulobá

— Para una noche—

Y... asi como viniste
te quieres alejar
Tu nada me ofreciste
Te tienes que marchar

Me aromas tu mi noche
que besos me dejaste
estrellas en derroche
caricias palpitantes

Dejas aqui en mi cuerpo
todo tu calor de noche
me dejas en la boca
toda tu aroma...noche...

Dejas en mi alma
un sello de frescura
el alma tuya... noche
eterna de ternura.....

Lunes 20 de agosto— 1979

Graceli

Decir.......

No sé si escribir pueda alguna prosa
o acaso sea algún soneto
solo quiero, que el perfume de mis rosas
perfumen para ti este momento.

De mi jardín, las flores olorosas
en un perfume suave y muy discreto,
te envuelva y te digan muchas cosas
entre ellas, mi mas grande secreto.

Todo esto con el mas grande respeto
a Dios,...que sabe de mis cosas
Te pido que analices todo esto,

y,... si encuentras que estas frases amorosas
~~amorosas~~ embellecen tu vida este momento
Tomalas Todas,... porque son mis rosas.

Septiembre 11-1,979

A una Carta

Aquella humilde carta que abrigaba
los mas puros y hermosas sentimientos
aquel papel en el que hablaba
aunque incierta y lejana la esperanza.

Aquella carta que decía con tristeza
"cuando te fuiste, me dijiste que volvías"
y yo que te creí, sigo esperando tu regreso
porque quise creer, que tu no me has mentido"

"Sin embargo, presiento en tu silencio
que ya me tienes a mi en el olvido
que algún otro amor, de mi ya te arrancó
otro amor que quizá a mi ya me borrado."

Es esta la tristeza que encerraba
aquella carta que nunca fue leída.
por aquél, que por su olvido escrita fuera
con un amor que no será correspondido

La carta aquella me ha inspirado
a convertir en verso, la tristeza
hacer, de aquella espera inútil, un poema
y la desilusión en canto se convierta.

Febrero - 1980

...Como...

Como vas a dejar de amarme
si nunca me quisiste
como vas a olvidarme
si nunca estuve en ti.
Voy a quedar muy triste
si ya no vuelvo a verte
¡Porque yo,.. si te quise!
¡Porque en mí, tú..si estuviste!

Como notar mi ausencia
si nunca foí presente
en tu recuerdo nunca
huella alguna se quedó
El sentimiento mío
que nunca comprendiste
no pudo romper el moro
que te tendio otro amor.

Octubre 26 - 1983

Noche de un lunes 30 de octubre 1,989

— *Nocturnando* — Nocturnando

Las nubes esparcidas
las nubes,.. como trocitos ~~de algod~~
de algodón,
en el cuadro combo azul-acerado
de los cielos.
Es el cerrar de ojos
de este día
cuyos párpados de ensueño
caen por ~~el~~ arrullo nocturnal,
el de los pájaros.
En la mecedora de los vientos
suavamente se columpian los aromas
son las damas,.. los galanes
limonarias y jazmines provincianos
que aguardan,... para cubrir
el gran manto de la noche

1,985

En busca...

Busqué y busqué
y en buscar se me fué el tiempo
en el camino te hallé
pero te encontré en dos tiempoo.

Que algo se hizo mal
en torno de mi destino
que nada se va a remediar
porque el paso de los años, se me vino.

Para un Recuerdo   1986

En el silencio de la noche
yo despierto con el rumor
de una canción lejana....
Mi pensamiento vuela a ti
amor que me negaste
el abrigo de tus brazos
y cerraste para mi tu corazón.

La tan lejana voz que asi cantaba
una canción que de amor
una noche de ronda...recordada
una romántica voz que enternecía
y....al sentir..lo lejos que tu estabas
mi corazón se estremeció
y de pena mi sueño entristeció.

Tu ausencia es algo que me envuelve
en un olvido triste y lento
aun asi,...me doy aliento
para decir, de ti, un bien perdido
mi remembranza de amor suave, sereno.
mi corazón asi,....te ha cumplido

... *NO SÉ* ...

Yo nunca quise que te fueras
Tu sólo dijiste que te vas
ni siquiera te dije que vinieras
Tan solo te acercaste hacia mi.

Yo nunca quise que me olvides
y tu ya me olvidaste, ya lo sé,
pero tampoco te exigí que me siguieras
eres libre de irte, también sé.

Yo no sé en que fallé
que hice mal, para perderte
pero creo que te amé
y pasaré tiempo en olvidarte.

Noviembre 1988

Quimera

Quisiera tenerte,... al alcance de mis manos
para palpar tu cuerpo,... llenarlo de caricias,
pero solo tocar puedo con mis ojos
tu imágen... a través de los recuerdos,
Quisiera .... con mis labios en los tuyos
Sentir tu aloma fundida con mis besos
pero solo puedo besarte con el alma
porque tú como siempre estás muy lejos.
Quisiera .... con mi cuerpo junto al tuyo
hacerte palpitar en fuego ardiente,
pero.. en mi corazón... solo... el fuego se consume
en el deseo infinito de tenerte.
Si escucharas mi voz, podría decirte.—
que te quise... te quiero... y te querré...
que tú fuiste, eres y serás
mi pasado,... mi presente... y... porvenir.

Noviembre 14 - 1989

Retazos

Ya nunca mas, volveré a verte
bella ilusión del alma mía
ya nunca mas volveré a mirarte
para ver en tus ojos la armonía,
pero.... voy a recordarte
con Tus ultimas frases de aquel día
y así... entonces.. no voy a olvidarte
porque de mi vida serás siempre la alegría. —

Lágrimas,... perlas de la vida
que fluyen rumorosas, cantarinas
cuando es felicidad.
Lágrimas... sublimes mensajeras
que desbordan todas sus Ternuras
formando cristalino manantial.
Lágrimas ... Frescores y dulzuras
cuando algo las inspira
como parte de un ideal.

Domingo 21 de Enero - 1990

Recopilaciones Hechas en Junio - 1776

Hoja Suelta

Mis oídos se llenan de alegría
si ciertas son las cosas que dijiste
si de verdad la noche de ese día
con palabras lindas me quisiste.

En el cielo sonó toda armonía
las brillantes estrellas que tú viste
arrullaron con suaves melodías,
el ideal que entre los dos existe.

En la luz de tus ojos vi que había
un sentir que en palabras convertiste
y sacó de soletargo al alma mía
en un ansia infinita de sentirte.

pensé....
Si fuera posible todavía
que el rosal de mi vida que está triste
para ti floreciera, vida mía.
con el amor que en palabras tú me diste.

Yo no sé si lo que escribo son cuartetos
o si pueden llamarse redondillas
ni sé tampoco si pueden ser sonetos
i solo sé que por ti, es poesía.

Noche de lunes 4 de febrero - 1980

IN THE PATH OF THIS LIFE . . .

In the path of this life, in my acts I am always in the hand of the great Universal Architect. To feel how the peacemaking relation exists, I recognize the grandeur of this God, to whom I mold my gratitude praising his name. [My] prayer [is] that in the end the continuity of his work will be, and the force of my will to be, more than what I was, of that which I am and will be: the strength of my roots in the heritage of my branches.[1]

I am grateful for this life, the reality of its lessons . . .
—Araceli Cab Cumí, July 2000

Otra faez

En el camino, de ésta vida, de mis actos siempre
está la mano del gran Arquitecto Universal, y al
sentir como existe la relación conciliadora, reconozco
la grandeza de este Dios, a quien, plasmo mi gratitud
loando su nombre en una petición, que al final
sea la continuidad de su obra y la fuerza de mi
voluntad de ser mas allá de lo que fui, de lo que
soy y seré: la fuerza de mis raices en la
heredad de mis ramas.
Agradezco de esta vida, la realidad de su enseñanza...

CHAPTER SIX

Endings?

I am grateful for this life, the reality of its lessons.
—*Araceli Cab Cumí, July 2000*

Retirement

At seventy-five Araceli may appear to have closed down her political career and be settling into retirement. In June 2002 Araceli's husband, Pablo, died after a long, debilitating illness that, although undiagnosed, resembled the slow fading of the mind characteristic of Alzheimer's disease. For the two years preceding his death Pablo was too ill to continue to farm his milpa. His dry goods stall in the Maxcanú market had closed several years ago for lack of business. While Pablo was ill, Araceli was absorbed in taking care of her husband. Now Araceli faces widowhood and retirement concerned about a future with diminishing financial resources.

In 1995 she wrote the following letter requesting a state pension to the governor of Yucatán, Federico Granja Ricalde of the PRI, whom she knew from her days in the Yucatecan Congress. With this letter Araceli submitted a file of documents verifying her many years of public service. She presented her letter and document file to the governor's secretary, a man who had previously helped Araceli with the formal application process in setting up her NGO.[2] The tone of Araceli's letter reads as polite and properly formal in Spanish, although in English it may seem somewhat subservient or stilted. Once again someone else typed her letter so Araceli's name is misspelled as "Aracely."

LETTER REQUESTING A PENSION
Aracely A. De J. Cab Cumí
Calle 25 No. 119
Maxcanu, Yucatan, Mexico
March 8, 1995
[C.] Engineer Federico Granja Ricalde[3]
Constitutional State Governor
Government Palace, Merida, Yucatan, Mexico
Attached to this letter, with total respect, I send you copies
of documents that verify my résumé in the activities that my
human capacity has permitted me to realize—a social and
political struggle in my native state at the levels where I
received the honor of being invited, to collaborate or express
ideas or judgments of the circumstances that have happened
in my life.

Confiding in your human and political capacity, in this
statement of motives, I solicit your intervention in my petition
requesting that I be granted a life pension.

My petition is sustained by the work that I have done, that
supports the merit of this request.[4] I am not a professional nor
do I have social security, nor do I have any other kind of aid. My
situation is that I need economic aid to survive and to attend to
the necessities of my routine labors. I work my land with all the
strength that my health allows me.

Hoping from you your spirit of solidarity, help, and
comradeship in order to consider [my request], I remain at your
behest in Calle 25, No. 119 in Maxcanu, Yucatan, Mexico.

Aracely A. de J. Cab Cumí

original page on page 244

A year after sending the letter, as Governor Granja Ricalde's term of office was ending, Araceli was notified to come retrieve her documents. Included in her documents was a card denying her request for a pension.

Through the intervention of her longtime friend and political ally, Blanca Estrada, Araceli did receive a one-time payment of 500 pesos (US$50) from the state government.[5]

Araceli concluded that a political enemy might have convinced the governor to deny her a pension. Disappointingly, the governor's secretary claimed no influence with the governor on her behalf despite his helpfulness to Araceli previously. Araceli's subsequent request in 1997 to the incoming governor of Yucatán, Victor Cervera Pacheco of the PRI, received no answer. She has made no further requests for a pension from the state government.

Since her husband Don Pablo had worked for a time as an agricultural laborer in the United States under the Bracero Program, Araceli is attempting to obtain the funds due her from her husband's pension.[6] Since Pablo often used variations of his name on official forms, Araceli's case to claim his pension has become more complicated. No doubt Don Pablo did not realize that such a detail as a name would complicate his wife's receiving the monies due her from his pension.

Making Peace, Coming to Terms

Araceli in the following poem and essay writes about coming to terms with a lifetime of complex emotions.

> THERE WAS A TOTAL ECLIPSE OF THE
> MOON AND I WISH TO SAY . . . 1996
>> *Great God . . .*
>> *that respecting your creation*
>> *I ask you please*
>> *that pain and sorrow*
>> *I exchange for love.*
>> *That my errors and my failures*
>> *Ask you pardon*
>> *That all the disappointments in me*
>> *would be successes for my loved ones.*
>> *All the crying and bitterness*
>> *would be reason for laughter and tenderness*
>> *and beautiful future lives.*
>> *That all the remorse, the despair, the rancor*

be cleansed with your pardon.
I never had a bad intention
neither did I take anything from anyone
nor do I blame those who took from me
illusions, ideals, and hope.
I ask you please that you listen
to the message of my words
and that knowing me as I am
you pardon me of that which is my fault.

Araceli, Thursday, September 26, 1996

original page on page 245

Araceli says that she wrote this poem thinking about her two children and how they reacted to her political career. She says that she fears she may have failed as a mother because she didn't communicate very well with Bertha and Fernando. In this spiritual poem Araceli asks for forgiveness of any errors she may have committed in her life.

Araceli continues her self-reflection in the following essay:

WITH ALL THAT I AM

With all that I am, with my ideas, with all that I think, feel, with all that my heart holds and yet passing over my defects, my errors and my failures. . . . my humanity is formed with a too romantic idealism. But reality is also too practical and material, where ideal and romantic words don't have a place because the condition, the comfort, the way of life are stronger, so you have so much, you are worth so much, hunger and misery are valued, unemployment and necessity are steps of power.

But I am not going to languish, I am as I am, and he who doesn't like it, well that isn't important to me, because I will continue walking and although my knees fail, I will arrive at the conclusion of my destiny. I will continue in pursuit of my ideal, and raising myself higher, I will pass over the apologies, excuses, and pretend not to heed the judgment of: the absurd, beyond the epoch and . . . I will proclaim, I am not frustrated, I love the past, I live in the present and I walk toward the future, with my romantic idealism . . . , I continue feeling ancient, in the modernization of all the economic, political, and social circumstances.

Well, between parentheses I say that to be a romantic idealistic, but over all, making it real, is like wanting to know what form the skeleton of a fly has, or how is the fossil of a cockroach, or like wanting to know what form the bony remains of a worm [is like]. To speak of good intentions is an insult, but more insulting would be to practice them.

    To speak of an honest struggle to achieve real accomplishments is unheard of, but even still more unheard of is to achieve these accomplishments and to recognize the honesty of the struggle

December 14, 1994

To be continued

original page on page 246

Araceli's preceding essay reads almost as a stream of consciousness. It is likely the most defiant of her works presented in this book. The essay is also one of the most strongly stated views of her self-acceptance, flying against the possible negative opinions of others. She presents herself in this essay as a romantic idealist—a criticism she has consistently had of herself. Araceli writes that to actualize such a philosophy of romantic idealism is like wanting to know the skeleton of a fly, as difficult and as futile. The "to be continued" with which Araceli concludes this essay indicates that her life is to be continued, not the essay.

Araceli closes this chapter by writing her own epitaph, a coming to terms with the events of her life thus far. She intentionally wrote her epitaph on her birthday, taking this day to reflect on her life and write about it.

EPITAPH

To God, in my epitaph
The worldly things
that I have had to live with the motives
that you know,
If a well-deserved pardon
you grant me in the end

Araceli at work at her dining room table.

> *then with a good compliment,*
> *I shall go from this life well loved*
> *and I go white and I go pure*
> *completely clean, completely sane . . .*
>   Araceli A. de Jesus Cab Cumí, December 9, 1997
>   *original page on page 247*

Araceli in her prayerful epitaph seems to have achieved a peace and self-acceptance as she enters the next stage in life acknowledging her own inevitable passing. The final poem in this chapter is an homage to her recently deceased husband, Pablo. She sent it to me the month following his death. The end of the poem notes his passing on June 13, 2002. Araceli wrote the poem, however, on December 15, 2001, during the time of Pablo's illness, knowing that his death was soon to come. The poem opens with this date preceding the title:

Saturday, December 15, 2001
To the Memory of Don Pablo del S. Patrón Cíh

This grandfather is now very tired of walking
through life, his strength is forgetting the routine,
now tired his gaze travels
other worlds.

He leaves behind a past, that muffled
the noises he no longer wishes, he denies the fajina[7]
and all its tasks, they remain forgotten
now he does not accept the responsibility.

The earthly path, has ended,
his fountain of singing waters is drained,
in his eyes, the light is going out,
in his life the echoes and the things that now don't rhyme.

He wishes to be, then rested
soon to leave all that he values here
and to go soon, where rested,
he may have only God as his eternal life.

Now, this caballero de pan
has left for the summit
where we hope that they will say to him
"here is your peace and your tenderness."

Thursday, June 13, 2002
Araceli

original page on page 248

    This poignant poem recalls Pablo as a grandfather and as a man who worked hard his entire life, a good man now at rest. Especially significant is her use of the phrase "caballero de pan" (literally "gentleman of bread"). The symbolic meaning of this phrase, however, describes a man considered admirable and dependable, one who does the right thing, whose values are culturally in tune, one on whom others can unquestionably rely. The phrase also incorporates notions of humility and lack of pretentiousness. It is a true compliment to Pablo's character.

    In its tone this poem to Pablo resembles the poem Araceli wrote to her

daughter, "To My Daughter, Bertha, in Memory of Her Childhood," discussed in chapter 2. In the two poems Araceli expresses a love for her family
that she thought she did not always demonstrate.

Conclusions

This chapter I entitled "Endings?" with a question mark because I think that
Araceli has not concluded her career as a writer or perhaps as a politician. She
continues to write, poetry especially. She is involved in the new leftist current
(Nueva Izquierda) of the PRD in Yucatán. The responsibilities of attending to
her husband in his long illness are now gone, replaced by the quiet sadness of his
death. Other than helping her daughter-in-law, Eney, with the household chores
while she works in the Maxcanú assembly plant, Araceli has fewer familial caretaking duties than she has had at any point in her life. She may now have more
time to think, reflect, and write. The time to write, however, is not underwritten
by any secure financial base. Araceli continues to worry about her income.

The Writers Continue

Other writers may be coming along in Araceli's family. With the following poem Araceli passes the pen to a potential next generation of writers in
her family, especially her two granddaughters, Edna Patrón May and Zoila
Espinosa Patrón.

> AND, . . . THE HISTORY CONTINUES, . . .
> OF MY CHILDREN, TO THEIR CHILDREN
>> *The soul of the people, the essence of provincial cradle*
>> *that will continue in a flow of ideas and narratives where*
>> *Maxcanú would be like perennial flame of the time*
>> *like the aroma of eternal copal,*[8] *like a voice that arrives*
>> *to the ears, an ancestral voice that rises up from the past*
>> *to be the echo of a well sketched future.*
>> *I am the prologue, . . . what, . . . who, . . . how, . . . when*
>> *will be the epilogue . . .*

> Araceli Cab Cumí
Summer, 2000
original page on page 249

Edna Patrón May, one of Araceli's grand-daughters, whose short story appears in this chapter.

Edna Patrón May

Edna is the teenage daughter of Eneyda (Eney) and Fernando, Araceli and Pablo's son. She lives with her parents and three brothers in the house compound her family shares with Araceli and Pablo. The two households are linked through their dining rooms by a common passageway. Family members pass freely from one house to the other as the two households intertwine.

That Araceli and Pablo share the house compound with their son and his family is a residence pattern that anthropologists term "virilocal" (See endnote 1, introduction). Customarily with a virilocal residence pattern the mother-in-law becomes the household manager of both households and, consequently, of her daughter-in-law's labor.

As a young bride Araceli lived with Pablo's parents. She found life very difficult in this shared household with her mother-in-law and within a year she and Pablo moved to their own house. Araceli and Eney, however, seem to get along companionably. Eney regards her parents-in-law with real affection. Now that she works four days a week in an assembly plant recently established in Maxcanú, Araceli and Eney increasingly share the cooking and other household duties of their joint household.

Because the two families live so closely together, I have gotten to know Eney quite well. On a visit to Maxcanú in 1999 she and I sat talking once again while we waited for Araceli to return from doing some errands. During our conversation Eney told me that her daughter Edna had written a short story that had won first prize in a writing competition at her grammar school. Because I was interested in Edna's story she found a copy for me. After reading it, I wondered if Edna's poignant story also belonged in this book. It seemed to me that her story represented a continuation of the writing tradition in Araceli's family. I mentioned my idea to Araceli who, after some thought, agreed.

When Araceli and I work in her home in Maxcanú, Edna is often a silent but attentive witness to our conversations. Edna says that her prize-winning story was inspired by the life of a neighbor in Maxcanú. She was eleven when she wrote the following story.

LA BURRITA[9]

Once upon a time there was a woman who was pregnant.
She waited with much anticipation to give birth.

Her husband also waited with much hope for the birth of his son or daughter.

After the nine months of waiting, a baby girl was born. BUT SHE WAS NOT NORMAL! She was mentally retarded. Her parents were very anguished, so much so that they didn't know what to do.

So with the passing of time the baby grew until she was a young woman. But she acted like a little girl of five years. Her parents were getting older and she continued growing, growing, and growing. Meanwhile she never married and she became a spinster. [Her parents] never did anything for her suffering.

But in spite of her mental retardation, she was pretty. Even though she did many silly things she passed the years forty to fifty-one to sixty-two. Even at sixty-nine years she hadn't stopped behaving as a little girl of five years.

In the town where she lived, they gave her the nickname of "la burrita" [the little donkey]. She was hurt by this. Sometimes she chased people to throw stones at them. But she never understood anything until ten years after her parents died.

When she entered a store they would give her all that she wanted because if they didn't, she would throw rocks at them.

But what makes her sad is that none of the MEN ever took her into account. For this reason she never married.

Edna Patrón May

February 1999

original page on page 250

Once Araceli had decided that Edna's story should be included in this book, she mentioned that one of her other granddaughters, Zoila, had also written a short story that she thought was quite good. I asked if I could see it and after reading Zoila's story with its modern interpretation of a traditional legend I agreed with Araceli. Both Araceli and I thought Zoila's story too belonged in this book, suggesting the possibility of another writer coming along in Araceli's family in addition to Edna.

Zoila Espinosa Patrón

Zoila is the daughter of Bertha, Araceli and Pablo's daughter and eldest child. She was born and has lived all of her life in an urban neighborhood in Mérida on a street where many of her neighbors were originally from Maxcanú. Zoila was fourteen when she wrote the following story.

GOSSIP

One fine day a woman hit her dog with a huge stick. Near them was Pablito, an eight-year-old boy, who upon seeing such a blow was nothing less than horrified.

A little while later when in his house, Pablito told his mother that he had seen Juana, their neighbor, beat her poor dog and almost kill him.

Pablito's mother was a talkative but not gossipy woman. She left her home and went to where her comadre Chona was and began to speak to her.

What she said was:

"Goodness, comadre! I heard that Juana beat her poor dog almost killing him. It was though instead of a stick she had used a machete."

Zoila Espinosa Patrón, another of Araceli's granddaughters, whose short story also appears in this chapter.

"Really?" said Chona. "What a lunatic!"

Chona went to Paulita's store and while paying for her groceries commented to her (Paulita who was a little deaf in her left ear) that just as she came in Juana was at the corner beating and hacking away at her dog.

"Ahh!" said Paulita. "Why is she doing it?" she asked. To this Chona hastened to answer:

"I don't know. I think perhaps the dog ate her food. And you know she is a very careless woman. So, bam, she hit him with a machete."

On the following day Paulita told Paquito, the cobbler, that she had heard a rumor that Juana, who lived on the other corner, had macheted her dog for eating [her food] because he was hungry.

Paquito didn't give credit to what he had heard but he took

care to spread the news among his customers. "The news" was that a woman was killing dogs with a machete so that afterward she could eat them. His customers in their turn told the whole neighborhood. Furthermore they began to spread the rumor that without a doubt one day this woman would do the same with some child who was walking his dog and would have the bad luck to go near her.

I hesitate to mention that upon hearing all this "news," the people of this small neighborhood in Mérida were terrorized. One of them didn't fail to tell the police that a cannibal woman was walking loose in their neighborhood. And therefore it was very dangerous for this woman to walk around freely.

The police arrived ready to arrest this "perverse and unhinged woman." But at the moment of seizing her, Juana fled, scared and frightened. She ran toward the backyards that were adjacent to the woods. Here they surrounded her instantly. In her fright she slipped on a pile of rocks hitting her head. It was a fatal blow. Here she lay dead on Friday June 6 at midnight under a plum tree. From then on they say that every June 6 at midnight a woman dressed in white appears screaming desperately "Why? Why?"

The End

Zoila Angelica Espinosa Patrón

July 1998

original pages on pages 251–52

Both Edna and Zoila write about women wronged by their communities. In Edna's story the community's perception of disability sets a woman apart, alienating her from community support and ultimately from the possibility of a man's affections and the potential for a family of her own. She becomes a feared and scorned outcast trapped by her own limited intellectual capacity and the community's inability to extend compassion to her.

Zoila writes about an extreme consequence of community gossip. In the urban neighborhood of her story no one questions what she or he has heard; each person adds to the ultimately destructive message passed around among neighbors. The story ends in terror and death for a woman who never understands why her community has turned against her. She returns yearly to haunt them with her disbelief and sadness.

The idea of a ghostly apparition of a woman returning to haunt is a culturally based idea that Zoila probably learned as a child. Common in folklore throughout Mexico is the story of la Llorona (the weeping woman) who haunts watercourses weeping for her drowned children. In some versions la Llorona seeks the children of others to replace her own. In other versions she drowns her own children or those of others. In Yucatán there is also the folk legend of the Xtabay (or Xtabi), a tall, beautiful woman with long hair who haunts the jungle, especially in the vicinity of ceiba trees. She looks particularly for men traveling alone. She seduces them and then strangles them with her long hair. In Zoila's story the wronged woman haunts her community, repaying it for its injustice to her.

Both Edna and Zoila have written stories of considerable sophistication, especially given that they were quite young when they authored their stories. Both clearly have talent as writers. Whether either of them will choose a career or realistically have the option of choosing a career that includes writing is uncertain. By the fall of 2003 Zoila had become a mother as she was completing high school. Edna continues her studies as a sixteen-year-old high school student, regarded by her family as the most serious of all the grandchildren.

In Honor of Zazil Espinosa Patrón

The intellectual tradition in Araceli's family shows itself in ways other than writing. In 1994 I met Zazil, Zoila's older sister and Araceli and Pablo's eldest grandchild. Zazil had accompanied her grandmother to hear a paper I presented at the Society for Applied Anthropology Meetings held in Cancún. Zazil's intense intellect seemed obvious to me that day as we all sat around eating lunch. Her mind roved through our conversation searching out questions and comments. I joked with her saying that she was probably a closet anthropologist.

Since lunch that day in Cancún, Zazil has been a creative participant in many of the conversations Araceli and I have had about Yucatán, politics, the Maya, and women. Zazil's comments are insightful and clarifying, especially regarding her grandmother. She is never reluctant to state her point of view, even in disagreement. So I consider Zazil to have contributed to this book, as have her sisters and cousin.

Zazil and Araceli have an especially strong bond. When Zazil was a

*Araceli Cab Cumí
and Zazil Espinosa
de Quintál, the eldest
of Araceli's grand-
daughters, a kindred
intellect and spirit.*

secondary school student she had conflicts with some of her teachers, as
Araceli says, because of her rebellious nature. As a result Zazil's family
thought it best if she changed schools and went to live with her grandparents. Zazil moved in with Araceli and Pablo for two years and completed
secondary school in Maxcanú. No doubt their closeness grew while they
shared a home.

As we worked on this book Zazil has sent me e-mail updates about
Araceli's recent political activities. She has also sent me scans of some of her
grandmother's writings and newspaper articles for this book. I appreciate
all of her efforts as a commentator and communicator.

Now in her mid-twenties, Zazil is married with four young children. She lives in a neighborhood in a newly developing area in the outskirts of Mérida. The following excerpt from my fieldnotes describes a bit the ambience Araceli, Zazil, and I have had together over the years.

FIELDNOTES
9/15/98 (LATE AFTERNOON)

I'm driving back from Maxcanú to Mérida with Araceli in the
front seat holding Iran, Zazil's infant daughter. Zazil is leaning
over from the back seat into the space between our seats.
The energy flowing among us as we talk makes it seem to me
that we are flying, taking off in this small car. Zazil's husband
sits all the way in a corner of the backseat. It is as though
he is shut out of the energy in the car created by a powerful
presence of women. Even little Iran seems part of that energy
and presence.

As Edna and Zoila have contributed to this book with their short stories, so has Zazil with her consistent intellectual companionship and personal friendship.

Conclusions

Araceli began writing as a quiet form of self-expression. Edna wrote her story as part of a grammar school exercise. Zoila wrote hers observing her own neighborhood. The quality of Araceli's writing in her essays and poems validates a claim to a status as an intellectual. As was discussed in the introduction Araceli, through her position embedded in the life of her Maya community, is able to express the worldview of that community and through her political activism mediate between her community and those social actors and institutions beyond it. For these reasons, as I argued in the introduction, I think that Araceli can be described rightfully as an organic intellectual as defined by Gramsci.

Although both of Araceli's granddaughters show promise as keen observers and recorders of the communities of which they are a part, it is uncertain if they will wish to or will have the opportunity to represent the

Araceli and three of her granddaughters, Edna Patrón May, Zazil Espinosa de Quintál, and Zoila Espinosa Patrón.

worldview of their communities and mediate between them and the wider society, that is, to become organic intellectuals. Both are still quite young and consumed by educational and family duties.

Although she has not written stories as her sister and cousin have, Zazil has demonstrated in our many conversations over the years that she has a perspective as a young Maya woman born of the city to represent the worldview of the urban Maya to those beyond her community. At her current stage in life, however, she is unlikely to be able to perform the political representation and activism that are also the mark of an organic intellectual. As a wife and mother of four young children, her time, as was Araceli's at such a point in her life, is devoted to family.

Whether Edna, Zoila, or Zazil will ever become organic intellectuals will depend not just on their own abilities and desires but also on the opportunities available to them. In present-day Yucatán they have more opportunities for education and employment and more contact with wider-ranging life experiences than did their grandmother. They still face, however, impediments caused by societal perceptions of gender and ethnicity. As young Maya women, Edna, Zoila, and Zazil have clear intellectual abilities. Whether their futures unfold as intellectuals and activists is a later-to-be-answered question.

ARACELY A. DE J. CAB CUMI.
CALLE 25 No. 119
MAXACNU, YUC., MEX. A 8 DE MARZO - 1995.

C. ING. FEDERICO GRANJA RICALDE
GOBERNADOR CONSTITUCIONAL DEL ESTADO.
PALACIO DE GOBIERNO-MERIDA YUC. MEX.

ADJUNTO A LA PRESENTE, Y CON TODO RESPETO, ENTREGO A USTED, --
COPIAS DE DOCUMENTOS QUE ACREDITAN UN POCO MI CURRICULUM, EN LAS-
ACTIVIDADES QUE MI CAPACIDAD HUMANA, ME HA PERMITIDO REALIZAR --
UNA LUCHA SOCIAL Y POLITICA, TANTO EN PROVINCIA NATAL COMO A NIVE
LES DONDE MI PERSONA RECIBIO EL HONOR DE SER INVITADA, PARA COLA-
BORAR O EXPRESAR LAS IDEAS O CRITERIOS DE LAS SIRCUNSTANCIAS QUE-
ME HAN TOCADO VIVIR.

CONFIADA EN SU CALIDAD HUMANA Y POLITICA, EN ESTA EXPOSICION -
DE MOTIVOS, SOLICITO SU INTERVENCION EN MI PETICION DE QUE SE ME-
CONCEDA UNA PENSION VITALICA.

MI PETICION SE SUSTENTA EN LA LABOR QUE HE REALIZADO, AVALA EL
MERITO DE ESTA SOLICITUD. NO SOY PROFECIONAL ASI COMO TAMPOCO TEN
GO SEGURO SOCIAL, NI ESTOY EN NINGUNA DEPENDENCIA DE APOYO, MI --
SITUACION ES PUES NECESITADA DE UN APOYO ECONOMICO PARA SOBREVI--
VIR Y ATENDER LOS MENESTERES DE MI LOBOR RUTINARIO. TRABAJO MI --
PARCELA CONTODO EL ESFUERZO QUE ME PERMITE MI SALUD.

ESPERANDO DE USTED SU ESPIRITU DE SOLIDARIDAD, APOYO Y COMPAÑE
RISMO PARA SER ATENDIDA, QUEDO A SUS RESPETABLES ORDENES EN LA CA
LLE 25 No. 119 DE MAXCANU YUC. , MEX.

ARACELY A. DE J. CAB CUMI.

Jueves - 26 - Septiembre - 1996
Había un eclipse total de luna y me puse a decir

Gran Dios......
que respetando tu creación
yo te pido por favor
que las penas y el dolor.
las trueque yo, por amar.
Que mis yerros y mis fallos
te piden a ti perdón
Que todo lo frustado en mí
sea logro para los míos..
todo el llanto y la amargura
sea motivo de risas y ternuras
y hermosas vidas futuras.
Que todos, los resquemores
los despechos los engaños
Se laven con tu perdón.
Nunca tuve mala intención
ni le quitó nada a nadie
ni culpo a los que me quitaron
la ilusión, el ideal y la esperanza
te pido por favor que escuches
el mensaje de mis palabras
y que conociéndome cual soy
perdones. lo que es mi culpa.....

Araceli.

Diciembre 14 - 1994

Yo con todo lo que soy, con mis ideas, con lo que pienso, siento, con lo que guarda mi corazón y aun pasando muy por encima de mis defectos, mis errores y mis fallas.... mi humanidad, se integra con un idealismo demasiado romántico. Mas la realidad también es demasiado práctica y material donde no encajan las palabras ideal y romántico, porque es mas fuerte la condición, el acomodo, el modus vivendi. tanto tienes tanto vales, el hambre y la miseria es cotizable, el desempleo y la necesidad son escalones de poder.

Pero no voy a decir, soy como soy, y al que no le guste, pues que me importa, porque seguiré caminando, y aunque mi rodilla reniegue yo llegaré a la conclusión de mi destino, Yo seguiré en pos de mi ideal, y alzándome muy en alto pasaré por encima de las disculpas, de las excusas y desoyendo el dictamen de: absurdo, fuera de época y... declararé, no estoy frustrada, amo el pasado, vivo el presente y camino hacia el futuro, con mi idealismo romántico..., seguiré siendo antigua, en el modernismo de todas las circunstancias, económicas, políticas y sociales.

Bueno, entre paréntesis digo que ser idealista romántica pero sobre todo, hacerlo real, es como si quisiera saber que forma tiene el esqueleto de una mosca, o que como es el final fósil de una cucaracha, o como quiere saber que formas tienen los gestos o ecos de un gusano.
Hablar de buenas intensiones es insólito, pero mas insólito sería practicarlas.
Hablar de una lucha honesta para llegar a logros reales, es inaudito, pero mas inaudito es, llegar a los logros. y sea reconocida la honestidad de la lucha.

Continuara.

A Dios, en mi epitafio

Las cosas que terrenales
tuve que vivir con motivos
que Tu conoces,
Si bien merecido el perdón
Tu me concedes al Fin
entonces con bien cumplido
me iré de esta vida bien amada
y me iré blanca y me iré pura
toda limpia, Toda sana........

Araceli A. ded. Cab Cumi

Diciembre - 9 - 1997

Sábado 15 de diciembre de 2001

A la memoria de **Don Pablo del S. Patrón Cíh**

Este abuelo de andar ya muy cansado
de la vida, va olvidando la rutina
su esfuerzo, ya todo fatigado
otros mundos, su mirar camina.

Deja un atrás, que ya amortiguado
los ruidos ya no quiere, se niega a la fajina
y todos sus aperos, se quedan olvidados
ya no acepta la responsabilidad, encima.

El camino terrenal, se ha terminado,
se agotó su fuente de aguas cantarinas,
en sus ojos, la luz se va apagando,
en su vida los ecos y las cosas ya no riman.

El quiere estar, entonces sosegado
presto a dejar todo lo que aquí estima
y acudir pronto, donde reposado,
sólo tenga a Dios, como su eterna vida.

Ahora, este caballero de pan
ha partido hacia las alturas
donde esperamos que le dirán
"aquí está tu paz y tu ternura".

Jueves 13 de junio de 2002
Araceli

una mas

Y,... la historia continúa,... de mis hijos, a sus hijos.

El espíritu del pueblo, la esencia de la cuna provinciana que seguirá en el fluir de ideas y relatos donde Marcaní esté como llama perenne de los tiempos como aroma del copal eterno, como la voz que llegue a los oídos, voz ancestral que al levantarse del pasado sea el eco de un porvenir mejor trazado.

Soy el prologo,... que,... quién, como,... cuando será el epílogo.....

" LA RETRASADA MENTAL "

Habia una vez una señora que estaba embarazada,
pues ella esperaba con mucho animo que naciera.

También
Su esposo tambien esperaba con mucho animo *Ilusión* que
naciera su hijo o hija.

Despues de los nueve meses de embarazo, *espera* nació
la niña. ¡ PERO LA NIÑA NO ERA NORMAL !
ERa retrasadmental, sus padres se agustiaron mucho,
tanto que no buscaban que hacer.

Asi fue pasando el tiempo la niña ya no era niña, era *no desarrollo como*
una muchachita, pero ella actuaba como una niñita de
de cinco años sus padres fueron envejeciendo y ella
seguia creciendo, creciendo y creciendo mientras nunca
se casó llego a ser soltera por que nunca hicieron
nada contra su padecimiento.

pero a pesar de su defecto
~~En que es retrasada~~ mental ella *era* es bonita , ~~pero~~ *aunque* hacia cada to-
terias,ella tuvo los siguientes años 40,51,62,hasta *los* 69 años
nunca dejo de comportarce como una chiquilla de cinco años.

En el pueblo donde vivia la apodaban " LA BURRITA " ,ella se
molestaba y a veces hasta los corretiaba para darteSde pedra-*les*
das, claro ella nunca entendia nada, Hasta esta edad ,que
hace diez años murieron sus padres.

Cuando entraba a una tienda le tenian que regalar todo
lo que deseaba de lo contrario se molestaba y les daba de
pedradas. *deseaba*

Pero lo que da tristeza es que a todos los " HOMBRES ~~LES~~
~~DABA ASCO~~ es por eso que nunca se casó.
NO la tomaban en Cuenta.
nunca la Tomaron en cuenta,
FIN
                    EDNA PATRON

deseaba   *embarazo*

CHISME.

Un buen día, una señora apaleó a su perro con
un palo enorme, cerca de ellos estaba Pablito, un niño
como de 8 años quien al ver tal paliza no pudo menos
que horrorizarse.

Un rato después, ya en su casa Pablito le contó a su
mamá que había visto a doña Juana, la vecina, apalear
a su pobre perro y que casi lo dejó muerto.

La mamá de Pablito era una mujer, un poco, comunicativa
(diferente a ser chismosa) y al salir de su vivienda fué
a donde su comadre Chona y entre plática y plática le
dijo:

—¡hay Comadre!, fíjese que me contaron que doña Juana
apaleó a su pobre perro tanto que casi lo mata, es
como si en lugar de palo hubiese utilizado machete.

— ¿De veras? dijo Chona ¡Que loca!

La Comadre Chona fué a la tienda de Doña Paulita
y mientras pagaba su mercancía le comentó a la tendera, quien
por cierto era un poco sorda del oído izquierdo,
que se acababa de enterar, que doña Juana la de la esquina
había apaleado y macheteado a su perro.

— ¡Ahh! - dijo doña Paulita - y ¿Porque lo haría? - Preguntó,
A lo que doña Chona se apresuró a contestar:

— No sé, Yo pienso que a lo mejor el perro se comió la
comida de doña Juana, ya ve que es una mujer muy des-
cuidada, y por eso ¡zaz! que lo "machetea".

Al día siguiente doña Paulita le contó a don Paquito
el zapatero, que había escuchado el rumor, de que doña
Juana, la que vivía en la otra esquina, había macheteado
a su perro para comérselo porque tenía hambre.

Don Paquito no daba crédito a lo que escuchaba, pero se
encargó de extender la noticia entre sus clientes "la noticia"
de que una mujer estaba matando perros a machetazos
para después comérselos, éstos (los clientes) a su vez
lo hicieron saber a la colonia completa y además
se empezó a esparcir el rumor de que no se

dudaba que algun dia, esa mujer ~~hiciera~~ hiciera lo mismo con algun niño que paseara a su perro, y que tuviera la mala suerk de pasar junto a ella.

Cabe mencionar que ante todas esas "noticias", la gente de esa colonia, de la ciudad de Mérida, estaba aterrorizada y no faltó quien diera parte a la policia que una mujer canibal andaba suelta por esos rumbos, y que por lo tanto era muy peligroso que andubiera libre.

La policía llegó, dispuesta a encerrar aquella "Perversa y desquiciada mujer" pero al momento de agarrarla, doña Juana huyó, asustada y asombrada tambien, corrió hacia los patios que colindaban con el monte, y allí la cercaron, en un instante, bastó un pequeño descuido de ella para que resbalara en un montón de piedras, pegandose en la cabeza. Fué un golpe fatal y allí quedó, inerte, un viernes 6 de Junio a media noche, bajo una mata de Cirhuelas.

Desde entonces cuentan que cada 6 de Junio a media noche se aparece una mujer vestida de blanco gritando desgarradoramente: ¿Porque? ¿Porque?

FIN.

Zoila Angélica Espinosa Potión

Verano del 98

julio 98

Conclusions

> I begin these essays today.
> —*Araceli Cab Cumí, August 28, 1994*

Araceli Cab Cumí, an Organic Intellectual

Araceli's poem, "I Begin These Essays Today," opens this book with its telling question, "Could we consider ourselves as important participants in such a world, born as we were poor in Maxcanú?" Her life, lived as triumph, has given the answer to this question. Her intellect, resilient spirit, and stalwart personality were her pathways out of poverty and despair into a vital and unusual life.

Araceli learned Spanish-language literacy in grammar school and then taught herself to read and write Yucatec Maya as an adult, giving her the tools to author her varied writings. She reared two children and was a significant influence in the lives of several of her grandchildren—three of whom may continue her activist or writing tradition. She built a career in partisan politics in a time and place where indigenous women were rarely part of that political process, notably being the only indigenous woman elected and then reelected to the Yucatecan State Congress. But it is Araceli's writings that may outlast her life and be her final triumph and answer to the question, "Could we consider ourselves as important . . . ?"

When Araceli and I first met, she presented herself as a Maya intellectual and political leader. Over the years as I have gotten to know her, Araceli's life and work seemed clarified to me by Gramsci's concept of the "organic intellectual." Gramsci, the late Italian philosopher, political theorist, and activist, wrote within the context of another time (pre–World War II) and place (the turmoil of an industrializing Europe). Yet I think his concept of the organic intellectual is elastic enough to apply to other times and social contexts. And although he considered socioeconomic class as a defining variable, absent considerations of other variables such as gender or ethnic identity, I think Gramsci's concept of the organic intellectual is relevant to understand Araceli, her life, and her work.

Gramsci considered all intellectuals to be part of a social group; that is, intellectuals, as a distinct, independent social category, did not exist. Further he distinguished between two kinds of intellectuals: traditional and organic. Gramsci defined as traditional intellectuals those employed in readily distinguishable institutional positions in literary or scientific organizations such as universities or state agencies.

Gramsci's theoretical innovation, however, was his notion of the organic intellectual. He defined organic intellectuals as the thinkers and organizers of a particular social group who were embedded within their group's living dynamic. Thus organic intellectuals were not defined by their employment or post within an institution, but by their sociocultural function as those able to articulate the worldview of the social group to which they belonged and within whose context they conducted their lives. By recognizing another category of intellectuals aside from the traditional, Gramsci acknowledged those gifted, articulate, reflective, and dedicated activists such as Araceli who labored not in literary or scientific organizations but within their own communities.

Gramsci maintained that from their locus within a social group, organic intellectuals were able to communicate the worldview of their group to those outside it. Such intellectuals positioned their group and individuals within it vis-à-vis the worldview they elaborated. Their representation of their group was mediated within a wider societal context that included other social actors and institutions. Thus to Gramsci, organic intellectuals by their positioning from within their group provided a basis for social critique, leadership, and political activism.

To Gramsci organic intellectuals were those capable of envisioning and organizing a new cultural, moral, and political leadership within an emerging social group. He, following the revolutionary Marxism of his times, thought that organic intellectuals should be organized as the backbone of a class-based revolutionary political party. Gramsci depended heavily on the Marxist idea of class conflict as an overarching variable that led organic intellectuals to act as societal critics seeking to bring about revolutionary change within the context of a revolutionary political party.

Yet without revolutionary political party engagement, however, I think that organic intellectuals can perform a mediated representation between their social group and the society of which it is a part. Further I think that organic intellectuals can create change-bringing ideas and initiate actions outside the context of class conflict as Gramsci envisioned it.

Since Gramsci's time, new or at least newly recognized bases of social organization and identity formation other than class have been conceptualized as important in understanding contemporary societies. In particular, ethnic, gender, indigenous, religious, and regional affiliations have emerged or at least been recognized as bases of social organization and collective identity.

I maintain that the contemporary indigenous peoples of the Americas represent one example of such emergent social groups. During the past several decades they have begun to organize as *indigenous peoples*, claiming and reshaping their identities. They have promoted cultural pride as contemporary peoples, often establishing their links to a preconquest indigenous past. They have undertaken political activism claiming their rights and demanding inclusion *as indigenous peoples* who are citizens of modern nations.

The Maya as the majority population in Guatemala and a significant minority in Mexico and Belize are an important component of the emergent indigenous peoples of the Americas. Most noticeably in Guatemala the various Maya groups have claimed their identities as K'iché, Kaqchikel, or Q'anjob'al (among others) and perhaps more importantly, have begun a pan-Maya movement to link the diverse Maya peoples of the nation. Similarly the Maya (principally the Tzeltal and Tzotzil) of the Mexican state of Chiapas have organized a social movement, growing out of a rebellion, in which they claim their indigenous identity and also their rights as *indigenous citizens* of the nation.

Although there are Maya groups in the Yucatán Peninsula who organize and claim citizen rights as *indigenous people*, the Yucatec Maya have not yet established a panregional movement based upon an identity as Mayas. Currently their efforts are quite local, limited to forming groups that focus upon Maya theater and literature or those that seek the resources of the state to better living standards or groups that acknowledge and honor a Maya heritage or ones that manage local resources as an identifiable Maya community.

Araceli Cab Cumí as a Maya writer, community activist, and partisan politician may be a precursor of emerging Maya identity–based social movements in Yucatán especially among Yucatec Maya women. She has positioned herself as a representative and spokesperson for the Yucatec Maya, especially Yucatec Maya women. Through her writings and speeches she movingly presents a worldview of a Maya woman, representative of other Yucatec Maya women. Most obviously as a political party member and congressional representative, Araceli has sought to mediate between her community and the sociopolitical institutions of Yucatecan society.

Community, Worldview, and Mediated Representation

In her writing, her poetry especially, Araceli locates herself in the Maya community she seeks to represent and thus is able to communicate its way of life to others. Araceli roots her political agenda as an organic intellectual in the lived experience of Maya women.

In her community of Maxcanú, Araceli is recognized for her political success and admired for her intelligence. She is especially revered among the women who consider her their leader and spokesperson. As the only Maya woman ever to be elected to the Yucatecan State Congress, she was in a pivotal position to express the worldview of her community, make a critique of the state policies affecting the Maya, and move an active agenda forward to better the lives of those she represents. In a Gramscian sense she is positioned to represent a Maya worldview to others outside her Maya community and able to undertake an activist agenda to build better lives for her fellow townspeople and constituents. Araceli has translated her loyalty to her community and her fellow townspeople not only through writings but also by being politically active on their behalf for much of her adult life.

Most obviously as a political party member and congressional representative Araceli has sought to mediate between her community and the sociopolitical institutions of Yucatecan society. In her activist agenda for women and in particular the Maya women she views herself as representing, she highlights several themes. She notes three in particular: first, that Maya women have great human potential and aspirations, especially an untapped or unrecognized intellectual capacity; second, that Maya women's roles within the family as wives and mothers are significant and should be recognized but, most importantly, expanded upon; and third, that Maya women have an appropriate role in agricultural production that ought to be supported and recognized. Although she is most directly concerned with Maya women, Araceli is a proponent for the rights of all women.

Especially important to Araceli is to underscore the human worth of Maya women. In her poetry and narrative essays particularly she demonstrates her humanity as a Maya woman, and by example that of other Maya women, who as individuals have a fully fleshed emotional life and the ability to express the complicated themes of human emotion.

In her writings Araceli is also critical of the position of Maya women in society as those most likely to experience poverty, discrimination, and exclusion. But she also as a community leader encourages agency especially on the part of women to take a hand in transforming their own lives despite the obstacles they face. Araceli especially stresses education as a path out of a life constricted by poverty and curtailed in hope.

Araceli's advocacy of the rights of Maya women, however, occurs within the context of an advocacy on behalf of all Maya, both women and men. In her political writings and speeches Araceli provides a critique of state policies and actions toward indigenous people. She analyzes the disadvantaged position of indigenous people vis-à-vis nonindigenous people and describes the loneliness of their social exclusion. From the basis of her critique Araceli paves the way for activism on behalf of her fellow Maya.

Araceli outlines her own policy platform for the Maya, which includes socioeconomic equity, recognition of the humanity and wisdom of the Maya, and their inclusion as *indigenous* peoples in all aspects of the life of Mexico as a nation and a culture. In her agenda for the Maya she especially emphasizes certain fundamental points. As basic rights for the Maya she calls for socioeconomic equity and a role for the Maya in public policy decision making. She also notes that Maya women have special socioeconomic concerns as wives and mothers. But Araceli also claims new kinds of socioeconomic participation for Maya women based on enhanced educational and professional opportunities that lie beyond their long-standing roles as wives and mothers.

As a writer, poet, and politician Araceli keynotes her Maya community by repeated references to Maya history and the legitimacy and relevance of Maya knowledge. She especially argues for the recognition of the humanity and wisdom of the Maya. She points out the importance of the tradition-rich Maya past to the Maya present. In highlighting the relevancy of Maya culture to contemporary life, she especially notes community-based approaches to solving problems and enhancing everyday life. Araceli also emphasizes the endurance of the Maya as an inspiration for the present originating from a Maya past.

Araceli argues also for the inclusion of the Maya *as Maya* in all aspects of society in Yucatán and, by extension, Mexico. She references the role of indigenous people in the creation and construction of Mexico as a nation. As such she argues for the recognition of the Maya as a part of the modern nation and their empowerment as citizens within the state and within the political system. Throughout her political career Araceli has sought inclusion, equity, and political rights for her fellow Yucatec Maya and by extension for the other fifty-five officially recognized indigenous peoples of Mexico.

A Muted Representation

Araceli's efforts to mediate between the community of which she is a part and the sociopolitical institutions of Yucatán were, however, muted by institutionalized resistance or nonrecognition of her role as an intellectual and leader. The representatives of political parties, male dominated and largely non-Maya, curtailed her career in politics. They only partly recognized her leadership and intellectual abilities, underplaying, or failing to recognize, her importance as a representative of a Maya community, particularly of Maya women. It seems that political parties wanted her presence as a Maya woman but not her participation as a Maya leader.

Yet despite the politics of exclusion and prejudice against women and indigenous people, politicians from four political parties (the PRI, PT, PRD and Frente Cardenista) have given some recognition to Araceli's talents and included her in their party organizations to some degree for almost thirty years. Her experience within the four parties, however, has varied.

The PRI, the long-dominant political party of Mexico, incorporated Araceli as a community activist and party member for many years. Yet despite her talent and loyalty to the party there seemed to be a glass ceiling set on her rise within the party. After serving her first term in Congress, the PRI proposed no higher office for her. Araceli was once again relegated to the party's rank and file.

After resigning from the PRI, Araceli was later reelected to Congress under the banner of the Frente Cardenista. Her tenure in the Frente, however, was very brief. She shortly changed allegiances to become a member of the PT. Of the four political parties with which Araceli has affiliated, the PT seemed to have offered her the best opportunities to represent her Maya community and move forward her agenda for them. In the PT Araceli had a clear leadership role in the organization of the party and a central voice in the policy making. The PT was also the only party ever to support her candidacy for national office when the party nominated her as its candidate for the Senate in 1993.

Araceli's political future became intertwined with that of the PT. The loss of power of the PT to the PRD led to its near demise as a politically significant party in Yucatán. Finally the conflict between the local leaders of the PT and those from the national PT organization hastened Araceli's withdrawal from partisan party politics.

Araceli's political future is now indeterminate. As an affiliate with the Nueva Izquierda faction of the PRD, she has become politically active again after a time on the political sidelines. Membership in a minority faction within a minority party, however, will no doubt limit Araceli's participation in the partisan politics of Yucatán.

Yet surmounting obstacles has been the leitmotif of Araceli's life. Although she has had a muted success with her mediated representation of her Maya community, Araceli's frustration and perhaps her occasionally expressed sense of personal failure are tempered by her expressions of a continuing hope for a better future for the Maya.

A Look to the Future: Recognition of an Intellectual

Gramsci's model of the organic intellectual is a theoretical innovation because it recognizes a new category of intellectuals and conceptualizes their role in their communities and in the wider society. Yet for all its relevance in conceptualizing another category of intellectuals and their societal role, Gramsci's model does not consider the reception of organic intellectuals by the wider society in which they live and work, in which they attempt to perform mediated representations of their communities.

The political-cultural context in which Gramsci formed his ideas was quite different from that in which Araceli sought to represent the worldview of her Maya community and perform a mediated representation of her community within the wider society of Yucatán. To Gramsci considerations of class and class conflict were paramount in understanding the

European society of his time. For Araceli her gender, indigenous identity, and the perception of her identity as a Maya woman by Yucatecan society were more influential variables in understanding her position as an organic intellectual within the contemporary society of Yucatán.

Institutionalized resistance and nonrecognition of her as a Maya woman leader muted Araceli's mediated representation of her Maya community. The recognition of Araceli's abilities as a political activist and politician were curtailed by others' bias toward women and indigenous people. Although four political parties did somewhat recognize her talents and include her in their party organization to some degree, recognition of Araceli as an *intellectual* has been scant within the wider society of Yucatán. Only her colleague, Diputada Blanca Estrada; the Spanish folklorist, Ascensión Amador Naranjo; a few academic colleagues in Yucatán; above all, her supporters in Maxcanú; and I seemed to have recognized and honored her as an intellectual. Beyond this small circle, however, few have.[1]

In the time and place that Araceli lives the notion of who can be defined as an intellectual is constricted by gender, class, and indigenous identity. Now that Araceli is older, in her seventies, I think that age too has become a factor in the nonrecognition of her status as an intellectual. An older Maya woman is not someone likely to be considered as an intellectual by Yucatecan society.

The nature of Araceli's engagement as an organic rather than traditional intellectual, I think, masks her achievements and talents in the eyes of many others. The position of traditional intellectuals, defined by Gramsci as those who occupy readily distinguishable positions in institutions in literary or scientific organizations, makes them more visible and recognizable as intellectuals. And in Yucatán as elsewhere in the Americas, traditional intellectuals are much more likely to originate in dominant classes, ethnic groups, and the male gender. Unaccustomed to recognizing the intellectual talents of people outside these categories, many are likely to disregard the achievements of such individuals.

Despite these societal restrictions concerning who is likely to be considered an intellectual, however, Araceli, as her life circumstances have allowed her, lives an intellectual life, writing her own works and reading widely, especially books by and about women. Apart from her grammar school education she is self-educated. She, as an indigenous Maya woman, has an identity as a political activist through her long career in politics. But beyond her political participation, she has an identity as a producer of knowledge through her writing. She frequently honors writing as a tool that allowed her to triumph over the obstacles she confronted. She cherishes the life of the mind and its expression through her writings. Now that she has retired from a full-time engagement in politics, her writings have become more important to her as part of her self-definition as an intellectual. She is a writer and poet as well as a politician and political activist. It is Araceli's hope and mine that this book will showcase her talents as a writer and open her world of understanding to others.

Appendix
Methodology

The saints aren't going to help me, you are!
—*Araceli Cab Cumí, conversation, July 1999*

As Araceli suggests in her opening phrase to this appendix, she recognizes my role in helping publish her work. I have long thought that she conceives this book as a final opportunity to gain the intellectual recognition she deserves.

My first goal for this book is to introduce an original and powerful writer to a wider audience. A secondary goal was to introduce a writer all the more rare because she is an indigenous Maya woman, one of a few to be published to date.

Anthropology is a personal science. Reflection upon oneself, one's work, or the people with whom one works is part of the process of doing anthropology. And so, I have written my reflections in the text when I thought they would illuminate its meaning, the relationship between Araceli and me, or our collaborative process of producing this book. I have been careful, however, to ensure that my reflections enhance the text rather than detract from Araceli's life narrative or her writings. The focus of this book is Araceli and her work. I did not want this book to become a confessional, as some current anthropology is, with the focus on the anthropologist and her or his angst—leaving one to wonder whose story is actually being told. It seems to me that it is one thing to inform the reader about the process of producing the text; it is another to make this process the text. It is important to acknowledge the difference.

In this book I have written only two "interventions," as I term them, focusing more on my thoughts in writing this book than on Araceli's writings or life narrative: one in chapter 4, "An Agenda for the Maya," and the other in chapter 6, "Endings?" In the first intervention I wrote about my response to Araceli's poem about Maya slavery after visiting Sisal, a port from which the enslaved Maya were shipped out to Cuba. Her poem sobered my memory of a relaxed, joyful vacation with my husband and overlaid it with haunting images of the Maya being sent away from their flat, beloved homeland. I thought others might understand Araceli's passionate poem better with the counterpoint of my experience. In the second intervention I sought to honor Zazil Espinosa Patrón, Araceli's eldest granddaughter, who supported and aided our efforts to produce this book. She, unlike her sister, Zoila, or her cousin Edna, has not written anything for this book but has been central to its production. Zazil deserves acknowledgment.

I described in the introduction how Araceli and I met in 1993 while she was a congressional representative whom I interviewed for the project "Women's Participation in Democratization: Transforming the Mexican State." Since then we have continued to stay in touch in all my subsequent, almost yearly, trips to Yucatán. Over the years we have had many conversations sitting around her dining room table in Maxcanú or in the cafés and restaurants of Mérida. Our ongoing discussions continued when we have visited Celestún, a Yucatecan seaside village; Oxkintok, the ancient Maya ruin; and on several occasions, the former Hacienda de Santa Rose de Lima, now a hotel and restaurant, all relatively near Maxcanú. From the beginning Araceli seemed to like talking to me and I certainly valued hearing her thoughts on women, politics, and indigenous issues. I also simply enjoy her company. She was one of three people including my friends, Sister Terry, a Maryknoll sister, and Thomas C. Gerhard (Sr. Tom), a North American retiree and longtime resident of Mérida, whom I always contact on my visits to Yucatán because I value their thoughts and enjoy their company. Sadly, my beloved friend, Sr. Tom, passed on in the spring of 2003.

During my absences from Yucatán, Araceli and I have communicated occasionally by exchanging letters and cards. Until 2000 I would call Araceli at a neighbor's home or at the telephone in a Maxcanú pharmacy. Then our communication eased when in 2000 Araceli got a semipublic telephone by her front gate so that calling on her birthday, to make arrangements to work together, or when hurricanes threatened Yucatán was much easier. Since the arrival of cybercafes in Mérida and the more widespread use of the Internet in schools, our communications have become more reliable. Her granddaughters Zazil and Anita and her grandson Pedro, who lives next door, all have access to computers and e-mail. Araceli says she wishes to learn to use a computer soon so that she can e-mail directly.

In 1996 we developed the idea for this book, the process of which I described in the introduction. Our first task was to organize the archive of Araceli's writings. We put each piece in a file folder labeled with its title (or first line if no title), separated the work into broad categories (poetry, political speeches, diary essays, and life narratives), and filed all the pieces chronologically. Next we made three copies of each document. The origi-nals and one copy remained with Araceli. I took one copy with me (and subsequently made another for translating). We stored the third copy in another location in Yucatán. We have followed this three-copy plan with all of Araceli's subsequent work.

Such an outline of our work suggests a more orderly process than what actually occurred. Araceli continues to write and so the final selection of her writings to appear in this book was steadily reviewed. We tried to select poems, essays, political speeches, and position papers that best represented the range and depth of her work. Consequently, we chose what we consid-ered the best expressions among writings similar in content (such as her three life narratives or the several poems she has written about Maxcanú) for inclusion in the book.

From 1996 to 2004 we taped 35½ hours of formal interviews, focusing on Araceli's life narrative and the contextual background for her writings. Over the eleven years that we have known each other we have also had countless untaped conversations, parts of which became my fieldnotes and ultimately contributions to the narrative of this book.

Until 1999 all the interviews were recorded either in Araceli's congres-sional office (the first two interviews) or her home in Maxcanú. Ultimately, however, I thought that interviewing Araceli in her home was becoming too distracting. Family life went on around us and Araceli's neighbors and politi-cal supporters would sometimes stop by because I was there. In such circum-stances interviewing became more communal—and while interesting, this did divert us from our task. With so many people coming and going I thought we were losing Araceli's more private thoughts. Although both Araceli and I were well focused and able to pick up the thread of a discussion once interruptions ended, I thought a quieter, more private atmosphere for our discussions about the book would be more productive.

Consequently in 1999 we began to work in the calm, quiet of the Hotel Santa Lucía in downtown Mérida and, in 2000, in its sister hotel, the Hotel San Juan, a block away. Araceli wrote the following acrostic at the end of one of our working sessions at the Hotel Santa Lucía. She gave a copy to the owner of the hotel, Sr. Juan Rosado Alcocer, who was pleased to have his hotel honored in a poem. Sr. Rosado Alcocer had been mayor of Valladolid in eastern Yucatán during the same period that Araceli was serving her first congressional term. Although they did not know each other during those days, Sr. Juan and Araceli reminisce about their early days in politics whenever their paths cross at one of his two hotels. She describes the Hotel Santa Lucía in the following acrostic:

HOTEL SANTA LUCÍA

H   *There would be memories, . . . remembrances*
O   *I will hear the lasting echo, . . .*
T   *Time, passing in these days*
E   *A stay saturated by words*
L   *Elaborated by mutual judgments.*

S   *Solace, a relaxing place*
A   *To walk, . . . whispers on the balconies*
N   *Home of the traveler's passage*
T   *Embroidered green, . . . the gardens*
A   *Harmony, . . . peace, . . . concentration.*

L   *Discrete flickering lights*
U   *Anointed by the voice of the serenades*
C   *Bohemian strings, romantic guitars*
I   *Unforgettable, . . . the conversations, . . . the days*
A   *Above all this, . . . many thanks!*

Monday the nineteenth,
Tuesday the twentieth, and
Wednesday the twenty-first of July 1999

Habrá recuerdos,...remembranzas
Oiré el eco perdurable,.........
Tiempo, transcurrido en estos días
Estancia saturada por palabras
Labradas por los criterios mutuos.

Solaz lugar de esparcimiento
Andar,... murmullo en los balcones
Nido de los pasos peregrinos
Tejido verde... los jardines
Armonía,... paz,... recogimiento.

Luces con discretos parpadeos
Ungidas por la voz de serenatas
Cuerdas bohemias,...romanticas guitarras.
Inolvidables,... las pláticas,... los días
Ante Todo esto,...¡muchas gracias!

Lunes Martes miercoles
19   20   21 de Julio-1999

A Cab C.

In this acrostic Araceli acknowledges our dedicated work together to produce this book. Her nostalgic description of the setting of the hotel was likely inspired by the Santa Lucía Park, a small gardenlike square across the street from the hotel where the city government sponsors poetry readings, music, and dance performances several nights a week and on Sunday mornings.

We found that working in these two small hotels in Mérida was much more productive and most of our longer discussions took place there in the quiet and privacy of Araceli's room or mine. In our nonworking time we both enjoyed walking around downtown Mérida, dining in its small restaurants, and running into people who knew one or both of us. I think that Araceli enjoyed her time in Mérida away from the daily routine and family responsibilities of life in Maxcanú.

A Note about Translation

Araceli writes everything, including her political treatises, with a simple, elegant poetic style, never elaborated or overblown. In my translation, I have tried to retain the lyrical flow of her work and the meaning and style of her original Spanish or her Yucatec Maya translations to Spanish. I have tried to do a nuanced translation, getting to the heart of the idiomatic meaning of words and phrases as used by people in Yucatán.

Both Araceli and I learned Spanish as a second language. Perhaps our common grounding in Spanish as a second language has helped the translation as we sought to clarify the meanings in Spanish so that they made sense in Araceli's Yucatec Maya and my English.

Translation seemed to work better when I stepped back from more literal translations and let the meaning flow, more easily read by taking some distance from the text. I first read each piece several times and then translated it noting any words or phrases I needed to clarify with Araceli and detailing those sections that would need explanatory endnotes. I then let the translation sit for a couple weeks and went on to the next piece. When I had completed the translations, I hired Juanita Mainster, a friend and former student in our department, to go over my translations with me to check for accuracy. Juanita was especially skilled at checking my translations because of her love of language and the depth of her knowledge of English and Mexican Spanish. I very much appreciate her dedication to checking my translations.

Some particular points of the translation need to be mentioned. Common Spanish writing convention allows for a longer sentence structure than does English. To ease the translation to English with its convention of shorter sentences I have sometimes put periods where Araceli has commas, semicolons, or colons. On rare occasions I have inserted a bracketed word or phrase to give a clearer, smoother reading to the English translation.

I have kept faithful to Araceli's paragraph breaks, use of sentence fragments, and placement of text on the page. Obviously these are all important to Araceli's mode of expression; they are part of the poetry of her writing. In some cases, I have retained the original Spanish word (for example, raza, querencia) when no suitable translation suggests itself in English. In such cases I have written an endnote to explain the term. Since Araceli salts her written Spanish with Yucatec Maya words, I have highlighted these by putting them in italics with an English translation in the endnotes. Throughout the text Yucatec Maya and Spanish words are italicized.

Notes

In Memoriam

1. Maria Isara Cumí Carbello was Araceli's mother. Román Ek, Donato Dzul, and Isamuel Zi were fellow Maya from Araceli's hometown of Maxcanú. She describes them as humble and poor but respected by other Maya for their wisdom and their generosity in sharing their knowledge. Guibaldo López Lara was a teacher and later school principal from Maxcanú. He willed his home for a school in the town. Dominga Cen from Halacho, Yucatán, and Maestra Paula Cruz Estrella from Progreso, Yucatán, were Araceli's colleagues and fellow political activists.

    Elvia Carrillo Puerto and Felipa Poot were social activists in early twentieth-century Yucatán. Elvia Carrillo Puerto of Motul, Yucatán, had a long career of activism in her native state during the 1920s. As an ardent supporter of women's rights Elvia Carrillo Puerto campaigned for women's suffrage. She was at the forefront of women's activism during its heyday in Yucatán from 1915 to 1924. Working with her brother Felipe Carrillo Puerto, who was the governor of Yucatán from 1922 to 1924, she established the Ligas Feministas (Feminist Leagues), uniting women all over Yucatán. When her brother was assassinated in January 1924, Elvia fled Yucatán to save her life and went to central Mexico where she reestablished her activist career. During the 1930s and 1940s she continued her political activism in Mexico City and in the state of San Luis Potosí where she ran unsuccessfully for governor, surviving an assassination attempt in the process. Elvia Carrillo Puerto died in 1965 in Mexico City, poor and largely forgotten (Lemaitre 1998; Peniche Rivero 1996; 2006; Soto 1990, 137, 140–41; 1979, 61–64).

    Felipa Poot was a Maya woman from Kinchil, Yucatán, who fought for women's rights as part of a civil rights movement in her region of western Yucatán. During her short life, she helped create a union, a worker cooperative, and a rural school. Felipa Poot was also president of the Ligas Feministas (Feminist Leagues) in Kinchil. She was assassinated on March 28, 1936, at age twenty-eight. Unfortunately little has been written about Felipa Poot. The journalists Jesus Canul (2001) and Jesus Solis Alpuche (1986) have written outlines of her life for the local press in Yucatán. The famous Mexican writer Manuel Luis Guzman (1984, 1077–89) wrote a largely fictionalized account of Felipa Poot centering on her death. The historian Ben Fallaw has written an article (2002) about Felipa Poot and mentioned her in his book (2001), analyzing her activism within an early twentieth-century context of political reform in Yucatán. I have written two articles reconstructing her life and analyzing her activism in terms of the Yucatecan women's rights movement (2006; 2004). Several years ago vandals destroyed a memorial to her in Kinchil for its metal (Canul 2001). A new plaque honoring Felipa Poot was recently placed in the secondary school in Kinchil.

2. Don Pablo del S. Patrón Cih was Araceli's husband. He died in June 2002. Araceli wrote a memorial poem for him that appears in the "Endings?" chapter of this book.

Dedication

1. Araceli dedicated this book to educators, to her family, and, as she says, "to people in her community who are forgotten or alone." Dr. Othón Baños Ramírez, Dra. Beatriz Castilla Ramos, and Dra. Beatriz Torres Góngora are all professors in the Centro de Investigaciones Regionales, Unidad de Ciencias Sociales at the Universidad Autónoma de Yucatán. Dr. Allan Burns is chair of the Department of Anthropology at the University of Florida. He invited Araceli and I to give presentations at the Wisdom of the Maya Conference held in Gainesville, Florida, in March 1994. Ms. Sharon Mújica from the University of North Carolina administers a summer field school in Yucatán and often invites Araceli to lecture to her students. Dr. Juan Castillo Cocom earned his doctorate with me in the graduate program in comparative sociology at Florida International University. He and Araceli have met several times and she honors him here as a fellow Yucatec Maya intellectual.

The primary school in her hometown of Maxcanú, the state cultural missions, and the National Institute for Adult Education all helped Araceli earn a formal education. Some of the individual teachers in these institutions were instrumental in encouraging her to run for political office.

Araceli has two sisters and two brothers. Her sister Maria lives in Mérida, the state capital of Yucatán about an hour's bus ride north of Maxcanú. Her other sister, Dalia, migrated to the United States some thirty years ago and lives with her husband and four children in Massachusetts. Araceli has a close relationship with Maria but unfortunately has lost contact with Dalia. Her brother Hugo lives in Maxcanú. He and Araceli have a cordial if somewhat distant relationship. Araceli's second brother, Medardo, died many years ago.

All of the other people to whom Araceli dedicates this book are local women from Maxcanú or neighboring communities in Yucatán. She has chosen to honor the humble, the forgotten, the alone, and those who overcame difficult life circumstances to survive and perhaps prosper. Araceli notes that all of these women stood up for themselves as women either within their families or in the public political arena. Araceli gave the following capsule descriptions of each woman. Aidee Ventura is Araceli's former schoolmate of whom she is especially fond. Now blind, Sra. Ventura lives alone. Carmela Dzul is a longtime friend and political supporter. Martina Catzim and Edelmira Catzim are neighbors and hard-working housewives. Teodora Rodriquez is Araceli's lighthearted cousin and a key political supporter. Isidra Chan is an elderly indigenous woman living in Maxcanú. Ernestina Lopez and Cristina Ku'mul are fellow activists. Maria Candelaria Uc is a neighbor who always fought to get her children an education. All of them are now professionals. Ismelda Ventura is a jolly woman who left her abusive husband to raise her children alone. Maria Teresa Canto C. is a former schoolteacher. Rosalia Pinzon R. is a woman who never married and a special friend of Araceli's. Maria Elena Martinez is a political ally of Araceli who was especially helpful in her efforts on behalf of the poor. Margarita Tun is a friend who has always lived very independently. Emilia Cime is a social activist from Motul, Yucatán. Nidelvia Ventura R. is a friend and political supporter of Araceli who now lives in Mérida.

Acknowledgments

1. In the acknowledgments Araceli introduces some major themes of her writing. These include her dedication to her fellow Maya and to women, her love and yearning for knowledge, and also the complex imagery of "hojas sueltas," the "discarded pages/loose papers/fallen leaves." All of these are discussed in greater detail throughout the book.

Introduction

1. Throughout Latin America, a barrio is a residential neighborhood. While not an officially designed place with clear boundaries, barrios nonetheless have social significance to their residents as home places.

2. Although not in proportion to their representation in the population, indigenous women in Mexico have been active politically at the community level and in social movements for some time. See Stephen 1991 and for Maya women in Mexico in particular see Re Cruz 1995; Forbis 1999; Kintz 1999; Logan 1995a; Martín 1998; and Ortiz 2001. Despite their political participation

at the community level and in social movements, however, the engagement
of indigenous women in partisan politics has been minimal. Political parties
seldom seek the participation of indigenous women nor do they routinely
include the agenda of issues that indigenous women are likely to wish to engage.

3. In Latin America there have been few Maya or other indigenous individuals
who have become published writers. Most commonly the works published are
indigenous people's life narratives presented through the intervening voice of a
transcriber or editor (for example, Barrios De Chungara 1978; Burgos-Debray
1984; Pozas 1962; Sexton 1981; 1985; Tirado 1991). See Logan 1997 for a critique
of this methodology. For a more collaborative, collegial approach between an
academic editor, Florencia E. Mallon, and an indigenous activist, Rosa Isolde
Reuque Paillalef, see Reuque Paillalef (2002), *When a Flower Is Reborn: The Life
and Times of a Mapuche Feminist.*

Indeed the best-known indigenous woman in Latin America, the 1992 Nobel
Peace Prize laureate Rigoberta Menchú Tum, is recognized in part because of the
"as told to" book, *I, Rigoberta Menchú* (Menchú 1984), first published in Spanish
as *Me llamo Rigoberta Menchú y así me nació la conciencia* (Menchú 1983). In
this work Ms. Menchú related her life narrative to the Venezuelan anthropologist
Elisabeth Burgos. Ms. Menchú has since authored her own book about her life,
Crossing Borders (1998), originally published in Spanish as *Rigoberta, La nieta de
los Mayas* (Rigoberta, The Granddaughter of the Maya).

Several other Maya women have published books with limited publication
runs. Maruch Sántiz Gómez, a Tzotzil Maya woman from Chiapas, Mexico,
published a trilingual (Tzotzil Maya, Spanish, and English) book of her
photographs accompanied by traditional Maya sayings, *Creencias de nuestros
antepasados* (1998).

In 2000 a collective of Guatemalan Maya women researchers, writers, and
photographers published a bilingual Spanish-English book about their lives,
*Voces e imagenes: Mujeres Maya Ixiles de Chajul/Voices and Images: Mayan Ixil
Women of Chajul* (ADMI 2000). Both books are now unfortunately out of print.
Other works of this sort no doubt exist but their limited publication runs and
lack of publicity curtail their audience.

Ignacio Bizarro Ujpán (pseudonym), a Tzutuhil Maya man from Guatemala,
with the translating and editing assistance of anthropologist James Sexton, has
published four books about his life and that of his community (1981; 1985; 1992;
2001). This collection remains the most complete record of a Maya life from the
perspective of an individual Maya.

Nonetheless the future for indigenous writers in Latin America is more
hopeful. In Guatemala particularly, Maya writers such as Gaspar Pedro González
(1995; 1998a; 1998b) and Estuardo Zapeta (1999) are beginning to emerge with
the advent of Maya cultural activism in that nation. The California-based Yax Te'
Foundation has been at the forefront of publishing contemporary Maya writers,

especially those from Guatemala (http://www.yaxte.org). Yax Te' publishes works in the various Maya languages of Guatemala as well as in Spanish or English translations, often in bilingual or trilingual editions. There is also an Asociación de Escritores en Lenguas Indígenas (Association of Indigenous Writers) that seeks to foster literatures in indigenous languages and recognize indigenous writers. As more Maya have the opportunity for higher education, academically trained Maya intellectuals will come to the fore as have Dr. Victor Montejo (1987; 1995; 1999) and Dr. Juan Castillo Cocom (2005).

4. Women's political resurgence in Yucatán is discussed more fully in chapter 3. Also see Martín 1998; 1999; 2001; Logan 1995a; 1995b.

5. There is a considerable literature about Mexican women's political participation. See Rodríguez 1998 for an overview of contemporary Mexican women's political engagement and Soto 1990 for a historical overview, especially of the early to mid-twentieth century.

6. Dr. Beatriz Castilla Ramos from the Centro de Investigaciones Regionales, Universidad Autónoma de Yucatán, and I met in 1984 when I first began to do research in Yucatán. Over the years we have become colleagues and friends. Beatriz customarily works on issues of women's employment and economic activities, not women's politics per se. I asked Beatriz to be codirector with me on this project because I respect her work and her thorough knowledge of Yucatán and its people. See Castilla Ramos (1998; 1999) and her most recent book, *Mujeres mayas en la robótica y líderes de la comunidad: Tejiendo la modernidad* (2004).

The project on which Beatriz and I were codirectors, "Women's Participation in Democratization: Transforming the Mexican State," was generously funded by a grant from the North-South Center, External Research Grant Program, University of Miami. We gratefully acknowledge their support. Over the summers of 1993–95 we did forty in-depth interviews with women activists, politicians, and state officials.

During the summer of 1995 I received a second grant from the North-South Center, External Research Grant Program, University of Miami, to focus on Yucatec Maya political participation, "Indigenous Engagement in Political and Social Change: The Yucatec Maya Case," Juan Castillo Cocom, codirector. This second grant allowed us to interview more Maya women politicians. Juan Castillo Cocom was at that time a doctoral candidate working with me in the graduate program in comparative sociology in the Department of Sociology/ Anthropology at Florida International University. A Yucatec Maya himself, Juan completed his doctorate in 2000 and now works in educational institutions and government agencies in Mérida, Yucatán.

7. Dr. Othón Baños Ramírez of the Centro de Investigaciones Regionales, Universidad Autónoma de Yucatán, is a longtime colleague and friend.

Customarily he researches policy-oriented issues pertaining to rural areas in the Yucatán Peninsula. See especially Baños Ramirez 1989; 1996; 2002.

8. Unfortunately, Beatriz was not able to attend either interview with Araceli because she became ill for a few weeks that summer.

9. Araceli and some of the women from Maxcanú proposed a cooperative garden in which they would raise crops for their own consumption and also for sale. They were especially interested in raising flowers to sell in Mérida's urban market. Unfortunately none of their efforts to seek funds through establishing their own NGO (nongovernmental organization) were successful. Much of the international funding that goes to Mexico is channeled through NGOs headquartered in Mexico City. As yet few NGOs operate in the Yucatán Peninsula and consequently the tristate region gets little funding in comparison to central Mexico.

10. Throughout this book I have used the opening line of Araceli's writings as the title for the particular work in those cases where she either hasn't given the work a title or when several works have the same or similar titles.

11. Antonio Gramsci (1891–1937) has become one of the most influential and frequently cited political theorists and cultural critics. Publication of his prison letters and six-volume notebooks in the late 1940s and early 1950s and their subsequent English translation in the 1960s and 1970s widened the audience for Gramsci's original, insightful, but complex thought. He is widely regarded as having influenced the social sciences especially in such areas as subaltern, postcolonial, and popular culture studies. His work is also frequently addressed in the discourse of North-South relations, modernity and postmodernity, theory, and praxis.

Gramsci grew up in Sardinia amidst poverty and with poor health that would plague him throughout his life. Coming from a family background of literacy and political engagement he intermittently attended school until he received a scholarship to the University of Turin. Gramsci subsequently left the university to engage more profoundly in politics by joining the Turin section of the Italian Socialist Party. After some leftists including Gramsci questioned the party's seemingly lackluster support of industrial workers engaged in a bitter labor dispute, he left the Italian Socialist Party to form, with other disenchanted leftists, the Italian Communist Party. Sent to the Soviet Union for eighteen months as a Communist Party representative, Gramsci married a Russian woman, Julca Schucht, in 1923. They had two sons but spent much time apart after Gramsci left the Soviet Union to return to Italy.

Upon his return he became a member of the Italian parliament and the general secretary of the Communist Party in Italy. He continued to write political philosophy as he had throughout his life. In 1926 Gramsci, along with thousands of other political leftists, was arrested by Mussolini's Fascist regime. During his imprisonment Gramsci's former landlady, his last cellmate, the economist Piero Sraffer, and especially his sister-in-law, Tatiana Schucht, aided him by supplying books and writing materials and ultimately smuggling his works out of prison. He was imprisoned until his death at age forty-six under guard in a clinic. His long years in prison destroyed his fragile health but he nonetheless wrote some of his most compelling and lasting works despite his illnesses and the watchfulness of his prison censors (Crehan 2002, 1–35; Hoare and Nowell Smith in Gramsci 1971, xv–xcvi).

There are three English-language biographies of Gramsci: Davidson (1977), Fiori (1990), and Germino (1990). English translations of Gramsci's writings are *Selections from the Prison Notebooks of Antonio Gramsci* edited by Hoare and Nowell Smith (Gramsci 1971); *Selections from Political Writings, 1910–1920* edited by Hoare (Gramsci 1977); *Selections from Political Writings, 1921–1926* edited by Hoare (Gramsci 1978); *Selections from Cultural Writings* edited by Forgacs and Nowell-Smith (Gramsci 1985); *Prison Notebooks* edited by Buttigieg (Gramsci 1992, vol. 1; 1996, vol. 2); *Letters from Prison* edited by Rosengarten (Gramsci 1994, vols. 1–2); and *Further Selections from the Prison Notebooks* edited by Boothman (Gramsci 1995). See Crehan's *Gramsci, Culture and Anthropology* (2002) for an interpretation of Gramscian theory as applied to anthropology.

12. Gramsci used the term "group" while meaning "class" in order to evade his prison censors who would have been suspicious if he had used "class" since this term would have referenced Marxist political philosophy.

13. For statements regarding Gramsci's definition and discussion of organic intellectuals see Hoare and Nowell-Smith (in Gramsci 1971, 3–23 and passim), Femia (1981, 130–33, 164, 186), and Crehan (2002, 131–56, 160).

14. For useful overviews and discussions of the cultural and political activism of contemporary indigenous peoples of the Americas, which underscore a view of them as newly emergent social groups, see Hector Diaz Polanco's *Indigenous Peoples in Latin America: The Quest for Self-Determination* (1997); Donna Lee Van Cott's *Indigenous Peoples and Democracy in Latin America* (1994); and Phillip Wearne's *Return of the Indian: Conquest and Revival in the Americas* (1996). For the Maya in particular, see Edward F. Fischer and R. McKenna Brown (1996), *Maya Cultural Activism in Guatemala*, and Kay B. Warren (1998), *Indigenous Movements and their Critics: Pan-Maya Activism in Guatemala*.

15. It would be erroneous to claim within the complicated sociopolitical context of Chiapas that the long-organized rebellion and its subsequent transformation into social movement was purely a Maya effort focusing on indigenous issues alone. There were and are other actors and other issues. See especially Neil Harvey's *The Chiapas Rebellion: The Struggle for Land and Democracy* (1998) and June Nash's *Mayan Visions: The Quest for Autonomy in an Age of Globalization* (2001) for discussion of the complex context of the Zapatista rebellion.

16. *Precursora* has a meaning in Spanish that belies the simplicity of its English translation as "precursor." In Spanish the term is often used to indicate someone honored as a perhaps forgotten visionary whose thoughts and actions influenced those who followed even if the continuity of their ideas was broken passing from one generation to the next. Precursoras' ideas are considered advanced beyond their times, often being rediscovered and achieving recognition and application only at some later time. In *Latin American Women and the Search for Social Justice*, Miller (1991) discusses women who were precursoras for the cause of women's rights in the region. One such precursora was Flora Tristan, a nineteenth-century Peruvian-French writer and social critic whom many now regard as a historical predecessor of socialist feminism.

17. See Gabbert (2004), *Becoming Maya*, and "Ethnicity in Yucatan" (2002) as well as Hervik (2002), *Mayan Peoples Within and Beyond Boundaries*, for a statement of these ideas. Hervik argues that to the people of Yucatán, "Maya" refers to the ancients and that contemporary Yucatecan people use the term "mestizo" (literally, "mixed") to refer to themselves. Gabbert circumscribes the term "Maya" as a scholarly invention indicative of a newly forming ethnic conscious that has not previously existed among the various "Maya" groups.

   For a distinctly Maya view on this theme refer to Juan Castillo Cocom's article (2005) that demonstrates the complexities of the issue of Maya identity as expressed by an emerging Yucatec Maya intellectual and scholar.

18. In *Maya Cosmos: Three Thousand Years on the Shaman's Path*, Freidel, Schele, and Parker (1993) argue for a Maya cultural continuity from the ancient to the contemporary based on an enduring Maya cosmovision most obviously represented through the performance of rituals.

19. See Almario's "Territorio, identidad, memoria coletiva y movimiento étnico de los grupos negros del Pacífico sur colombiano: Microhistoria y etnografía sobre el Río Tapaje" (2002); Rappaport's *Politics of Memory* (1990); and the Andean Oral History Workshop's (THOA) "Indigenous Women and Community Resistance: History and Memory" (1990) for expressions of this view.

20. In her 1994 poem "I Have Here," Araceli gives a Maya perspective on links between ancient and contemporary Maya peoples. In her 1992 congressional speech, "The Solidarity of Indigenous People," she expresses the relevance of Maya values to contemporary life. Both the poem and speech appear in chapter 4.

21. See Fischer (2002), *Cultural Logics and Global Economies: Maya Identity in Thought and Practice*, and Nash (2001), *Mayan Visions: The Quest for Autonomy in an Age of Globalization*, for interpretations and discussion of Maya responses to globalization.

22. See Freidel, Schele, and Parker (1993), *Maya Cosmos: Three Thousand Years on the Shaman's Path*, and Schele and Freidel (1990), *A Forest of Kings: The Untold*

Story of the Ancient Maya, for accessible, reader-friendly accounts of ancient Maya cultures, especially their architectural styles, political structure, religion, and philosophy.

23. See Coe (1992), *Breaking the Maya Code,* for an accessible, well-written account of the process by which a group of international scholars decoded ancient Maya writing.

24. For an overview of the ancient Maya, refer to Coe (2005), *The Maya.* Although no such thorough overview yet exists for the contemporary Maya, more specialized publications abound. Village-level ethnographies such as Re Cruz (1996), *The Two Milpas of Chan Kom,* Kintz (1990), *Life under the Tropical Canopy,* and Fischer and Hendrickson (2003), *Tecpan Guatemala,* are useful introductory sources to the contemporary Maya.

25. The term, "Zapatista," adopted by the Chiapan rebels, references an early twentieth-century hero of the Mexican Revolution, Emiliano Zapata. Himself a person of, in part, indigenous (Nahua) heritage, he led an armed agrarian reform movement in central Mexico. Ultimately betrayed and assassinated, Zapata and his movement have become emblematic of the Mexican Revolution and are revered national symbols. He was a fitting choice as a namesake for the indigenous rebels of Chiapas since they fight as Zapata fought for many of the same rights, especially regarding land usage and ownership. Womack (1968), *Zapata and the Mexican Revolution,* remains a basic text about Zapata.

26. See Restall (1998), *Maya Conquistador,* and Farriss (1984), *Maya Society under Colonial Rule,* for analyses of Maya cultural transformations throughout the conquest and colonial periods. Both books focus upon a Maya view of the conquest and subsequent colonialism. Restall validates a continuing Maya cultural presence by recontextualizing the calamity of conquest, noting the continuities between the pre- and postconquest Maya societies and analyzing the reconstituted social order as conceived by the Maya along class rather than ethnic lines. Farriss notes that within the context of the particular colonial regime installed by the Spanish in Yucatán, Maya cultural survival was possible because of the Maya "capacity to forge something new out of existing elements in response to changing circumstances" (1984, 9). See Edward F. Fischer's *Cultural Logics and Global Economies: Maya Identity in Thought and Practice* (2002) for an analysis of how contemporary Guatemalan Maya peoples employ a flexible, creative interpretation of their culture to express and defend their identity in a rapidly transforming world. Fischer also demonstrates how structural shifts in international relations have opened new options for expressions of indigenous identity.

27. See Harvey (1998), *The Chiapas Rebellion: The Struggle for Land and Democracy,* and Nash (2001), *Mayan Visions: The Quest for Autonomy in an Age of Globalization,* for detailed accounts of current indigenous (largely Maya) resistance in the Chiapas highlands of Mexico. See Ortiz (2001), *Never Again a World*

Without Us, for the views of women involved in the Zapatista movement. For an important historical account of the nineteenth-century Yucatec Maya rebellion and subsequent resistance see Reed (2001, Rev. ed.), *The Caste War of Yucatán.*

28. Fischer and Brown (1996), *Mayan Cultural Activism in Guatemala,* provide a fine-tuned examination of contemporary Maya cultural florescence in Guatemala from both the perspective of scholars and indigenous Maya intellectuals. Warren (1998), *Indigenous Movements and Their Critics,* critically examines indigenous identities and their links to political activism among the Maya groups of Guatemala.

29. Since Araceli and I were not doing an interview on that afternoon, only organizing her files, I was not taping our conversation. Consequently I have paraphrased Araceli's response to my question here in the text.

30. Araceli's use of this complex phrase is also discussed in chapter 5.

31. Araceli maintains that Mexican state policy does not support the survival of the Yucatec Maya language or indigenous languages in general. Bilingual educational policy focuses on Spanish literacy not indigenous language proficiency. A state-sponsored chain of radio stations broadcasting in indigenous languages is managed from Mexico City with little participation or control by local indigenous peoples from the areas where the stations broadcast. A family friend of my former student (Juan Castillo Cocom), the well-known Yucatec Maya politician Max Yam Cocom, reported that when he tried to introduce legislation in the Yucatecan Congress to make the state officially bilingual, Yucatec Maya and Spanish, his fellow largely non-Maya legislators simply laughed.

The issue of speaking Yucatec Maya is a complex one. There is discrimination against those who speak Maya; yet individuals from non-Maya elite families who have been raised by Maya-speaking nannies are often proud of their ability to speak Yucatec Maya. Some wealthy and politically powerful individuals have told me that they learned Yucatec Maya because they needed fluency to communicate with their workforce and political constituents. Yucatec Maya and Maya-Spanish bilingualism is more common in rural areas while Spanish is the dominant language of the cities.

Araceli's own family history reflects an unfortunate diminishing use of Yucatec Maya in her region of the state. Her grandparents spoke only Maya; her parents were bilingual but spoke Maya in their home. Araceli uses both languages in her home and community. Her two adult children speak Spanish and understand Yucatec Maya somewhat. Their children, Araceli's grandchildren, neither speak nor understand Yucatec Maya.

Araceli notes that contemporary Yucatec Maya is much influenced by Spanish and adds that if an authentic Maya were spoken no one would understand it. Yucatec Maya in turn has influenced Spanish as spoken in Yucatán since many local people pepper their predominately Spanish speech with Maya words and phrases.

32. The Guatemalan Maya Nobel Peace Prize laureate Rigoberta Menchú Tum (1984) writes that she learned Spanish as an adult out of necessity to communicate to a wider audience particularly about the genocide of Maya peoples in Guatemala during that nation's three-decade-long civil war.

33. Felipe Carrillo Puerto was governor of Yucatán from February 1922 until his assassination on January 3, 1924. Known as a socialist reformer he sought to bring change to a wealthy but socially retrograde Yucatán. Felipe Carrillo Puerto took a special interest in attempting to improve the lives of women and the Maya. In his reform efforts he was aided by various members of his family including his sister Elvia Carrillo Puerto—one of the people to whom Araceli dedicated this book. He was a charismatic man who lived an eventful and unconventional life. Today he is one of the most revered figures in Yucatecan history, subject of song, poetry, and legend. Every January 3 his death is commemorated at a special ceremony at the cemetery in Mérida where he is buried. It was for this ceremony that Araceli was asked to write a speech in Yucatec Maya during her first term in Congress in 1974. Much has been written about Felipe Carrillo Puerto and there are contesting interpretations of his history but some useful sources include Joseph (1982), Mantilla and Sandoval (1994), and Sarkisyanz (1996, 1995).

34. Araceli used books published by the Mexican Secretariat of Public Education and the dictionary by Cordemex, the state agency that until its demise bought, processed, and marketed the Yucatecan henequen (*Agave fourcroydes* Lem.) crop. During the early twentieth century this crop underwrote the wealth of Yucatán's economy. Crops similar to henequen produced more cheaply elsewhere, and ultimately synthetic fibers, replaced Yucatán's henequen. Its demise in the 1930s devastated the state's economy.

35. Araceli gives the following as an example. *P'ak* in Yucatec Maya is "tomato," but *paak* is "to weed." Without the proper spelling, especially accent placement, two similar but distinctly different words could easily be confused.

36. The Yucatec Maya were one of the few ancient peoples of the Americas to have their written literature survive conquest and colonialism. Ancient Yucatec Maya is a complicated language combining symbols for syllables (sounds) as well as symbols for entire words. Ancient Yucatec Maya writing was decoded and thus made translatable only in the late twentieth century (Coe 1992).

Contemporary written Yucatec Maya, however, is formed from the common alphabet of European languages, Roman script. The Franciscans first introduced Roman script to Yucatán in the mid-sixteenth century. Consequently contemporary Maya who write their own language do so utilizing the alphabet of Roman script, not the ancient Maya alphabet. Recently in Guatemala the alphabetization (based on Roman script) of the various Guatemalan Maya languages was standardized. As Sigal (2000, ix) notes a similar standardization of Yucatec Maya has not yet been undertaken. Thus even so basic an element of written language as word division is problematic in Yucatec Maya because of the lack of standardization.

37. Julia Alvarez, the Dominican American writer, has addressed the issue of writing in a second language as one's predominant form of expression, particularly in her 1998 book, *Something to Declare*. Two essays in this book, "My English" and "Dona Aida, with Your Permission," especially focus on this theme.

38. Ariel Dorfman 1998, 25.

39. Araceli Cab Cumí, Life Narrative no. 2, 1995.

40. During the mid-1990s Araceli gave bilingual (Yucatec Maya–Spanish) lectures nearly each summer to the students of the Summer Intensive Introductory Course in Yucatec Maya sponsored by the Consortium in Latin American Studies at the University of North Carolina at Chapel Hill and Duke University. I introduced Araceli to Sharon Mújica, director of this program, at the Wisdom of the Maya Conference sponsored by Dr. Allan Burns at the University of Florida in March 1994. Sharon subsequently invited Araceli to give bilingual lectures to the students for several summers.

Chapter One

1. "Campesino" (or the feminine form "campesina") is a word that has no single word-precise translation into English. "Campesino" encompasses the idea of rural people, peasant farmers, or both. But in Mexico it means more. It represents a rooted, rural way of life and an identity with that life that transcends occupation.

2. Because the three life narrative accounts Araceli has written are quite similar, I have chosen to include in its entirety only the most complete one. The other two life narratives are Life Narrative no. 1, October 1, 1994, "My childhood was sad," and Life Narrative no. 3, summer 1996, "Speech to University of North Carolina Students." The diarylike essays are included as follows: the August 28, 1994, essay ("I Begin These Essays Today") opens the book. The September 8, 1994, essay ("And Well . . . What Can I Think?") appears in chapter 4 and the December 14, 1994, essay ("With All That I Am") in chapter 6. The July 6, 1995, essay ("And . . . Well . . . What Can I Say about Myself?") closes chapter 3.

3. Araceli wrote this life narrative to present to the students of the Summer Intensive Introductory Course in Yucatec Maya sponsored by the Consortium in Latin American Studies at University of North Carolina at Chapel Hill and Duke University. This program focuses on teaching Yucatec Maya to graduate students. During the Wisdom of the Maya Conference held at the University of Florida in

March 1994, I introduced Araceli to Sharon Mújica, organizer of the Duke-UNC summer program. Sharon subsequently invited Araceli to give a presentation to the students the following summer. Araceli participated in the seminar for several years. Given the language emphasis of the summer program, Araceli wrote one life narrative in both Yucatec Maya and Spanish.

4. See note 1, chapter 1.

5. In Araceli's original text she wrote "*mi caminar.*" Literally this phrase means "my walk." Given the context of the rest of the sentence it reads better in English to say "my step."

6. "Sacbe" means "white road" in Yucatec Maya. Constructed of the limestone so common to the Yucatecan peninsula, the ancient Maya built these roads or causeways to link their cities. Some scholars (Coe 1999, 141) maintain that the sacbe served ceremonial purposes instead, however, and were not transportation arteries.

7. "Chacnobitán" is the Yucatec Maya word for the Yucatecan peninsula. The word "Yucatán" is a Spanish construction originating from the Maya word.

8. See Meyer and Sherman (1995) for an overview of Mexico's complex history.

9. Huipils are the common everyday dress of many Yucatec Maya women and a style of dress commonly identified with Yucatán as a distinct region of Mexico. A huipil consists of a knee-length tunic worn over an underskirt.

   Most frequently the huipil tunic is embroidered with colorful floral designs around the yoke and hem. The hem of the underskirt is most commonly cut-out lace. The tunic and underskirt are usually white but nowadays women also wear pale pastels of yellow, blue, pink, or green. The yoke and hem embroidery on modern huipils also shows variation in design with fruits or geometric designs now used in addition to flowers. Nowadays the hem design of the underskirt can also vary with the use of a wide variety of kinds of lace or knotted fringe.

   The huipils women wear every day are likely to be mass produced so that the embroidery is done by machine, or lace bands are sewn on or preprinted floral borders are used in place of the embroidery. For everyday use many women just wear the tunic without the underskirt.

   A huipil can be the most simple of garments or the most elaborate depending upon its customization, the materials used, and elegance of the tunic embroidery and underskirt design. The huipil together with shawl, gold filigree jewelry, and flowers or combs in a swept-back hairstyle constitute the "traje de la mestiza" as this distinct ensemble of Yucatec Maya women is called. So adorned with intricate gold earrings and necklaces and draped with a shawl, a huipil is a garment suitable for the most formal of occasions. Women politicians in Yucatán whether they are indigenous or not often wear the "traje de la mestiza" to formal occasions or when representing the state at events elsewhere in the nation or

abroad. Thus Yucatecan women from the poorest to the most wealthy wear
this garment. See Oztoy (1996) for further analyses of this important, distinctly
Yucatecan style of women's dress.

10. "Huaraches" is a term in Mexican Spanish for sandals. The word itself is drawn
from Nahuatl, one of the indigenous languages from central Mexico. In addition
to the leather sandals of long habit, sandals are now made of plastic. Many
individuals in Yucatán wear huaraches. Most low-income or rural people wear
these leather or plastic sandals all the time.

11. *Dignidad* is translated as "dignity" but the Spanish word carries more meaning
than a simple, literal English translation would imply. One's dignidad is one's
sense of being and worth as a person. As such one's dignidad is honored
and taken very seriously. Affronts to one's dignidad are regarded as deeply
wounding insults.

12. "Raza" is literally translated as "race." In Mexico the term is sometimes used in
place of "ethnic group." Some Mexican political activists use it to refer to anyone
who is Mexican or of Mexican heritage. Some activists use "raza" as a rallying cry
to mobilize Mexicans or those of Mexican heritage.

13. "Cenote" is a Spanish interpretation of the original Yucatec Maya word
tz'onot. The term refers to the sinkholes that dot parts of the Yucatecan
countryside. Cenotes form when soil erosion or the collapse of cave roofs
expose groundwater.

14. Araceli lists a rather eclectic collection of eight famous historical women about
whom she has read. Guinevere was an English queen of the Middle Ages from
the famed court of King Arthur. Joan of Arc was a fifteenth-century leader
of the French resistance during the Hundred Years' War, canonized in 1920.
Cleopatra was a first-century Egyptian queen renowned for her leadership
and her involvement with the Imperial Roman leaders Julius Cesar and Mark
Antony. Messalina was a powerful first-century Roman empress and reputed
libertine. Lucrezia Borgia was a late fifteenth- to early sixteenth-century Italian
noblewoman and important political figure. La Belle (Carolina) Otero was
a Spanish-born singer and actor of the late nineteenth and early twentieth
centuries who achieved international fame. Mata Hari was an early twentieth-
century exotic dancer and femme fatale who was accused by France of spying
for Germany during World War I. Isadora Duncan was an early twentieth-
century American innovator of modern dance.

15. "Querencia" has no ready English translation. It refers to a deeply rooted
sense of place, a place strongly significant to individuals to which they feel
an emotional attachment.

16. Araceli here references some issues that she thought we had not covered in the
1993 interviews (the two interviews I first did with Araceli as part of the project

about Yucatecan women's engagement in politics) and that she notes that she wishes to mention now.

17. Araceli makes the distinction that *kinder* is like babysitting where the children just play. But in contrast the little children (*párvulos*) in preschool learn the beginning basics of writing and reading.

18. Araceli was a diputada suplente to the Yucatecan State Congress from her home district in southwestern Yucatán. Araceli ran on a slate with a prominent ladino male politician as his suplente, that is, the person who serves in office if the elected person for some reason cannot serve out the term of office to which he or she was elected.

19. The diputado titular is the first candidate on a ticket, the one who if the ticket wins will actually serve in office.

20. Domitila Barrios de Chungara is a well-known activist from Bolivia whose 1978 book *Testimony of Domitila, A Woman of the Bolivian Mines: Let Me Speak!* written with Moema Viezzer has become a classic in gender studies and Latin American studies literature. Ms. Barrios de Chungara spoke at the UN conference that Araceli attended in Mexico City.

21. The PRI (Partido Revolucionario Institucional, Party of the Institutional Revolution) is the political party that has dominated Mexican politics since the 1920s. Other political parties began to challenge PRI hegemony in the 1980s. The process of political transformation of Mexico into a multiparty democracy was at least symbolically culminated by the presidential victory of an opposition party in the 2000 elections. In these elections Vicente Fox from the PAN (Partido de Acción Nacional, National Action Party, a right-of-center party) won the presidency.

22. The plurinominal designation in the Mexican electoral system indicates a rule whereby minority parties are allocated seats in state congresses based on the party's percentage of the total vote count in each state. Araceli was thus elected as a member of the minority Partido del Frente Cardenista para la Reconstrucción Nacional (Party of the Cardenista Front for the National Reconstruction).

23. The term "ladino" as I use it here refers to a vaguely defined distinction that presumes to distinguish the indigenous peoples from those who are not, that is, those of European ancestry or at least partly of such ancestry. Yucatecans themselves, however, do not commonly use the term "ladino" although it is readily employed in other parts of Mexico (Chiapas and Veracruz) and Guatemala. Anthropologists also use "ladino" when discussing ethnic relations and social structure in these regions. As used by indigenous people "ladino" sometimes takes on an additional quite negative meaning as someone crafty and exploitative who cannot be trusted. Yucatecans generally refer to all the people of the state as "Yucatecos," sometimes using "Maya" to refer to those thought to be

indigenous. Additionally Maya women are sometimes referred to as "mestizas," meaning literally "mixed," as someone from a biethnic background. North American social scientists often use "mestizo" to refer to Mexicans of mixed European and indigenous ancestry although the term is not used by Mexicans themselves. The haziness of ethnic group distinctions in Yucatán makes any definition unsatisfactory and likely to displease at least some. See Reed (2001, 379–80n5) for a discussion of the historical difficulties in using the term "ladino." See Gabbert (2002) for a discussion of contemporary terms used in Yucatán to distinguish among its diverse people.

24. Rigoberta Menchú Tum, the K'iché Maya activist from Guatemala who won the 1992 Nobel Peace Prize, has also expressed her desire to have a Maya name. Until she was nineteen years old her name was Mi In (translated into Spanish as "Día Sereno" and English as "Serene Day"). When she and her father went to register her, however, municipal officials told them that she needed to have a Catholic saint's name. Thus "Mi In" became "Rigoberta" (*Día Sereno* 1998).

25. Araceli chose the English spelling of her daughter's name, "Bertha," instead of the Spanish, "Berta."

26. Sister Terry, a Maryknoll sister and my longtime friend in Yucatán, explained to me that the Roman Catholic Church no longer follows this practice but instead honors nearly all names that parents or godparents select.

27. Abandonment such as experienced by Araceli, her siblings, and her mother is an unfortunate but not rare occurrence. Yet the perspective of the men who leave their families is seldom discussed. Without men's perspective on their own actions, however, the circumstances of abandonment cannot be fully understood. I am thankful to my husband and colleague, W. A. Martín Gonzalez, for this insight.

28. Such an arrangement is termed "virilocal" residence by anthropologists. The pattern of newly married couples living in the same house or house compound as the husband's parents or wife's parents ("urilocal" residence) has been a common residential pattern. For many people their extended families of relatives and in-laws have been and still are the most important social and economic safety net. Migration to urban and tourist resort areas, however, is changing the common residence as families move away from the villages and towns where their parents live. Increased economic independence among some families has also made virilocal or urilocal residence less preferable to some, or at least less common.

29. A much-debated issue in the literature of Latin American women's political participation concerns the motivation for women's engagement in politics. Within the literature on women's political participation in Latin America scholars have long debated the influence and significance of women's domestic

roles in their political activities. Some have maintained that women's domestic responsibilities are fundamental to their political activism (Bouvard 1994). Conversely some have claimed that domestic responsibilities limit women as political actors because women in these circumstances become active out of their concern for others and not for themselves as women (Feijóo 1991; Jacquette 1991a, 1991b). Others argue that political participation arising from familial and community concerns does not exclude activist women from having or gaining a perspective that includes self-awareness or self-actualization as women or as individuals (Logan 1984; Martín 1998, 1999).

30. See Castillo Cocom's enlightening analysis of this event and its importance to politics and indigenous identity in Yucatán (2005).

31. For further analyses of the Mexican Revolution see Knight 1986; Meyer and Sherman 1995; Womack 1968.

32. Rural schoolteachers in Mexico have been very important generators of change. By bringing formal education to remote or underserved rural areas of their nation they have not only educated people but also empowered them. A theme in Araceli's life is that despite the prejudice against indigenous people in Mexico many people have recognized her talent and encouraged her. The schoolteachers and the cultural missions workers in Maxcanú helped her complete her education and then she become a literacy instructor herself. They encouraged her participation in art classes and musical events. These same people recognized her leadership abilities and encouraged her entrance into politics. See Foweraker (1993) and Cook (1996) for contemporary views regarding the importance of rural schoolteachers in Mexico. See Redfield (1950) for a historical view of the role of schoolteachers in rural Yucatán in particular. See Vaughan (1992) for a historical view especially of women who became rural schoolteachers.

Chapter Two

1. "Traje" in Spanish means "apparel" or "suit of clothes." Araceli uses "traje" as the shortened form of "traje de la mestiza" to indicate the distinctive clothing of Yucatec Maya women. See note 9 in chapter 1 for a full explanation of Maya women's clothing and note 6, this chapter, for an explanation of "mestiza."

2. Henequen is a large bromeliad, (*Agave fourcroydes* Lem.). It was the mainstay crop that sustained Yucatán's economy in the early twentieth century. Still in limited production, henequen fibers were most often used for making rope and twine. Now its fibers are woven into household objects such as rugs and placemats. The henequen plant is related to the blue agave, *Agave tequilana* A. Weber, from which tequila is produced.

3. There are other versions of how Maxcanú got its name. According to Professor Santiago Pacheco Cruz, "Maxcanú" evolved from the Maya word "Meexcanul" meaning "hair ornament" or "beard of Canul," a common Yucatec Maya surname. Also according to Professor Santiago Pacheco Cruz, "Maxcanú" can be broken into three syllables indicating three words in Yucatec Maya (*maax, can, u*) translated as "their (his, her, or your) four monkeys." *Monos* (monkeys) is a derivative of "maax," *cuatro* (four) is derived of "can," and *su* (their, his, her, or your) is a derivative of "u" (Pacheco Cruz 1980, B1). The differences in the origin of "Maxcanú" as a place name are likely caused by the lack of standardization of the written form of the Yucatec Maya language plus the ambiguities characteristic of the oral tradition in which the stories originally emerged.

   All three versions (the two reported in this chapter and that of Santiago Pacheco Cruz), however, share the double or triple entendre common in Yucatecan place names. See Burns (1983, 1), *An Epoch of Miracles: Oral Literature of the Yucatec Maya*, for a discussion of this place-naming pattern and the humor it sometimes implies.

4. Stephens 1988, 104.

5. Vaquerías are given in towns throughout Yucatán and are widely anticipated as a joyous community event. Despite the origin of the word "vaquería" in the Spanish word *vaca* for cow, the festivals are not based on cattle-raising activities but rather are celebrations of rural life in general.

6. "Mestizas" is translated from Spanish literally as "hybrid" from the verb *mestizar*, "to cross breeds," and the noun *mestizaje*, the "crossing of races." In Yucatán, however, "mestizas" is used to refer to indigenous women. The masculine equivalent, "mestizo," correspondingly is not commonly used to reference indigenous men. Thus "traje de la mestiza" refers to the distinctive clothing that many Yucatec Maya women wear. See note 1, this chapter, and note 9 in chapter 1. Also see the special editions of the *Journal of Latin American Anthropology* (Hale 1996; Rahier 2003) for a full discussion of the term "mestizaje" in its regional and historical variations of meaning and social significance in Latin America (although none discuss its use in Yucatán). Within the 1996 edition see particularly the article by de la Cadena for a discussion of mestizas in Peru, which describes a use of the term somewhat similar to its use in Yucatán.

7. Jaabin according to Araceli is a tree symbolic of Yucatán. In Spanish it is *habin*, described as a tropical hardwood with the scientific name of *Piscidia communis leguminosa* (*Diccionario Maya Cordemex* 1980).

8. Subinche according to Araceli is a flowering, fragrant tree especially known for its attraction for honeybees. The Yucatec Maya–Spanish dictionary Araceli and I use (*Diccionario Maya Cordemex* 1980) does not have a Spanish-language equivalent for this tree.

9. Tajonal as described by Araceli is a shrub with yellow flowers also known for its attraction of honeybees.

10. Dzidzilche Araceli describes as a tree especially attractive to honeybees. The Yucatec Maya–Spanish dictionary Araceli and I use (*Diccionario Maya Cordemex* 1980) does not have a Spanish-language equivalent for this tree.

11. Petenes are jungle plains of Yucatán.

12. Novenario is the nine days and nights of prayers said honoring certain ceremonies or rites of passages of the Roman Catholic faith.

13. In Araceli's original text she uses the word *cariño*, which I have translated as "love." "Cariño" is, however, a word that has no exact translation into English. Cariño is a deeply rooted and profoundly felt affection and caring. It is more specific and nuanced than the general term "love" implies.

14. See Irma Oztoy (1996) for an interpretation of Yucatec Maya women's clothing as cultural preservation. As cited in Natividad Gutierrez (1999, 193), another Yucatec Maya woman writer, M. L. Góngora Pacheco, said about the importance of the huipil, "As a woman writer, I think that the huipil was created by a ray of light, which symbolizes the whiteness of the cloth. Part of the neck is divided in four sections, meaning the four cardinal points from which emerges the center, which is our head" (interview, November 13, 1992, Ixmiquilpan).

15. Salvador Alvarado, originally from Sonora in northwest Mexico, came to Yucatán as a general in 1915 to reestablish Mexican government control of the state. During his rule as military governor of Yucatán, he brought many needed reforms including the end of the debt peonage that virtually enslaved many Maya. With their emancipation from this form of all-but-in-name slavery thousands of Maya moved from the henequen haciendas into towns. Araceli's grandparents as well as those of her husband, Pablo, were among those who arrived to make new lives in Maxcanú.

Salvador Alvarado was also known for his support of women's rights, hosting the Second and Third Feminist congresses ever held in Latin America in January and November 1916, respectively. He and his successor as governor, Felipe Carrillo Puerto, are likely the two most revered figures in Yucatecan history because of the reforms they brought to a socially archaic Yucatán. Much has been written about Salvador Alvarado but two basic sources are Joseph (1982) for the period of his rule in Yucatán and Soto (1990) for his women's rights reform efforts.

Manuel Gonzalez, a foreman of Maya heritage from a hacienda near Maxcanú, joined the forces of General Salvador Alvarado to establish Mexican government control in Yucatán in 1915. The general rewarded him with the military command of Maxcanú. Gonzalez established a well-organized control of the area until his assassination in 1921 (Joseph 1982, 118). Gonzalez is especially remembered in

Maxcanú for his enforcement of the law that ended the debt peonage that enslaved many Maya. See chapter 4 for more on the issue of debt peonage.

16. See Ana Castillo (1996), *The Goddess of the Americas,* for further reference on the significance of the Virgin of Guadalupe as a religious and cultural symbol, especially as a contemporary popular symbol to Mexicans and Mexican Americans.

17. "Bomba" literally in Spanish means "pump," "bomb," or "shell." As used in Yucatán it also refers to this distinctly Yucatecan brand of humor.

18. Copal is dried pine resin that Maya peoples have used since ancient times as a cleansing incense, often used in religious or community ceremonies. Copal produces a strong, fresh pine fragrance when it is burned.

19. "Señorío" has no exact English translation. As Araceli uses the term here it denotes a term of respect for a man as in "a great man."

20. In his essay, "Wisdom Sits in Places: Notes on a Western Apache Landscape," Keith H. Basso notes that ethnographers have seldom inquired about the "cultural constructs of geographical realities" (1996, 53). Yet Araceli's "place-based" poetry demonstrates the potential richness of this line of pursuit. As Basso writes, "Places possess a marked capacity for triggering acts of self-reflection, inspiring thoughts about who one presently is, or memories of who one used to be, or musings on who one might become. And that is not all. Place-based thoughts about the self lead commonly to thoughts of other things—other places, other people, other times, whole networks of associations that ramify unaccountably within the expanding spheres of awareness that they themselves engender" (55). In discussing the Maya in particular June Nash notes a kind of "situational identity" linked to a locale considered as a sacred environment (1995, 24).

Chapter Three

1. "Razas" (plural) has no definitive translation into English. A translation of "razas" as "races" has too biological a sense; "razas" indicates ethnic groups or those with a strong and deeply rooted sense of collective cultural identity.

2. "Mayab" is the plural of "Maya" as written in Yucatec Maya with the ending letter "b" indicating a plural as "s" or "es" does in Spanish and English.

3. Life Narrative no. 2, summer 1995, "It Was December 9, 1932."

4. Ibid.

5. Comadres, literally "comothers," are women who are mothers and god-mothers to the same child. The comadre is the ritual sponsor of the other woman's child for the ceremonial life passage events basic to Christian

religious practice. The bond between such women linked as they are as fictive kinswomen is potentially strong.

6. Ejido is a form of communally owned if not communally worked land. "Ejidal" is the adjective form.

7. Indigenismo is a philosophical, cultural, and public policy movement promoting the integration of the indigenous peoples of Mexico into the nation. Indigenismo arose especially during and after the Mexican Revolution (1910–20). While appearing to favor indigenous peoples and better the material conditions of their lives, indigenismo has been criticized because it did not empower indigenous people nor did it foster a true respect for their cultural differences. Mexico now has an official pluriethnic state policy that recognizes and respects indigenous people as *indigenous*, not as poorly assimilated and inferior others.

8. See Harvey (1998) for an analysis of Mexico's agrarian policies and indigenous peoples.

9. See Diaz del Castillo (1963, 59–63) for a full account of this intriguing vignette of Yucatán and Mexican history.

10. The painter Francisco Castro Pacheco was not the only one to notice Araceli's exceptionality during her early days as a congressional representative. The famous Mexican writer Martin Luis Guzman interviewed her for his magazine in 1975 and the interview was likely published soon after. Unfortunately Araceli gave all her copies away years ago. We have not been able to locate a copy of this important document.

11. Nelson (1999, 189) reports a similar response in Guatemala to Rigoberta Menchú's winning the Nobel Prize for Peace. Using the phrase "*se rayó la mula*" (literally "striping the mule," "the striped mule," i.e., a zebra), meaning idiomatically to get lucky, those critical of Ms. Menchú considered it luck that she won the Nobel rather any merit of her own. Thus in both cases the successes of Maya women activists are attributed to only a lucky, freakish accident. In both cases comparing Araceli's and Ms. Menchú's successes as Maya women by referencing un burro and la mula (the burro and the mule, animals associated as stubborn beasts of burden) casts these expressions as racist.

12. "Solar," literally the "place where the sun hits," does not have a one-word equivalent in English. The word implies a combination of home, house, and plot of land on which a house sits.

13. Nixtamal is ground corn. People commonly take corn to be ground at special mills to produce the corn-dough base from which tortillas are made.

14. These are Yucatec Maya names for various features in the natural world that have special significance for agriculture. Kankabales are lands with reddish earth where peanuts and jicamas especially are grown. Tsk'eles are extensions

of flat-rocked land where farmers plant chiles and tomatoes. Chultunes are seasonal water holes in areas with porous rocks. Haltunes are seasonal water holes in areas with smooth rocks. Aktunes are depressions in the earth where because the land is sheltered, a microclimate is created where milder tropical crops such as bananas and mameys can flourish.

15. Araceli spells her name with a single "l" and an "i," not a double "ll" and a "y" as appears at conclusion of this speech. Her speech was typed by one of the student volunteers in Congress who misspelled her name.

16. See Soto (1990, 72–81) for description of the feminist congresses.

17. Both title translations are inexact, altering their original meaning. *Me llamo Rigoberta Menchú y así me nació la conciencia* literally means "I am called Rigoberta Menchú and so my consciousness was born." Omitting the second part of the original title not only diminishes its power but also leaves out the reference to a central theme of Rigoberta Menchú's life narrative—the story of how and why she became an activist. *Rigoberta, La nieta de los Mayas* is literally "Rigoberta, Granddaughter of the Mayas," a title much more in keeping with the author's rootedness in Maya culture than the more prosaic title *Crossing Borders*.

18. Cristina is a Miami-based television talk show with the Cuban American media star Cristina Saralegui as its host. The show is syndicated throughout Latin America and has an avid following. Araceli's granddaughters watch it regularly although their grandmother is critical of the values she sees projected on the program.

19. As used here, "temperament" means "too strong tempered."

Chapter Four

1. "Caminante" means "traveler."

2. *Oxkintok* is an ancient Maya site that lies in a dramatic setting of a hilltop plateau of the Pu'uc hills. Araceli routinely uses the term *las ruinas* (the ruins) to refer to ancient Maya sites as is common practice in Mexico when discussing the settlements of ancient indigenous peoples. Labeling such settlement sites as ruinas has such common, long-standing usage that it implies no intentional disrespect. Entsil is the largest pyramid within Oxkintok.

3. X-pukil-Tun is a cave near Maxcanú.

4. X-Kan-Maya, Chuyub-balam, and X-Ulmil are small ancient Maya sites near Maxcanú.

5. According to Araceli's description, Uklan is an Atlas-like mythical Maya ancestor.

6. X-la-pak is an ancient Maya site along with Labna and Sayil that are located in the same region as Maxcanú. All three are relatively close to the largest and most famous ancient Maya site in the region, Uxmal.

7. Chak-xix, Chakal, Aktun Kopo, and Aktun On are caves near Maxcanú.

8. See Burns (1983, 1–2 and passim) for interpretations of the deer as a symbol to the Yucatec Maya.

9. The reference to "driver" is that Felipe Carrillo Puerto was a driver of horse wagons. The poet who termed him the "driver of Motul" was Antonio Mediz Bolio, a Yucatán poet who became well-known shortly after the epoch of Felipe Carrillo Puerto. He is still revered locally as a most Yucatecan of poets.

10. "Camino" I have translated as "way" as best following what I think is Araceli's intention here. "Camino" can also be translated as "road," "highway," "path," "pass," "passage," "trip," or "journey."

11. Henequen is the bromeliad, *Agave fourcroydes* Lem., once the mainstay monocrop that sustained the Yucatecan economy in the early twentieth century.

12. Araceli's name is misspelled here. An assistant, likely a university student performing mandatory social service as a degree requirement, typed her speech and made the error. Although her name legally is "Aracely," she dislikes the "y" as a foreign spelling and signs her name "Araceli" as a less than perfect second choice.

13. FIRA and FIRCO are acronyms for government programs whose complete names Araceli does not remember. They were, however, government-sponsored agrarian social welfare programs that provided small subsidies to individual producers of various basic crops.

14. SRH is the acronym for Secretaría de Recursos Hidráulicos (Secretariat of Hydraulic Resources), a federal agency that had the responsibility of water control mechanisms such as dams.

15. PRONASOL is the acronym for Programa Nacional de Solidaridad, a federal government program that during the presidency of Carlos Salinas (1988–94) sold state-owned enterprises and sought to use the resultant funds to alleviate poverty and foster development. Accusations that many of the funds were used to bolster the political position of PRI plagued "Solidaridad," as this program was more commonly known.

16. The translation here is difficult. In Araceli's original text she refers to "*una escuela digna*" and "*un techo honroso*," which would be literally "a dignified school" and "an honorable technological school." Both of these terms were used to identify certain kinds of school programs as part of a federal educational reform. Here Araceli seems to be using the terms as a metaphor unifying material and spiritual needs.

17. In the typed text of Araceli's handwritten original the verb *encausar* (to prosecute, indict, or sue) is used. But in checking with her, she told me she meant the verb to be *encauzar* (to channel, to conduct through channels, to guide, lead, or direct). The office worker who typed Araceli's handwritten original made what is likely a typographical error.

18. Araceli's quote at end of the speech is taken from a slogan of the Frente Cardenista (PFCRN) to which she was affiliated prior to her switch to the PT (Partido de Trabajo).

19. Fajina was originally a form of cooperative communal labor used by the Maya for projects that benefited the community as a whole. Under Spanish rule the fajina became a practice whereby the Spanish commanded the labor of indigenous peoples as an obligation owed to them as the new masters of the land.

20. Another acrostic Araceli composed, "Hotel Santa Lucía," appears in appendix A.

21. Like all writers Araceli occasionally misspells. In her original *siempre* (always) is written as "*siem*." In reviewing the text with Araceli she confirmed that she had intended to write "siempre."

22. *Gestas* has no exact English translation. It refers to a monumental historical social struggle. When Araceli clarified her use of the term to me, I thought "revolutions" was the most accurate translation.

23. Nopal (*Opuntia cochenillifera*) is a common kind of cactus found throughout Mexico and the southern United States. A hearty, easily grown plant, its tender young green paddles are cut in strips, cooked, and eaten as vegetables. Served in this way, nopals appear and taste somewhat like green beans. In drier areas of Mexico nopals are sometimes planted closely together to make a fence around a yard.

24. "Casta" is literally "caste." Araceli uses the term here more in the sense of "ethnic group." In Yucatán, however, "casta" has a special reference. During the 1840s the Maya, especially of the eastern part of the peninsula, rebelled. The rebellion is commonly referred to as the War of the Castes (Guerra de las Castas), referencing that the cultural and socioeconomic gap between the campesino Maya and much of the local Spanish-speaking population was so great they appeared to be from different castes.

25. See Nelson Reed's revised edition (2001) of his original work (1964), *The Caste War of Yucatán*, for a well-written account of the Caste War. See also Dumond (1997) and Rugeley (1999, 2001) for accounts of the Caste War that stress a variety of factors, such as origins of the war, and for a more nuanced reading of the event, especially regarding regional divisions within the Maya ranks. Regarding the issue of Maya slavery see Reed (2001, 142, 183, 200, 220–21, 302–3; 1964, 180).

26. See Nash (1995) for a discussion of reclaimed collective cultural practices among the Maya settlers of the Lacandón region of Mexico.

Chapter Five

1. "Trine" is a rarely used word in English derived from the Latin *trinus* meaning "threefold" or "a set or group of three."

2. If Araceli's poetry is its own muse, there are certainly other poets whose muse is uncertain. Emily Dickinson (1830–86), the nineteenth-century American poet, was largely unpublished until after her death. A perplexing question for interpreters of her poetry is the depth of human emotion evident in her poetry contrasted with a life lived in seclusion seemingly apart from much interaction with others. Students of her poetry are left to ponder from where her emotional understanding arose.

3. By the phrase, "Believing myself in your life . . . the complement," Araceli indicates that she is the completion of the other.

4. By "that one" Araceli refers to the love to whom she writes, indicating that the loved one didn't read what she wrote.

5. Here Araceli uses *en* as a physical place. To ease the reading of this poem in English, I translated "en" as "with" and "for."

6. "Noctornando" is a word Araceli invented. It combines a reference to night (*nocturno*) with an active verb ending (*-ando*). A literal translation, "nighting," has no meaning as expressed in English. Since "noctornando" contains the notions of night and activity, I translated it as "thinking in the night" in keeping with the tone of the poem.

7. The phrase "jasmines of the province" again references the idea that Yucatán is a distinct and special place.

8. When Araceli gave me her writings to photocopy, she had already redrafted this poem. The original of the poem she discarded when she rewrote it in 1996. So I have never seen the poem as she originally wrote it. Araceli tells me that she substantially redrafted this poem. Such a rewrite is unusual since Araceli seldom revises her work, especially after so long a time. She usually writes a draft in one sitting, making changes as she goes. Araceli finishes her work by rewriting the final version to get a clean copy.

9. Redondillas are a seven-syllable quatrain with alternate rhyming.

10. In his book *An Epoch of Miracles* (1983) and also in an article "Modern Yucatec Maya Oral Tradition" (1992), Allan F. Burns discusses the Yucatec Maya oral tradition and the importance of its performance in detail.

Chapter Six

1. This last line is a possible reference to the ceiba tree, sacred to the ancient Maya and important as a symbol to the contemporary Maya.

2. NGOs (nongovernmental organizations) are citizen-organized groups that seek to provide services or obtain resources most often for socioeconomic development or political reform. They are customarily issue oriented: low-income housing, environmental protection, women's rights, etc. The "nongovernmental" indicates that these organizations operate outside of state agencies. Most NGOs get funding from private foundations, governmental grants, and international organizations such as the United Nations. NGOs represent a rapidly growing sector concerned with development globally.

3. The "C." before the governor's name stands for "ciudadano" or "fellow citizen."

4. Araceli's original text is "*Mi peticion se sustenta en la labor que he realizado, avala el merito de esta solicitud.*" I have translated this sentence as "My petition is sustained by the work that I have done, that supports the merit of this request." "Avala" is literally a guarantor, a cosigner as in rental properties, one who would stand behind someone else.

5. On at least one other occasion Blanca Estrada had helped Araceli get financial aid. When Araceli visited Florida International University in 1994, Blanca Estrada convinced the governor to give her some additional travel funds to supplement the funds given her by my university.

6. The Bracero Program (1942–64) was established to bring Mexican laborers to the United States to help with the labor shortage caused by World War II. Millions of Mexican workers came to the United States in this joint (Mexico–United States) state-sponsored migration. The bracero workers have had to bring legal action to win the pensions promised them but not delivered due to state ineptitude and corruption. Araceli is working through a local attorney to obtain her husband's pension.

7. Fajina (literally "toil," "task" or "work") is the custom of obligatory unpaid labor performed by a collective of individuals from a community for the benefit of the community. In Mexico schools, roads, and other projects from which the entire community benefits are sometimes built with fajina labor from the local community. In such cases, the government provides the construction materials. For many communities the fajina provides a way for needed community projects to be done without waiting for government funds to cover the costs of the entire project, that is, labor.

8. Copal is pine resin. Since ancient times the peoples of Mesoamerica have burned copal as incense in religious or cleansing rituals. Copal was widely traded

throughout the Maya regions. Many regard its refreshing, distinct scent as fresh and cleansing.

9. The original title of Edna's story was "La retrasada mental," which translates into English as "The Mentally Retarded One." Since this title gives the appearance of an insensitivity I doubt Edna intended, I have changed the title to "La burrita" (Little Donkey), referencing the protagonist's nickname in Edna's story.

Conclusions

1. The bias against recognition of an indigenous person as possessing intellectual talents seems deep-seated. Historical accounts of Yucatán often mention the dim view taken by non-Maya society regarding the intellectual capacities of the Maya. During the Caste War, Reed (2001:28) writes of the amusement of some non-Maya that Jacinto Pat, a Maya leader, bought and read a book.

   Historically many non-Maya thought the Maya to be intellectually and technologically backward. They believed that the Maya could not possibly be descended from the people who had constructed the impressive cities whose ancient ruins dot the peninsula. Others considered Maya agricultural techniques to be inefficient. The Maya not only left huge quantities of land untilled (necessary for the swidden agriculture of the tropics with its quickly depleted soil) but also based their agricultural system on the "limiting" concept of communal land ownership (Patch 1991, 57).

Works Cited

ADMI
> 2000 *Voces e imagenes: Mujeres Maya Ixiles de Chajul/Voices and Images: Mayan Ixil Women of Chajul.* Guatemala City: Victor Herrera de Magna Terra Editores.

Almario G., Oscar
> 2001 Territorio, identidad, memoria coletiva y movimiento étnico de los grupos negros del Pacífico sur colombiano: Microhistoria y etnografía sobre el Río Tapaje. *Journal of Latin American Anthropology* 7 (2): 198–229.

Alvarez, Julia
> 1998 *Something to Declare.* Chapel Hill, NC: Algonquin Books of Chapel Hill.

Baños Ramírez, Othón
> 1989 *Yucatán: Ejidos sin campesinos.* Mérida, Yucatán: Ediciones de la UADY.

> 1996 *Neoliberalismo, reorganización y subsistencia rural. El caso de la zona henequenera de Yucatán: 1980–1992.* Mérida, Yucatán: Ediciones de la UADY.

> 2002 *La modernidad rural mexicana a fines de milenio: El caso de Yucatán.* Mérida, Yucatán: Ediciones de la UADY.

Barrios de Chungara, Domitila, with Moema Viezzer
> 1978 *Testimony of Domitila, A Woman of the Bolivian Mines: Let Me Speak!* New York: Monthly Press.

Basso, Keith
> 1996 Wisdom Sits in Places: Notes on a Western Apache Landscape. In *Senses of Place,* ed. Steven Feld and Keith H. Basso, 53–90. Santa Fe, NM: School of American Research Press.

Bizarro Ujpán, Ignacio
> 1992 *Ignacio: The Diary of a Maya Indian from Guatemala.* Ed. and trans. James D. Sexton. Philadelphia: University of Pennsylvania Press.

> 2001 *Joseño: Another Mayan Voice Speaks from Guatemala.* Ed. and trans. James D. Sexton. Albuquerque: University of New Mexico Press.

Bouvard, Marguerite Guzman
    1994 *Revolutionizing Motherhood: The Mothers of the Plaza de Mayo.*
        Wilmington, DE: Scholarly Resources.

Burns, Allan
    1983 *An Epoch of Miracles: Oral Literature of the Yucatec Maya.* Austin:
        University of Texas Press.

    1992 Modern Yucatec Maya Oral Tradition. In *On the Translation of Native
        American Literatures,* ed. Brain Swann. Washington, DC: Smithsonian
        Institution Press.

Canul, Jose T.
    2001 En el olvido, procer kinchilena de la lucha indígena. *Por Esto!*
        April 10, 2001.

Castilla Ramos, Beatriz
    1998 La industria maquiladora yucateca en el contexto de la globalización.
        Infomaquila (Revista de la Asociación de Maquiladoras, Mérida,
        Yucatán) 2.

    1999 Yucatán: La otra frontera o la desaparición de sistema agroexportador.
        Certeza 3 (13, agosto–septiembre).

    2004 *Mujeres mayas en la robótica y líderes de la comunidad: Tejiendo la
        modernidad.* Mérida, Yucatán: Ayuntamiento de Mérida; Instituto de
        Cultura de Yucatán; Universidad Autónoma de Yucatán.

Castillo, Ana
    1996 *Goddess of the Americas/La Diosa de las Americas: Writings on the Virgin of
        Guadalupe.* New York: Riverhead Books.

Castillo Cocom, Juan
    2005 It Was Simply Their Word: Yucatec Maya PRInces in YucaPAN and the
        Politics of Respect. *Critique of Anthropology* 25 (2): 131–55.

Coe, Michael D.
    1992 *Breaking the Maya Code.* New York: Thames and Hudson.

    2005 *The Maya.* 7th ed. New York: Thames and Hudson.

Cook, Maria Lorena
    1996 *Organizing Dissent: Unions, the State, and the Democratic Teachers'
        Movement in Mexico.* University Park: Pennsylvania State University Press.

Crehan, Kate
    2002 *Gramsci, Culture and Anthropology.* Berkeley: University of California
        Press.

Davidson, Alastair
    1977 *Antonio Gramsci: Towards an Intellectual Biography.* London: Merlin Press.

Día Sereno
    1998 *Día Sereno.* Film for the Humanities and Sciences Series.

Diaz de Castillo, Bernal
  1963 *The Conquest of New Spain*. Baltimore: Penguin Books.

Diaz Polanco, Hector
  1997 *Indigenous Peoples in Latin America: The Quest for Self-Determination*. Trans. Lucia Rayas. Boulder, CO: Westview.

Diccionario Maya Cordemex
  1980 *Diccionario Maya Cordemex*. Mérida and Mexico City: Ediciones Cordemex.

Dorfman, Ariel
  1998 Empower Children: Teach Them a Foreign Language. *Miami Herald* July 3, A25 (originally in the *New York Times*).

Dumond, Don E.
  1997 *The Machete and the Cross: Campesino Rebellion in Yucatan*. Lincoln: University of Nebraska Press.

Fallaw, Ben
  2001 *Cárdenas Compromised, The Failure of Reform in Postrevolutionary Yucatán*. Durham, NC, and London: Duke University Press.

  2002 The Life and Death of Felipa Poot: Women, Fiction, and *Cardenismo* in Post-Revolutionary Mexico. *HAHR* 82 (4).

Farriss, Nancy M.
  1984 *Maya Society under Colonial Rule*. Princeton, NJ: Princeton University Press.

Feijóo, Maria del Carmen
  1991 The Challenge of Constructing Civilian Peace: Women and Democracy in Argentina. In *The Women's Movement in Latin America*, ed. Jane Jacquette. Boulder, CO: Westview.

Femia, Joseph V.
  1981 *Gramsci's Political Thought*. Oxford: Clarendon Press.

Fiori, Giuseppe
  1990 *Antonio Gramsci: Life of a Revolutionary*. London and New York: Verso.

Fischer, Edward F.
  2002 *Cultural Logics and Global Economies: Maya Identity in Thought and Practice*. Austin: University of Texas Press.

——, and R. McKenna Brown, eds.
  1996 *Maya Cultural Activism in Guatemala*. Austin: University of Texas Press.

——, and Carol Hendrickson
  2003 *Tecpan Guatemala: A Modern Maya Town in Global and Local Context*. Boulder, CO: Westview.

Forbis, Melissa M.
1999 Hacia la Autonomía: Zapatista Women and the Development of a New World. Paper presented in session "Defining the Political: Maya Women's Activism" at the 98th annual meeting of the American Anthropological Association, Chicago.

Foweraker, Joe
1993 *Popular Mobilization in Mexico: The Teachers' Movement, 1977–87.* Cambridge and New York: Cambridge University Press.

Freidel, David, Linda Schele, and Joy Parker
1993 *Maya Cosmos: Three Thousand Years on the Shaman's Path.* New York: William Morrow.

Gabbert, Wolfgang
2002 Ethnicity in Yucatán. *Anthropology News* 43 (7): 54.

2004 *Becoming Maya, Ethnicity and Social Inequality in Yucatán since 1500.* Tucson: University of Arizona Press.

Germino, Dante
1990 *Antonio Gramsci: Architect of a New Politics.* Baton Rouge and London: Louisiana State University Press.

González, Gaspar Pedro
1995 *A Mayan Life.* Rancho Palos Verdes, CA: Yax Te' Foundation.

1998a *Return of the Maya.* Rancho Palos Verdes, CA: Yax Te' Foundation.

1998b Sq'anej Maya'/*Palabras Mayas.* Rancho Palos Verdes, CA: Yax Te' Foundation.

Gramsci, Antonio
1971 *Selections from the Prison Notebooks of Antonio Gramsci.* Ed. and trans. Quintin Hoare and Geoffrey Nowell Smith. New York: International Publishers.

1977 *Selections from Political Writings, 1910–1920.* Ed. Quintin Hoare. London: Lawrence and Wishart.

1978 *Selections from Political Writings, 1921–1926.* Ed. Quintin Hoare. London: Lawrence and Wishart.

1985 *Selections from Cultural Writings.* Ed. David Forgacs and Geoffrey Nowell-Smith. London: Lawrence and Wishart.

1992 *Prison Notebooks.* Vol. 1. Ed. Joseph A. Buttigieg. New York: Columbia University Press.

1994 *Letters from Prison.* 2 vols. Ed. Frank Rosengarten. Trans. Ray Rosenthal. New York: Columbia University Press.

1995 *Further Selections from the Prison Notebooks.* Trans. and ed. Derek Boothman. Minneapolis: University of Minnesota Press.

1996 *Prison Notebooks.* Vol. 2. Ed. Joseph A. Buttigieg. Trans. Antonio Callari and Joseph A. Buttigieg. New York: Columbia University Press.

Gutiérrez, Natividad
    1999 *Nationalist Myths and Ethnic Identities.* Lincoln and London: University of
        Nebraska Press.

Guzmán, Martín Luis
    1984 Maestros Rurales. In *Obras Completas.* Vol. 1, 1077–89. México, DF: Fondo
        de Cultura Económica.

Hale, Charles R., ed.
    1996 Mestizaje. *Journal of Latin American Anthropology* special edition 2 (1).

Harvey, Neil
    1998 *The Chiapas Rebellion: The Struggle for Land and Democracy.* Durham, NC,
        and London: Duke University Press.

Hervik, Peter
    2002 *Mayan Peoples Within and Beyond Boundaries.* New York: Routledge.

Jacquette, Jane
    1991a Introduction. In *The Women's Movement in Latin America,* ed. Jane
        Jacquette. Boulder, CO: Westview.

    1991b *Conclusion. In The Women's Movement in Latin America,* ed. Jane
        Jacquette. Boulder, CO: Westview.

Joseph, G. M.
    1982 *Revolution from Without. Yucatán, Mexico and the United States, 1880–1924.*
        Cambridge: Cambridge University Press.

Kintz, Ellen
    1990 *Life under the Tropical Canopy: Tradition and Change among the Yucatec
        Maya.* New York: Holt, Rinehart and Winston.

    1999 Modernization, Policy and the Actions of Yucatec Maya Women: Coba,
        Quintana Roo, Mexico. Paper presented in session "Defining the Political:
        Maya Women's Activism" at the 98th annual meeting of the American
        Anthropological Association, Chicago.

Knight, Alan
    1986 *The Mexican Revolution.* Cambridge and New York: Cambridge University
        Press.

Lemaitre, Monique J.
    1998 *Elvia Carrillo Puerto: La monja roja del mayab.* Monterrey, Nuevo León:
        Ediciones Castillo.

Logan, Kathleen R.
    1984 *Haciendo Pueblo: The Making of a Guadalajaran Suburb.* Tuscaloosa, AL:
        University of Alabama Press.

    1995a Women's Participation in Democratic Transformation: Yucatán. *SECOLAS
        Annals* 26:77–89.

    1995b Urban Women as Political Activists: Mérida, Yucatán, Mexico. In *Urban
        Life: Readings in Urban Anthropology,* ed. Walter Zenner and George
        Gmelch. 3rd ed. Prospect Heights, IL: Waveland Press.

1997 Personal Testimony: Latin American Women Telling Their Lives. *Latin American Research Review* 32 (1): 199–211.

Mantilla Jorge, and Guillermo Sandoval

1993 *Felipe Carrillo Puerto, Ensayo biográfico (vida y obra)*. Mérida, Yucatán: Ediciones de la Universidad Autónoma de Yucatán.

Martín, Kathleen R.

1998 From the Heart of a Woman: Yucatec Maya Women as Political Actors. *Sex Roles* 39 (7/8): 559–71.

1999 *An Indigenous Maya Feminism. SECOLAS Annals* 31:136–47.

2001 Never Again a Mexico without Us: Indigenous Peoples and the 21st Century. In *Ethnicity and Governance in the Third World,* ed. John Mbaku, 165–94. London: Ashgate.

2004 *Gender and Maya Activism in Early 20th Century Yucatán*. SECOLAS Annals 36:31–47.

2006 *Felipa Poot, una precursora y su vida, un portal. In Dos mujeres que vale la pena*, ed. Piedad Peniche Romero, 41–62. Mérida, Yucatán: Instituto Cultural de Yucatán.

Menchú, Rigoberta

1983 *Me llamo Rigoberta Menchú y así me nació la conciencia*. Ed. Elisabeth Burgos. Barcelona: Argos Vergara.

1984 *I . . . Rigoberta Menchú, An Indian Woman in Guatemala*. Ed. Elisabeth Burgos-Debray. Trans. Ann Wright. London: Verso.

1998 *Crossing Borders*. London and New York: Verso.

Meyer, Michael C., and William L. Sherman

1995 *The Course of Mexican History*. New York and Oxford: Oxford University Press.

Miller, Francesca

1991 *Latin American Women and the Search for Social Justice*. Hanover and London: University Press of New England.

Montejo, Victor

1987 *Death of a Guatemalan Village*. Willimantic, CT: Curbstone Press.

1995 *Sculpted Stones*. Willimantic, CT: Curbstone Press.

1999 *Voices from Exile: Violence and Survival in Modern Maya History*. Norman: University of Oklahoma Press.

Nash, June

1995 The Reassertion of Indigenous Identity: Mayan Responses to State Intervention in Chiapas. *LARR* 30 (3): 7–41.

2001 *Mayan Visions: The Quest for Autonomy in an Age of Globalization*. New York and London: Routledge.

Nelson, Diane M.
  1999 *A Finger in the Wound: Body Politics in Quincentennial Guatemala.*
       Berkeley: University of California Press.

Ortiz, Teresa
  2001 *Never Again a World without Us.* Washington, DC: EPICA.

Oztoy, Irma
  1996 Maya Clothing and Identity. In *Maya Cultural Activism in Guatemala,* ed.
       Edward F. Fischer and R. McKenna Brown, 142–55. Austin: University of
       Texas Press.

Pacheco Cruz, Santiago
  1980 Radiografías de Yucatán, Diario de Yucatán. *!Por Esto!* March 24, B1.

Patch, Robert W.
  1991 Decolonization, the Agrarian Problem, and the Origins of the Caste War.
       In *Land, Labor and Capital in Modern Yucatán: Essays in Regional History
       and Political Economy,* ed. Jeffery T. Brannon and Gilbert M. Joseph, 51–82.
       Tuscaloosa, AL: University of Alabama Press.

Paz, Octavio
  1961 The Sons of La Malinche. In *The Labyrinth of Solitude: Life and Thought in
       Mexico,* 65–88. Trans. Lysander Kemp. New York: Grove Press.

Peniche Rivero, Piedad
  1996 Las ligas feministas en la revolución. *Unicornio, Por Esto!* July 7.

———, ed.
  2006 Dos mujeres que vale la pena. Mérida, Yucatán: Instituto Cultural de
       Yucatán.

Pozas, Ricardo
  1962 *Juan the Chamula.* Berkeley: University of California Press.

Rahier, Jean Muteba, ed.
  2003 *Mestizaje, Mulataje, Mesticagem* in Latin American Ideologies of National
       Identities. *Journal of Latin American Anthropology* 8 (1).

Rappaport, Joanne
  1990 *Politics of Memory: Native Historical Interpretation in the Colombian Andes.*
       Cambridge and New York: Cambridge University Press.

Re Cruz, Alicia
  1996 *The Two Milpas of Chan Kom: Scenarios of a Maya Village Life.* Albany:
       State University of New York Press.

Redfield, Robert
  1950 *A Village That Chose Progress: Chan Kom Revisited.* Chicago: University of
       Chicago Press.

Reed, Nelson
    1964 *The Caste War of Yucatán*. 1st ed. Stanford, CA: Stanford University Press.
    2001 *The Caste War of Yucatán*. Rev. ed. Stanford, CA: Stanford University Press.

Restall, Matthew
    1998 *Maya Conquistador*. Boston: Beacon Press.

Reuque Paillalef, Rosa Isolde
    2002 *When a Flower Is Reborn: The Life and Times of a Mapuche Feminist*. Ed.,
        trans., and intro. Florencia E. Mallon. Durham, NC, and London: Duke
        University Press.

Rodríguez, Victoria E., ed.
    1998 *Women's Participation in Mexican Political Life*. Boulder, CO: Westview.

Rugeley, Terry, ed.
    1999 *Yucatán's Maya Peasantry and the Origins of the Caste War*. Austin:
        University of Texas Press.
    2001 *Maya Wars: Ethnographic Accounts from Nineteenth-Century Yucatán*.
        University of Oklahoma Press.

Sántiz Gómez, Maruch
    1998 *Creencias de nuestros antepasados*. México, DF: Centro de la Imagen,
        CIESAS, and Casa de las Imagenes.

Sarkisyanz, Manuel
    1995 *Felipe Carrillo Puerto. Actuación y muerte*. Mérida, Yucatán: Congreso
        Estado de Yucatán.
    1997 *Felipe Carrillo Puerto*. Mérida, Yucatán: Talleres Gráficos del Sudeste, S.A.
        de C.V.

Schele, Linda, and David Freidel
    1990 *A Forest of Kings: The Untold Story of the Ancient Maya*. New York: William
        Morrow.

Sexton, James, ed.
    1981 *Son of Tecun Uman: A Maya Indian Tells His Life Story*. Tucson: University
        of Arizona Press.
    1985 *Campesino: The Diary of a Guatemalan Indian*. Tucson: University of
        Arizona Press.

Sigal, Pete
    2000 *From Moon Goddess to Virgins*. Austin: University of Texas Press.

Solis Alpuche, Jesus
    1986 Hace 50 años: Felipa Poot. *Diario del sudeste* (March 20, 21, 23, 25–29, 31;
        April 1–3).

Soto, Shirlene
  1979 *The Mexican Women: A Study of Her Participation in the Revolution, 1910–1940.* Palo Alto, CA: R & E Research Associates.
  1990 *Emergence of the Modern Mexican Woman.* Denver, CO: Arden Press.

Stephen, Lynn
  1991 *Zapotec Women.* Austin: University of Texas Press.

Stephens, John L.
  1988 *Incidents of Travel in Yucatan.* Vols. 1–2. Condensed ed. Azcapotzalco, México, DF: Panorama Editorial, S.A. de C.V. (originally published by Harper and Brothers, New York, 1843).

THOA (Andean Oral History Workshop) compiled by Silvia Rivera Cusicanqui
  1990 Indigenous Women and Community Resistance: History and Memory. In *Women and Social Change in Latin America*, ed. Elizabeth Jelin, compiled by Silvia Rivera Cusicanqui, 151–83. New York and London: ZED Books.

Tirado, Thomas C.
  1991 *Celsa's World: Conversations with a Mexican Peasant Woman.* Special Studies, no. 27. Tempe: Center for Latin American Studies, Arizona State University.

Van Cott, Donna Lee, ed.
  1994 *Indigenous Peoples and Democracy in Latin America.* New York: St. Martin's Press.

Vaughan, Mary Kay
  1992 Women School Teachers in the Mexican Revolution: The Story of Reyna's Braids. In *Expanding the Boundaries of Women's History*, ed. Cheryl Johnson-Odin and Margaret Strobel, 278–302. Bloomington and Indianapolis: Indiana University Press.

Warren, Kay B.
  1998 *Indigenous Movements and Their Critics. Pan-Maya Activism in Guatemala.* Princeton, NJ: Princeton University Press.

Wearne, Phillip
  1996 *Return of the Indian: Conquest and Revival in the Americas.* Philadelphia, PA: Temple University Press.

Womack, John, Jr.
  1968 *Zapata and the Mexican Revolution.* New York: Knopf.

Zapeta, Estuardo
  1999 *Las Huellas de B'alam.* Guatemala City: CHOLSAMAJ.

Index

The letter *n* following a page number indicates a note on that page. The note number follows the *n*. Page numbers in **bold type** indicate reproductions of the original pages. Italicized page numbers refer to photographs.

Kathleen Rock Martín
is associate professor of
anthropology at Florida
International University, Miami.